A GEORGE ELIOT CHRONOLOGY

A George Eliot Chronology

TIMOTHY HANDS

G.K.HALL &CO.

70 LINCOLN STREET, BOSTON, MASS.

5179459

© Timothy Hands 1989

Published 1988 in the United States by
G. K. HALL & CO.
70 Lincoln Street
Boston, Massachusetts 02111

First published 1989 by
THE MACMILLAN PRESS LTD
Houndmills, Basingstoke
Hampshire RG21 2XS

Printed in Hong Kong

Library of Congress Cataloging-in-Publication Data
Hands, Timothy.
  A George Eliot chronology.
  (Macmillan author chronologies)
  Bibliography: p.   35.
  Includes index.
  1. Eliot, George, 1819–1880—Chronology.   2. Novelists,
English—19th century—Chronology.
I. Title.   II. Series.
PR4687.H3   1989   823'.8   88–1791
ISBN 0–8161–8983–8

For Jane

Contents

General Editor's Preface   ix

Preface   xi

List of Abbreviations   xiii

A GEORGE ELIOT CHRONOLOGY   1

Bibliography   170

Index   175

General Editor's Preface

Most biographies are ill adapted to serve as works of reference – not surprisingly so, since the biographer is likely to regard his function as the devising of a continuous and readable narrative, with excursions into interpretation and speculation, rather than a bald recital of facts. There are times, however, when anyone reading for business or pleasure needs to check a point quickly or to obtain a rapid overview of part of an author's life or career; and at such moments turning over the pages of a biography can be a time-consuming and frustrating occupation. The present series of volumes aims at providing a means whereby the chronological facts of an author's life and career, rather than needing to be prised out of the narrative in which they are (if they appear at all) securely embedded, can be seen at a glance. Moreover, whereas biographies are often, and quite understandably, vague over matters of fact (since it makes for tediousness to be forever enumerating details of dates and places), a chronology can be precise whenever it is possible to be precise.

Thanks to the survival, sometimes in very large quantities, of letters, diaries, notebooks and other documents, as well as to thoroughly researched biographies and bibliographies, this material now exists in abundance for many major authors. In the case of, for example, Dickens, we can often ascertain what he was doing in each month and week, and almost on each day, of his prodigiously active working life; and the student of, say, *David Copperfield* is likely to find it fascinating as well as useful to know just when Dickens was at work on each part of that novel, what other literary enterprises he was engaged in at the same time, whom he was meeting, what places he was visiting, and what were the relevant circumstances of his personal and professional life. Such a chronology is not, of course, a substitute for a biography; but its arrangement, in combination with its index, makes it a much more convenient tool for this kind of purpose; and it may be acceptable as a form of 'alternative' biography, with its own distinctive advantages as well as its obvious limitations.

Since information relating to an author's early years is usually scanty and chronologically imprecise, the opening section of some volumes in this series groups together the years of childhood and adolescence. Thereafter each year, and usually each month, are dealt with separately. Information not readily assignable to a specific month or day is given as a general note at the beginning of a year's or month's entry. The first entry for each month carries an indication of the day of the week, so that when necessary this can be readily calculated for other dates. Each volume also contains a list of persons frequently referred to, with brief relevant details, and a bibliography of the principal sources of information. In the chronology itself, the sources of many of the more specific items, including quotations, are identified, in order that the reader who wishes to do so may consult the original contexts.

NORMAN PAGE

Preface

George Eliot was a writer with a fondness for chronologies: a calendar of ecclesiastical history was amongst the earliest of her literary projects; later, she employed detailed historical time charts to integrate the personal foreground with the political background of novels such as *Middlemarch* and *Felix Holt*.

In this *Chronology*, following the example of Eliot's husband and first biographer J. W. Cross, I have tried to let the authoress tell the story of her life wherever possible, quoting not only from Cross's *George Eliot's Life as Related in her Letters and Journals*, but also from Gordon S. Haight's standard and comprehensive *George Eliot: A Biography*, and the same author's monumental edition of *The George Eliot Letters*. Quotations have generally been taken from Cross's more readily available volumes; but, where Cross's dating or editing appear questionable, I have generally preferred the reading of Haight. Some standardisation of punctuation – especially with regard to the italicisation of titles – has occasionally been necessary.

Compression is inevitable in a work of this kind. Details of foreign holidays have generally been abridged, though references to further sources are provided, and the guest lists of the Saturday evening parties and Sunday afternoon At Homes at which Eliot did so much of her entertaining have usually been excluded. Most of all (though the reader may not guess it) references to Eliot's recurrent bouts of minor illness and all but hypochondriacal *malaise* have been curtailed – as the authoress herself remarked to Barbara Bodichon: 'George and I have both been suffering more than usual, but we are always grumblers, so there is no use in dwelling on what is so far from exceptional' (*Letters*, VIII, 358).

Since historical and political change are so central to Eliot's fiction, the more important historical dates of the period, taken from Helen Rex Keller's *Dictionary of Dates*, as well as the births and deaths of the major Romantic and Victorian writers, have been added to the text. The reader seeking a more detailed chronological analysis of the cultural and historical background of the period is referred to S. H. Steinberg's classic *Historical Tables*.

A question mark indicates reason for caution before confidently assigning the event mentioned to the date shown. A singular verb

xi

without subject always infers George Eliot as the subject of the sentence (as in 'Begins *Middlemarch*'), whilst a similarly subjectless plural verb implies George Henry Lewes (or, in 1880, John Walter Cross) and George Eliot as the subject (as in 'Leave for Weimar'). The unrelated personal pronouns to which this compressed sentence structure occasionally gives rise should cause the reader only the most momentary difficulty. Unless otherwise stated, 'Blackwood' refers to John Blackwood, 'Chapman' to John Chapman, 'Cross' to John Walter Cross, and 'Trollope' to Anthony Trollope. Other abbreviations are listed on a subsequent page. The Bibliography and Index contain introductory notes of their own.

The Yale University Press have kindly given permission for quotation from *The George Eliot Letters*. I am also most grateful to Mark Brafield, for expert assistance with the period 1852–8; Catherine Hands, for help with the index; Norman Page, who has been a most helpful General Editor; and Jane Smart, who did much of the typing.

T.H.

List of Abbreviations

I, II, III   Respective volumes of J. W. Cross, *George Eliot's Life, as Related in her Letters and Journals*, 'New edition', 3 vols (Edinburgh, 1885)

DNB   *Dictionary of National Biography*

GE   George Eliot

GHL   George Henry Lewes

Haight   Gordon S. Haight, *George Eliot: A Biography* (Oxford, 1968).

Letters   *The George Eliot Letters*, ed. Gordon S. Haight, 9 vols (New Haven, Conn., and London, 1954–78).

Pinney   *Essays of George Eliot*, ed. Thomas Pinney (London, 1963).

A George Eliot Chronology

Early Years (1819–1839)

1819 (Mon 22 Nov) GE born at South Farm, Arbury, near Nuneaton, Warwickshire, daughter of Robert Evans, 'the one deep strong love I have ever known' (*Letters*, ɪ, 284) and his second wife Christiana, *née* Pearson, to whom GE was not especially close. GE the youngest of his five surviving children: Robert (half-brother to GE, b. 1802), Frances (or Fanny, half-sister, b. 1805), Christiana (or Chrissey, b. 1814), and Isaac (b. 1816).

(29 Nov) Baptised at Chilvers Coton church. Six Acts introduced in Parliament.

1820 (29 Jan) Death of George III. Accession of George IV (Regent since 1811).

(Mar) The Evans family move to Griff, a neighbouring village.

1821 (16 Mar) Birth of twins William and Thomas Evans (lived only 10 days).

(17 Aug) Death of Queen Caroline.

1824 Attends Mrs Moore's dame school at Griff House with her brother Isaac, at this stage an inseparable playmate and friend. In this or the following year, Isaac sent to school at Foleshill, near Coventry, and GE sent to join her sister Chrissey at Miss Lathom's boarding school, Attleborough, near Nuneaton, where she remains a pupil until 1827.

(19 Apr) Death of Byron.

1825 (27 Sep) Opening of Stockton and Darlington railway.

1826 (18 May) Begins first journey away from home, visiting Derbyshire and Staffordshire in the company of her father and mother.

1827 (?) GE, unable to finish reading Scott's *Waverley*, begins to write out the story for herself.

(30 Apr) Canning forms a Ministry following the resignation of Lord Liverpool on grounds of ill health.

(8 Aug) Viscount Goderich becomes Prime Minister following the death of Canning.

1828   Sent to Mrs Wallington's boarding school, Nuneaton. Maria Lewis, the principal governess, of earnest Evangelical outlook, takes an immediate interest in GE, soon becoming her 'most important early influence' (Haight p. 8). GE becomes thoroughly acquainted with the Bible at this school, and witnesses Nuneaton's Evangelical arousal by John Edmund Jones, whose ministry, which begins this year, was to suggest much of 'Janet's Repentance'.

(8 Jan) Resignation of Viscount Goderich, succeeded as Prime Minister by the Duke of Wellington.

(9 May) Corporation and Test Repeal Act passed.

(5 July) O'Connell elected to Parliament.

(15 July) Corn Law Act passed, introducing sliding scale of charges for import of wheat.

1829   (13 Apr) Catholic Emancipation Act receives royal assent.

(22 Nov) Tenth birthday.

1830   (26 June) Death of George IV. Accession of William IV.

(15 Sep) William Huskisson killed by the *Rocket* at opening of Liverpool and Manchester Railroad.

(16 Nov) Duke of Wellington resigns as Prime Minister. Succeeded by Earl Grey.

1831   (1 Mar) Reform Bill introduced.

1832   Sent to the Miss Franklins' school, Coventry, where she acquires greater social accomplishments and experience, as well as furthering her academic proficiency and developing her talents as artist and pianist. Makes her first acquaintance with many English authors. Reading most notably includes Shakespeare, Milton, Watts, Pope, Young, Cowper, Southey, Moore and Byron. Especially distinguishes herself in English composition.

(7 June) Reform Bill receives royal assent.

(21 Dec) Two days of rioting, witnessed by GE, and subsequently influential on the composition of *Felix Holt*, begin at Nuneaton during the election for the North Warwickshire constituency.

1833   (14 July) Keble's Assize sermon, marking the beginning of the Oxford Movement.

(23 Aug) Act for Abolition of Slavery passed.

(29 Aug) Shaftesbury's Factory Act passed.

1834 (16 Mar) School notebook, containing essay on Affectation and Conceit, and story 'Edward Neville' (Haight, pp. 553–60) begun.

(16 July) Viscount Melbourne forms Ministry following resignation of Grey.

(25 July) Death of Coleridge.

(14 Aug) Poor Law Amendment Act approved.

(15 Nov) Melbourne's Ministry dismissed.

(22 Nov) Fifteenth birthday. About this time has Evangelical conversion experience: 'One feels certain that it struck Mary Anne suddenly and hard' (Haight, p. 19). Begins to neglect her personal appearance in order to demonstrate her anxiety for the state of her soul.

(9 Dec) Peel forms Ministry.

1835 (8 Apr) Peel's Ministry resigns.

(18 Apr) Melbourne forms his second Ministry.

(July) Health of GE's mother is declined sufficiently for Robert Evans to take her out in a four-wheeled carriage rather than a gig.

(Dec) Leaves the Miss Franklins' school.

(31 Dec) Robert Evans suffers acute attack of kidney stone, an illness from which he never completely recovers.

1836 (6 Jan) Apologises for failing to send Maria Lewis details of her mother's health, the reason being her father's sudden illness.

(3 Feb) Death of her mother. GE soon begins to supply the loss in her father's life.

(25 Dec) Receives Holy Communion for the first time.

1837 (30 May) Acts as bridesmaid for Chrissey at her wedding to Edward Clarke, a medical practitioner at Meriden, near Coventry. Becomes her father's housekeeper as a result of Chrissey's departure.

(20 June) Death of William IV. Accession of Queen Victoria.

1838 Reading, especially of religious works, very considerable at this time. Reputation as a learned lady begins to spread in the neighbourhood, Henry Harpur, squire of Chilvers Coton, lending her some of the *Tracts for the Times*, and Maria Newdegate offering the use of the Arbury Hall library.

(26 May) Invites Maria Lewis to stay with her in the coming holidays.

(18 Aug) Sends Maria Lewis details of a recent week-long visit to London with Isaac, with whom she went to services at St Bride's and St Paul's, but refused to attend the theatre.

(4 Sep) Writes to Martha Jackson, declaring that it is the duty of Christians 'to aim as perseveringly at perfection as if they believed it soon to be attainable' and condemning a recently heard oratorio concert in Coventry (*Letters*, I, 9).

(18 Sep) Anti Corn Law League founded.

(6 Nov) Tells Maria Lewis, 'I am generally in the same predicament with books as a glutton with his feast' (I, 43), current reading including Robert Leighton's *A Practical Commentary upon the First Two Chapters of the First Epistle of St Peter* and *The Life of William Wilberforce* by R. I. and S. Wilberforce. Repeated condemnation of the Coventry oratorio symptomatic of her religious zeal at this period: 'It would not cost me any regrets if the only music heard in our land were that of strict worship' (I, 44).

(Dec) Publication of Charles Hennell's *An Inquiry into the Origins of Christianity*.

1839 Visited at Griff for two to three weeks early in the year by her Methodist aunt, Elizabeth Evans, with whom she debates predestination. The germ of *Adam Bede* develops from Elizabeth Evans's story of persuading a young child-murderer to die penitent.

Later in the year, begins to compile a chronological chart of ecclesiastical history.

Begins Italian lessons with Joseph Brezzi.

(6 Feb) Solicits her aunt Elizabeth to send news of herself.

(27 Feb) Writes to Maria Lewis, copying out in the letter Ryland's hymn 'Sovereign Ruler of the Skies'.

(5 Mar) Tells her aunt Elizabeth, 'I feel that my besetting sin is . . . ambition, a desire insatiable for the esteem of my fellow-creatures' (I, 49).

(16 Mar) Sends a lengthy and earnest letter to Maria Lewis questioning the expedience of reading fiction: 'As to the discipline our minds receive from the perusal of fictions, I can conceive none that is beneficial but may be attained by that of history' (I, 52–3).

(20 May) Disapproves of the Tractarian movement in letter to

Maria Lewis. Reading John Hoppus, *Schism as Opposed to Unity of the Church*; Joseph Milner, *The History of the Church of Christ*; and William Gresley, *Portrait of an English Churchman*.

(July) Visited at Griff by Jessie Barclay, a schoolfriend, one of several such visitors at this time.

(17 July) Sends Maria Lewis a poem, 'As o'er the Fields', 'the crude fruit of a lonely walk last evening, when the words of one of our martyrs occurred to me' (I, 57).

(4 Sep) Sends Maria Lewis another early work, the sonnet 'Oft, when a child' (*Letters*, I, 30).

(Nov) With her father, and accompanied by Jessie Barclay, visits London for five days, making her first journey by railway.

(22 Nov) Twentieth birthday. Reading Wordsworth: 'I never before met with so many of my own feelings expressed just as I could like them' (I, 61).

1840

Robert Evans begins to consider retirement. GE returns increasingly to the works of the Romantic poets, many not studied since the time of her conversion experience.

January
'As o'er the Fields' appears in the *Christian Observer*, GE's first published work.
10 (Fri) Penny post established.
14 Reading includes Milton's 'Nativity Ode' and Anna Jameson's *Winter Studies and Summer Rambles in Canada*. Tells Martha Jackson that she has been reflecting on 'the duty of perfect contentment with such things as we have' (*Letters*, I, 37).

February
10 (Mon) Queen Victoria marries Albert of Saxe-Coburg.
13 Reading includes G. P. R. James, *The Life and Times of Louis XIV*; Edwin Sidney, *The Life of Sir Richard Hill*; and William Scrope, *Days and Nights of Deer Stalking*. Tells Maria Lewis, 'A foreign war would soon put an end to our national humours, that are growing to so alarming a head' (I, 81).
26 Writes to her uncle Samuel, 'I have been much exposed to temptation from contact with worldly persons . . . I have great

need of your prayers, and I fear not that I shall be denied
them' (*Letters*, I, 40).

March
Buys Keble's *Christian Year*. Begins taking German lessons.
13   (Fri) Tells Maria Lewis of progress with the chart of ecclesiasti-
     cal history, and asks advice on the formation of a clothing
     club. Mentions attack of hysteria at a party.
30   Sends Maria Lewis an outline of the historical chart, and refers
     enigmatically to the recent breaking-off of a romance (probably
     with a young man not of her own religious suasion). She
     repressed her feelings by a 'prayer to be free from rebelling
     against Him whose I am by right' (*Letters*, I, 46). Some High
     Church reading at this time, including the *Tracts for the Times*
     and the *Lyra Apostolica*.

April
?6   (Mon) Proposes that Martha Jackson always suggest in her
     letters a subject for intellectual debate: 'You will polish and
     sharpen me, will you not? Alas: I need melting and remoulding'
     (*Letters*, I, 48).
10   Writes a lengthy letter of sympathy to Edith Kittermaster,
     following the death of her sister Jane.

May
28   (Thurs) Rereading Byron's *Childe Harold*. Discovers that a rival
     chart of ecclesiastical history has just been published – plans
     for her own chart subsequently abandoned. Tells Maria Lewis,
     'I am a negation of all that finds love and esteem' (*Letters*, I,
     51).

June
2   (Tues) Birth of Thomas Hardy.
10   Asks Maria Lewis to obtain Italian books for her in London.
18   Arrives with her father at Wirksworth, Derbyshire, where they
     stay with her uncle Samuel and aunt Elizabeth at the beginning
     of a week's tour. Comparative lack of enjoyment of this visit
     indicative of the growth of her religious doubts: 'I think I
     was simply less devoted to religious ideas' she subsequently
     recalled (*Letters*, III, 176).
19   Move on to stay with William Evans.

22   Return to Griff.
23   Writes to Maria Lewis about her recent journey.

July
 6   (Mon) Tells Maria Lewis that she and her father intend moving
     to Coventry.
23   Reading *Don Quixote*, and asks Maria Lewis to obtain a copy
     of *The Faerie Queene*.
30   Under the *nom de plume* of Clematis asks Martha Jackson (or
     'Ivy') to visit her.

August
10   (Mon) Tells her uncle Samuel, 'I cannot for her own sake
     regret that my dear Aunt is so near the very brink of Jordan'
     (*Letters*, i, 61).
12   Reading Isaac Taylor's *Ancient Christianity, and the Doctrines of
     the Oxford Tracts for the Times*.

September
17   (Thurs) Praises Shelley's 'The Cloud' in letter to Maria Lewis.
23   Begins four-day visit with Isaac to his fiancée Sarah Rawlins
     at Edgbaston, near Birmingham.
24   Hears performance of *Messiah* in Birmingham.

October
 1   (Thurs) Reading includes Tasso, and Schiller's *Mary Stuart*.
     Delighted by Wordsworth's 'Power of Sound'.
20   Writes to Martha Jackson, 'Every day's experience seems to
     deepen the voice of foreboding that has long been telling me,
     "the bliss of reciprocated affection is not alloted to you under
     any form"' (*Letters*, i, 70).
27   Reading poetry by Felicia Hemans, and John Harris's *Great
     Teacher*. Tells Maria Lewis that she has adopted *Certum pete
     finem* ('Seek a sure end') as her motto.

November
22   (Mon) Twenty-first birthday.

1841

January

15 (Fri) Inspects possible new house (Bird Grove, at Foleshill) with her father, who agrees to purchase it.

27 Visits the Nicholas Chamberlaine Hospital, an almshouse near Griff. Reports having recently read Erskine Neale's *Life-Book of a Labourer*.

February

8 (Mon) With her father, buys furniture for their new home.

March

4 (Thurs) Tells Martha Jackson that she has read Buckland's *Treatise on Geology* with much pleasure.

9 Regrets that preparations for the move to Foleshill have prevented her writing sooner to her uncle Samuel.

17 Isaac drives GE to Foleshill to prepare for her father's arrival.

19 Robert Evans arrives at Foleshill.

April

11 (Sun) Receives Easter Day communion with her father at Trinity Church, Coventry, where they become regular attenders.

May

20 (Thurs) Suggests that Maria Lewis might become governess to the Whittem family. Tells Martha Jackson of her delight in reading Isaac Taylor's *Physical Theory of Another Life*.

June

3 (Thurs) Robert Evans takes GE and Chrissey to see their half-sister, Fanny Houghton, at Baginton, near Coventry.

7 Travels to Edgbaston with Isaac.

8 Acts as bridesmaid at Isaac's wedding to Sarah Rawlins. The couple honeymoon in the Lakes and Scotland before returning to live at Griff.

9 Visits Chrissey at Meriden.

20 Drives to Kenilworth with her father to hear Henry Montagu Villiers (later Bishop of Durham) preach his final missionary sermon in the parish.

July

21 (Wed) Agrees with Maria Lewis's determination to advertise for a position.

31 Tells Maria Lewis 'I am beginning to be interlaced with multiplying ties of duty and affection that, while they render my new home happier, forbid me to leave it on a pleasure-seeking expedition' (I, 89).

August

12 (Thurs) Tells Maria Lewis of the force of her realisation that she is *'alone* in the world' (I, 88).

21 Thanks Maria Lewis for obtaining books for her (including Chalmers' *Sermons*) in London.

September

Reading John Pye Smith's *Relation between the Holy Scripture and Some Parts of Geological Science*: 'the main subject of the work . . . is fully satisfactory to me' (*Letters*, I, 110).

3 (Fri) In a letter to Maria Lewis analyses the parable of the sower, and recommends Henry Hallam's *Introduction to the Literature of Europe*, remarking, 'I love words; they are the quoits, the bows, the staves that furnish the gymnasium of the mind' (I, 91).

6 Formation of Peel's second Ministry.

October

2 (Sat) Sends her uncle Samuel favourable news of her father and brother.

16 Asks Maria Lewis if she would object to becoming governess to a Nonconformist family, and bewails her own lack of social involvement: 'I am supine and stupid . . . while the haggard looks and piercing glance of want and conscious hopelessness are to be seen in the streets' (*Letters*, I, 116).

November

2 (Tues) Taken to visit Charles and Caroline Bray at their house, Rosehill, overlooking Coventry, by Charles Bray's sister, Elizabeth Pears, a neighbour of the Evanses at Foleshill. Immediately becomes attracted to them. 'It is impossible to overestimate the importance of Mary Ann's introduction to the Brays . . . She was quickly brought from provincial isolation into touch

with the world of ideas' (Haight, pp. 44, 46). Reads Charles Hennell's *Inquiry* as a result of this introduction.

13   Writes to Maria Lewis, 'My whole soul has been engrossed in the most interesting of all inquiries for the last few days, and to what results my thoughts may lead, I know not – possibly to one that will startle you' (I, 103).

December

16   (Thurs) Recommends Carlyle's *Sartor Resartus* to Martha Jackson.

27   Maria Lewis (who had stayed over Christmas) and Robert Evans temporarily leave Foleshill.

1842

January

1   (Sat) Urges Maria Lewis to return to Foleshill and to stay for as long as she wishes. Maria Lewis arrives in the evening.

2   GE refuses to accompany her father and Maria Lewis to church, her first familial display of her religious change of heart, causing several subsequent pleas to change her mind, from both family and friends.

14   Maria Lewis leaves Foleshill for her new school at Nuneaton.

16   Again refuses to accompany her father to church.

24   Robert Evans pays his son-in-law Edward Clarke £250 to purchase a house, the commencement of money troubles which may have suggested those of Lydgate in *Middlemarch*.

28   Discusses her new religious feelings in letter to Elizabeth Pears: 'I wish to be among the ranks of that glorious crusade that is seeking to set Truth's Holy Sepulchre free from a usurped domination' (I, 106).

February

18   (Fri) Tells Maria Lewis, 'having had my propensities, sentiments, and intellect gauged a second time, I am pronounced to possess a large organ of "adhesiveness", a still larger one of "firmness", and as large of "conscientiousness"' (I, 107–8).

24   Has her conduct reproved by her brother Isaac.

28   Writes to her father, announcing her determination not 'visibly

to unite myself with any Christian community' and offering
to leave Foleshill should he wish (*Letters*, i, 128).

March

3   (Thurs) Robert Evans plans to leave Foleshill, chiefly as a result
of his daughter's conduct.

6   Writes to Cara Bray, regretting condemnation of the Evans
family in an interview of that morning.

12   Advises Cara Bray that it would be unwise for Elizabeth Pears
to seek an interview with Robert Evans. Considering leaving
her father and supporting herself by teaching in Leamington.

23   Robert Evans, succumbing to the pleas of Rebecca Franklin
and Elizabeth Pears, sends GE to live with Isaac at Griff. GE
recalls, 'I came hither . . . in compliance with my Father's
wish that I should retire for a time from a neighbourhood in
which I had been placed on the very comfortable pedestal of
the town gazing-stock' (*Letters*, i, 138).

26   Robert Evans postpones the sale of his house.

31   GE tells Elizabeth Pears that 'on a retrospection of the past
month, I regret nothing so much as my own impetuosity' (i,
112).

April

11   (Mon) Writes to Francis Watts, professor of theology at Spring
Hill College, Birmingham, discussing her doubts, and expressing her desire to translate R. A. Vinet's *Mémoire en faveur de
la liberté des cultes*.

20   Tells Cara Bray that Robert Evans has agreed to GE's return
to him after a time.

30   Following an agreement to attend church with her father
(whilst tacitly withholding assent from the worship), GE
returns to Foleshill. Cross records, 'In the last year of her life
[GE] told me that, although she did not think she had been to
blame, few things had occasioned her more regret than this
temporary collision with her father, which might, she thought,
have been avoided by a little management' (i, 113).

May

1   (Sun) Visits Cara Bray at Rosehill, and is shown letters from
her brother, Charles Hennell.

15   Attends church with her father.

22   Again attends church with her father.
27   Invites Maria Lewis to visit Foleshill in the coming holiday.

June
12   (Sun) Death of Thomas Arnold.

July
3   (Sun) Sara Hennell arrives for a six-week stay at Rosehill. GE introduced to her during this month, and visits Rosehill when able to leave her father. Cross remarks, 'The two ladies – Cara and Sara . . . – now became like sisters to Miss Evans, and Mr Bray her most intimate male friend' (i, 114).
30   Edward Clarke and his family, still in financial difficulties, arrive for a three-day visit to Foleshill.

August
3   (Wed) Tells Francis Watts, 'It seems to me that the awful anticipations entailed by a reception of all the dogmas in the New Testament operate unfavourably on moral beauty' (*Letters*, i, 144).
12   Sara Hennell leaves Rosehill.
30   Thanks Sara Hennell for writing to her.

September
16   (Fri) Reading the *Aeneid*.

October
Elizabeth (or 'Rufa') Brabant and Charles Hennell visit Rosehill, GE finding great pleasure in their company.
20   (Thurs) Tells Sara Hennell that she has again met W. B. Ullathorne at Rosehill.

November
4   (Fri) Resumes correspondence with Martha Jackson, left off because GE feared that her new opinions might give offence. Reports that her life is now 'peaceful and happy to a degree that I little anticipated some months ago' (*Letters*, i, 152).
23   Sends birthday greetings to Sara Hennell, the first of many exchanges of birthday letters between them.

December
25   (Sun) The assembled Evans family discuss the desirability of GE's further association with the Bray circle.

1843

January
Begins to translate an unspecified work by Spinoza for Cara Bray.

February
22   (Wed) Cara Bray records Robert Evans's refusal to carry out Isaac Evans's plan of moving from Foleshill to Meriden, so that GE may be removed from the Brays' influence.

March
?15   (Wed) Assures Sara Hennell of sympathetic thoughts during the final days of Mary Hennell's life.
16   Death of Mary Hennell.

May
In the middle of this month, tours for five days with the Brays and Sara and Charles Hennell, visiting Stratford, Malvern and Worcester.

July
13   (Thurs) Sets out with the Brays, the Hennells and Rufa Brabant for three-week holiday, visiting Bristol, Tenby, Pembroke and Swansea. Rufa Brabant and Charles Hennell renew their engagement during this trip.

August
2   (Wed) Returns to Foleshill.

September
15   (Fri) Dines with Robert Owen at Rosehill: 'I think if his system prosper it will be in spite of its founder' she reports to Sara Hennell (i, 119).
16   Thanks Sara Hennell for procuring her a copy of *Hymns and Anthems*, edited by W. J. Fox.

October

9   (Mon) Sends Sara Hennell a lengthy letter about loss of faith, stressing 'the *truth of feeling*, as the only universal bond of union' (I, 122).

28   Arrives in London, where she enjoys some sightseeing both before and after the Brabant–Hennell wedding.

November

1   (Wed) Acts as bridesmaid at the wedding of Rufa Brabant to Charles Hennell at Finsbury.

7   Goes to stay at Devizes, Wiltshire, with Dr Brabant, who may have suggested features of Casaubon in *Middlemarch*.

8   Sends Cara Bray a favourable account of her reception by the Brabants.

20   Again enthuses about the Brabants in a letter to Cara Bray: 'I am in a little heaven here, Dr Brabant being its archangel . . . I am never weary of his company' (*Letters*, I, 165). Her relationship with Brabant, 'an intellectual friendship drawn by over-ready expansiveness into feelings misunderstood' (Haight, p. 52), begins to assume a proleptic character.

30   Tells Cara Bray that her return to Coventry is imminent, though concealing the problems caused by Dr Brabant's affection for her.

December

4   (Mon) Returns to Coventry from Devizes, indignant at Dr Brabant's ungenerous behaviour after his wife's insistence that GE should leave the house.

1844

January

Agrees to complete Rufa Hennell's translation of D. F. Strauss's *Das Leben Jesu* (*The Life of Jesus*).

February

22   (Thurs) Cornelius Donovan gives GE and Charles Bray a lesson in phrenology.

March

3 (Sun) Asks Sara Hennell to clarify who is providing the funding for the Strauss translation, and whether the manuscript is to be sent directly to the publisher.

18 Hears Daniel O'Connell speak in Coventry.

April

Delighted to hear from Charles Hennell that arrangements for the publication of *Life of Jesus* have been satisfactorily concluded, and requests Sara Hennell to send further passages for translation.

June

18 (Tues) Thanks Cara Bray for sending an account of her visit to Clapton, East London.

30 Leaves with the Brays for seventeen-day holiday at the Cumberland lakes, visiting James Martineau and his family in Manchester on the journey home. For Cara Bray's account of the trip see *Letters*, i, 178–80.

July

22 (Mon) Begins three-day trip with Bray to London, where they visit a phrenologist, James Deville.

28 Birth of Gerard Manley Hopkins.

September

14 (Sat) Writes to Sara Hennell regretting the long gap since they last saw each other.

October

Begins giving German lessons to Mary Sibree.

31 (Thurs) Tells Sara Hennell that she hopes to have finished vol. i of *Life of Jesus* by the end of November. Apologises to Martha Jackson for the long gap in their correspondence.

1845

March

Meets a young artist, whose name remains unknown, at Baginton, and passes two days in his company. Agrees to exchange letters, but refuses to become engaged to him.

26 (Wed) Visited by the young artist, but her interest in him
    subsides.
27 Writes to break off their relationship.

April
6   (Sun) Writes to Sara Hennell: 'My unfortunate "affaire" . . . I
    have now dismissed . . . from my mind, and only keep it
    recorded in my book of reference, article "Precipitancy, ill
    effects of"' (*Letters*, i, 185). Also oppressed by her translation
    work.
?16 Tells Sara Hennell that vol. ii of *Life of Jesus* is now completed.
17 First meeting with Harriet Martineau: 'She is a charming
    person – quite one of those people whom one does not
    venerate the less for having seen' (*Letters*, i, 189).
21 Writes to Martha Jackson, giving details of her translation
    work and mentioning her ended involvement with the young
    artist.
29 Thanks Sarah Hennell for her painstaking assistance with the
    copy-editing of *Life of Jesus*.

May
25 (Sun) Writes to Cara Bray, giving her comments on Disraeli's
    Sybil.

June
2   (Mon) Begins three-day trip to London with Bray.
12 Goes with the Brays to see Macready in *Julius Caesar* at
    Birmingham.

September
25 (Thurs) Delighted with first section of proof of *Life of Jesus*.

October
9   (Thurs) Newman received into the Roman Catholic Church.
12 Forced to withdraw from the Brays' projected trip to Scotland
    because of the bankruptcy of her brother-in-law Edward
    Clarke.
14 At the last minute, intervention by Bray enables GE to
    accompany the Brays on their holiday, visiting Liverpool
    (where they renew contact with the Martineaus), Glasgow,
    Loch Lomond, Loch Katrine, Stirling, Edinburgh and Abbots-

ford. Cara Bray remarks, 'We were all in ecstasies, but Mary Anne's were beyond everything' (*Letters*, i, 201).

24 Learns of her father's broken leg.

28 Arrives home.

December

18 (Thurs) Complains to Sara Hennell about quality of printing of Greek in *Life of Jesus* proof.

1846

Acute famine in Ireland, caused by failure of the potato crop.

January

26 (Mon) Explains to Sarah Hennell that the illness of herself and her father has impeded translation work.

February

14 (Sat) Cara Bray reports that GE has not enjoyed 'dissecting the beautiful story of the crucifixion' and is nervous about public reception of her translation. Her father's illness has also been a cause of anxiety (i, 139).

March

Corresponds with Sara Hennell about the use of the words 'sacrament' and 'dogmatics'.

4 (Wed) Tells Sara Hennell that she has not enjoyed translating Strauss's accounts of the crucifixion and resurrection of Jesus, or the bursting asunder of Judas.

April

Decides to commence vol. iii with the Passion, finishes correcting proofs, and sends *Life of Jesus* to Strauss for his approval and a preface.

27 (Mon) Delighted by Strauss's preface to her translation.

May

26 (Tues) Begins eleven-day visit to Sara Hennell in Clapton.

June
Bray buys the Coventry *Herald*.
15 (Mon) *Life of Jesus* published by Chapman. Varied reading
    following the completion of this translation includes Shake-
    speare, Milton, Wordsworth, Dickens, Thackeray, Carlyle,
    Goethe, Disraeli, Rousseau and Sand.
26 Corn Importation Act receives royal assent.

July
Visits Dover with her father for a fortnight, and becomes considerably distressed by the deterioration in his health.
 6 (Mon) Lord John Russell forms his first Ministry following the
    resignation of Peel.

September
25 (Fri) Sara Hennell remarks that GE 'must be writing her novel',
    an engimatic speculation (*Letters*, i, 233).

October
 5 (Mon) Reports herself in high spirits to Sara Hennell, asking
    her to write more frequently.
21 Writes a burlesquely humorous letter to Charles Bray, imagin-
    ing herself proposed to by Professor Bücherworm of Moderig
    University.
30 Review of *Christianity in its Various Aspects*, by Quinet, of *The
    Jesuits*, by Quinet and Michelet, and of *Priests, Women and
    Families*, by Michelet alone, appears in the Coventry *Herald*.

November
 4 (Wed) Review of Gilbert à Beckett's *Comic History of England*
    appears in the *Herald*.
 5 Tells Sara Hennell that she would like to complete her collection
    of Xenophon's works, and reassures her about the extent of
    her regard for Brabant: 'If ever I offered incense to him it was
    because there was no other deity at hand' (*Letters*, i, 225).
15 Expresses her qualified satisfaction with the review of *Life of
    Jesus* in the *Prospective Review*: 'The praise it gives to the
    translation is just what I should have wished' (i, 150).
26 Discusses St Luke's account of the Emmaus Road in letter to
    Sara Hennell.

December

4 (Fri) 'Introductory', the first instalment of 'Poetry and Prose from the Notebook of an Eccentric' appears in the Coventry *Herald*.

20 Thanks Sara Hennell for the opportunity of seeing her manuscript *Heliados*.

25 Over Christmas GE makes her final break with Maria Lewis, who is staying for a fortnight.

1847

January

15 (Mon) 'How to Avoid Disappointment', the second instalment of 'Poetry and Prose from the Notebook of an Eccentric', appears in the *Herald*.

February

5 (Fri) Third instalment, 'The Wisdom of a Child', appears in the *Herald*.

12 The *Herald* publishes the fourth instalment, 'A Little Fable with a *Great Moral*'.

19 The *Herald* publishes the final instalment, 'Hints on Snubbing'.

26 'Vice and Sausages', a satirical piece on the Coventry police inspector John Vice, appears in the *Herald*.

28 Tells Sara Hennell, 'Mr Chapman . . . was always too much of the *interesting* gentleman to please me. Men must not attempt to be interesting on any lower terms than a high poetical genius' (*Letters*, i, 231).

April

24 (Sat) Begins five-day visit to London with Charles Bray.

28 Attends performance of Mendelssohn's *Elijah* at the Exeter Hall.

29 Sees Bellini's *I Puritani* at Her Majesty's Theatre.

May

10 (Mon) Gives Mary Sibree an account of her London trip.

June

17 (Thurs) Sara Hennell begins a two-day visit to GE, remarking

that GE 'grows better and wiser every time I see her' (*Letters*, i, 235).

August
At the beginning of this month, declines to visit Germany with Dr Brabant.

September
16   (Thurs) After rereading Charles Hennell's *Inquiry*, sends Sara Hennell a lengthy appreciation of the work: 'I think the *Inquiry* furnishes the utmost that can be done towards obtaining a real view of the life and character of Jesus' (i, 165).
27   Takes her father to the Isle of Wight to improve his health.

October
 3   (Sun) Sends the Brays a cheerful account of her Isle of Wight visit.
 6   Takes her father to Brighton.
 9   Returns from the Isle of Wight.
13   Describes Alum Bay and Brighton in letter to Sara Hennell. Reading Richardson's *Sir Charles Grandison* with enthusiasm.

November
27   (Sat) Tells Sara Hennell of two new readers of Strauss – a Leamington lady (probably Caroline Congreve) and John Sibree, remarking, 'I confess to a fit of destructiveness just now which might have been more easily gratified if I had lived in the days of iconoclasm' (*Letters*, i, 241).

1848

January
Reading George Sand's *Lettres d'un voyageur*.

February
11   (Sat) Sends lengthy letter, including discussion of *Tancred* and Judaism, to John Sibree, with whom she had begun to correspond late in 1847.
21   Death of Leonard Clarke, nephew, aged nine months.

22 Revolution breaks out in France, leading to the establishment of the Second Republic.

March
8 (Wed) Pleased to note John Sibree's agreement with her enthusiasm for the French revolution, also giving her own opinions on British reform: 'there is nothing in our Constitution to obstruct the slow progress of *political* reform. This is all we are fit for at present . . . we English are slow crawlers' (I, 181).

April
10 (Mon) Demonstration in London following the presentation of the Chartist petition.
11 Has tooth withdrawn after chloroform.
14 Delighted to hear of Sara Hennell's encounter with Emerson.
17 Worried by deterioration in her father's health.
26 Reports to Sara Hennell a decided improvement in her father's health.

May
?14 (Sun) Writes to congratulate John Sibree on abandoning his training for the ministry: 'It was impossible to think of your career with hope, while you tacitly subscribed to the miserable *etiquette* . . . of sectarianism' (I, 183).
25 Tells Fanny Houghton that their father's health is now sufficiently recovered for him to be able to contemplate a recuperative visit to the coast.
29 Takes her father to St Leonards, Sussex.
31 Tells the Brays that her father's health fared better on the journey down than her own did.

June
5 (Mon) Reading Scott's *Fair Maid of Perth* to her father.
8 Writes to the Brays and Hennells deploring the impeachment of the French revolutionary Louis Blanc, and angry because 'society is training men and women for hell' (I, 190).
11 Reports decline in her father's health to Bray, recording also her disapproval of *Jane Eyre*.
16 Returns with her father from St Leonards.
23 Tells Sara Hennell, 'I am entering on a new period of my life, which makes me look back on the past as something incredibly

poor and contemptible.' Comments also on the fall of the
French Socialist party: 'Paris, poor Paris – alas! alas!' (I, 190,
191).

July
Robert Evans's health continues to decline, GE nursing him through
the coming months to her own physical disadvantage.
13   (Thurs) Introduced by the Brays to Emerson: 'the first *man* I
     have ever seen' (I, 191). The party visit Stratford, Emerson
     becoming much impressed by GE: 'That young lady has a
     calm, serious soul' (Haight, p. 66)

August
12   (Sat) Death of George Stephenson.

September
11   (Mon) Cara Bray tells Sara Hennell that Robert Evans's death
     appears imminent.

1849

January
Tells Sara Hennell, 'I am suffering perhaps as acutely as ever I did
in my life' (I, 194).

February
 4   (Sun) Writes to Sara Hennell, admiring Macaulay and Sand,
     and reporting, 'My body is the defaulter – consciously so. I
     triumph over all things in the spirit, but the flesh is weak, and
     disgraces itself by headaches and backaches' (I, 196). Tells her
     sister Fanny, 'We may satirise characters and qualities in the
     abstract without injury to our moral nature, but persons hardly
     ever' (I, 195–6).
 9   Sends lengthy appreciation of Rousseau and Sand to Sara
     Hennell.

March
10   (Sat) Begins to translate Spinoza's *Tractatus theologico-politicus*
     (the translation has not been found).
16   Review of J. A. Froude's *Nemesis of Faith* appears in the *Herald*.

22   Froude congratulates GE on her review, with some affection.

April
18   (Wed) Tells Sara Hennell of her admiration for *Nemesis of Faith*
     and recommends Froude's *Shadows of the Clouds*.
25   Reports her father much deteriorated in health.

May
 6   (Sun) Reading F. W. Newman's *The Soul*, and expresses her
     enthusiasm for the author in a letter to Sara Hennell.
10   Tells Elizabeth Pears that Robert Evans has remembered her
     with gratitude and affection, adding that 'my chair by father's
     bedside is a very blessed seat to me' (i, 203).
31   Death of Robert Evans: 'What shall I be without my father? It
     will seem as if a part of my moral nature were gone' (i, 205).

June
 5   (Tues) Requests Bray's advice and help.
 6   Robert Evans buried at Chilvers Coton.
 7   Meets J. A. Froude.
12   Leaves with the Brays for continental tour, visiting France,
     Italy and Switzerland, in which she eventually decides to
     winter. Begins her Journal.

July
25   (Tues) The Brays return home, leaving GE at Geneva.
27   Sends Bray an account of her life in a *pension* owned by a
     Madame de Vallière.

August
 5   (Sun) Sends the Brays and Sara Hennell further details of her
     new environment, also asking them, 'Pray that the motto of
     Geneva may become mine – "Post tenebras lux"' (i, 213).
20   Tells the Brays and Sara Hennell that she has not yet decided
     whether or not to spend the winter in Switzerland.
28   Informs the same correspondents that she has now decided
     on staying: 'I am really good for nothing yet, and I feel that
     my future health and actions entirely depend on my recovering
     thoroughly my strength and spirit' (*Letters*, i, 301).

September
6   (Thurs) Implores Fanny Houghton to write to her.
13 Asks the Brays to give her address only to friends as close as themselves.
20 Informs the Brays that she will return to England in the spring, also including details of her friendship with Madame de Ludwigsdorff. Reports that Charles Bray has remarked 'there is much that is morbid in your character . . . with a dwelling on yourself, and a longing to think of yourself unhappy' (*Letters*, i, 307).
21 Birth of Edmund Gosse.

October
4   (Thurs) Tells Fanny Houghton and the Brays that she has decided to lodge with F. D'Albert-Durade, a Genevan painter.
9   Moves to lodge with D'Albert.
11 Gives the Brays a favourable description of her new surroundings. Reports that she has had a letter from Mary Sibree: 'a good sweet girl, but her ideas want testing' (*Letters*, i, 315).
22 Thirtieth birthday.
24 Enthuses about D'Albert in a letter to the Brays: 'I have not heard a word or seen a gesture of his yet that was not perfectly in harmony with an exquisite moral refinement' (i, 233–4).
26 Tells Sara Hennell, 'I have always had a hankering after this sort of life, and I find it was a true instinct of what would suit me' (i, 237).

December
4   (Tues) Tells the Brays that lack of health has obliged her to suspend work on the Spinoza translation, and confesses to Sara Hennell that she is becoming 'passionately attached' to her life in Geneva (i, 241).
22 Sends seasonal greetings to the Brays and Sara Hennell.

1850

January
28 (Mon) Urges the Brays to write to her.

February

4 (Mon) Requests a letter from Fanny Houghton, who has not written for five months.

9 Thanks Fanny Houghton for her letter, and announces intention of returning to England in late March or early April.

15 Tells the Brays that D'Albert is painting her portrait, and that 'I go to the Genevese churches every Sunday, and nourish my heterodoxy with orthodox sermons' (i, 247).

March

1 (Fri) Informs Bray that she may now leave Geneva as early as mid-March.

18 Accompanied by D'Albert, leaves Geneva for England.

25 Reunited with the Brays at Rosehill, but re-encounters with her family subsequently distress her.

30 Tells Fanny Houghton, 'I am sad at the sight of my own country, and feel more of an outcast here than at Geneva' (*Letters*, i, 333).

April

Spends most of April and beginning of May visiting relations at Griff and Meriden.

4 (Thurs) Tells Martha Jackson that her homecoming has been painful and that she is uncertain whether she will remain in England or return to Geneva.

11 Asks Sara Hennell to send details of the accommodation offered by Chapman, also remarking, 'Oh the dismal weather, and the dismal country, and the dismal people' (i, 252).

23 Death of Wordsworth.

May

1 (Wed) Tells Cara Bray that although Chrissey has been kind to her, she is delighted to feel of no importance to the rest of the Evans family, and has no motive for living amongst them.

4 Begins an eight-day stay at Rosehill.

7 Entertains D'Albert at Rosehill for four days.

June

4 (Tues) Makes Rosehill her base for the next six months.

July
2   (Tues) Death of Peel.

September
2   (Mon) Death of Charles Hennell.
30 Papal Bull issued creating Roman Catholic bishops in England.

October
Introduced by Chapman to R. W. Mackay. Agrees to review the latter's *Progress of the Intellect*.

November
18 (Mon) Delivers review of *Progress of the Intellect* to Chapman, lodging with him for two weeks, and deciding to make writing her career.
30 Meets Eliza Lynn Linton at Chapman's. Tells the Brays that she has enjoyed her stay at Chapman's and is to visit him again in January.

December
2   (Mon) Returns from London.

1851

January
Review of Mackay's *Progress of the Intellect* appears in the *Westminster Review*.
8   (Wed) Returns to lodge with Chapman, increasing her artistic and social knowledge, but deepening his domestic difficulties.
24 Attends lecture by Faraday.
26 Dines at Mackay's with the Chapmans, Arnott and Leslie.
28 Tells the Brays of her visits to lectures by Faraday and F. W. Newman.

March
3   (Mon) Lord John Russell returns to office, following Stanley's failure to form a Ministry.
13 Sees collection of paintings by Turner owned by B. G. Windus.
24 Leaves Chapman, perhaps as a result of some indiscretion, but continues to correspond with him. Returns to Rosehill.

April

4 (Fri) Returns to Chapman letters from his wife reproving his conduct with GE, enclosing comments of her own. Agrees to continue to provide a *catalogue raisonné* of Chapman's more important publications, though insisting that he make clear to his wife that the work is undertaken at his request.

18 Chapman receives letter from GE consenting to abridge Strauss for £100 (a project Chapman never pursued), and revealing that she is beginning to get greater enjoyment from work on the catalogue.

29 Chapman forwards to his wife a letter from GE, and hopes that GE and Susanna Chapman will now become better disposed towards each other.

May

Chapman buys the *Westminster Review*.

1 (Thurs) Great Exhibition opens.

9 Agrees to write an article on W. R. Greg's *The Creed of Christendom* and Charles Hennell's *Inquiry* for the *Westminster*. Sends Chapman an account of James Martineau's *The Rationale of Religious Inquiry* for inclusion in his catalogue.

27 Chapman arrives for a fortnight at Rosehill, proposing that GE should assist him in editing the *Westminster*.

31 Meets Thornton Leigh Hunt at Rosehill, where he stays the weekend.

June

2 (Mon) Writes the prospectus for the *Westminster*.

5 GE and Chapman make a 'solemn and holy vow' to bind them to 'the right' (Haight, p. 91).

9 Suggests to Chapman that he should give out that he employs an editor whilst himself retaining editorial responsibility.

12 Advises Chapman on how the proofs of the prospectus might have been circulated more diplomatically.

15 Gives Chapman further advice on attracting supporters for the *Westminster*.

20 Sends Chapman her verdict on several *Westminster* contributions, and advises against inviting Charlotte Brontë to write an article on modern novelists: 'She would have to leave out Currer Bell, who is perhaps the best of them all' (*Letters* I, 355).

August
1   (Fri) Agrees with Chapman's suggestion that GHL be invited to contribute an article on modern novelists.
13 Chapman discusses the *Westminster* prospectus with GE, visiting London in company with the Brays. Her introduction to Spencer also dates from this visit.
15 Chapman takes GE and Sara Hennell to the Great Exhibition.
16 GE returns to Rosehill, though still advising Chapman from a distance on *Westminster* plans.
28 Tells Mary Sibree, 'there are but two words of very vital significance for you and me and all mortals – *Resignation* and labour' (*Letters*, i, 359).
29 Meets the phrenologist George Combe at Rosehill, Combe noting in his journal GE's extraordinary ability.

September
18 (Thurs) Advises Chapman that a translation of Comte's *Cours de philosophie positive* by W. M. W. Call will probably be more successful than one by Harriet Martineau.
20 Article on W. R. Greg's *The Creed of Christendom* appears in the *Leader*. Chapman and his wife begin a three-day stay at Rosehill.
29 Returns to lodge with Chapman, gathering contributions for the first number of the *Westminster*'s new series, and enormously broadening her intellectual and social acquaintances. Involvement with Herbert Spencer begins to develop.

October
3   (Fri) Sends Cara Bray news of her employment: 'I am training myself up to say adieu to all delights, I care for nothing but doing my work and doing it well' (*Letters*, i, 363).
4   Tells Charles Bray of her meeting with Herbert Spencer, whose *Social Statics* she recommends.
6   First, unimpressed, encounter with GHL – 'a sort of miniature Mirabeau in appearance' (i, 261).
8   Tells Charles Bray that the Swedish novelist Frederika Bremer, currently staying with Chapman, is extremely unprepossessing.
9   Repents of her attitude to Frederika Bremer in a letter to Sara Hennell.
11 Again visits the Great Exhibition.

22   Brings the Brays and Sara Hennell up to date with subscriptions
     to, and articles for, the *Westminster*. Tells them of the pleasure
     given to her by Carlyle's *Life of Sterling*.

November
 2   (Sun) Reading J. H. Newman's *Lectures on the Present Position
     of Catholics*.
22   Sees *The Merry Wives of Windsor* with Spencer and Chapman.
     GHL in the same box.
27   Tells Cara Bray of GHL's witticisms on the *Merry Wives*
     performance.

December
 7   (Sun) Combe urges Chapman to use GE's judgement as an
     aid to his own.
19   Death of J. M. W. Turner.
23   Tells the Brays that pressure of work will regrettably prevent
     her from joining them for Christmas: 'It is the first Christmas
     day I shall have passed without any Christmas feeling' (i, 267).

1852

January
Appearance of first number in new series of the *Westminster*,
containing review by GE of Carlyle's *Life of John Sterling*. Though
praised for its content, the series remained a financial liability.
19   (Mon) Visited by H. G. Atkinson and Harriet Martineau –
     repulsed by the vulgarity of the latter's looks and gestures.
     Has lengthy conversation with Pierre Leroux at a *soirée*.
22   Advises Charles Bray to read article on physiognomy in the
     Quarterly Review.
30   Sends birthday greetings to Charles Bray.
31   Attends party at Mackay's.

February
 2   (Mon) Tells the Brays of her pleasure in the company of Bessie
     Parkes, with whom her friendship develops this year. W. J.
     Fox visits in the evening.
 9   Sara Hennell begins a nine-day visit to GE and Chapman.
15   Dines with Peter Taylor and his wife Clementia at Sydenham,

Kent (now South London). Bessie Parkes visits and 'is very pretty in her attentions' (*Letters*, II, 11).

16   Tells Cara Bray that 'The thick of the work is just beginning' on the *Westminster* (I, 272).

25   Attends meeting of Association for the Abolition of Taxes on Knowledge, hearing Cobden, 'in whom I was woefully disappointed' (I, 272).

27   Lord Derby forms Ministry.

28   Visits a Miss Lynn to discuss lodgings, but subsequently considers it undesirable to fix on a London residence immediately.

March

1   (Mon) Death in Florence of Edward Lombe, underwriter of several articles for the *Westminster*

6   Tells Clementia Taylor, 'until the end of March I fear I shall be a prisoner from the necessity for constant work' (I, 273).

April

During the next five months Comte contributes a series of articles to the *Leader*, subsequently edited by GHL (with GE's assistance) as *Comte's Philosophy of the Sciences*. Notice of *Memoirs of Margaret Fuller*, perhaps by GE, appears in 'Contemporary Literature of America' section of the *Westminster* (for a discussion of the authorship see Pinney, pp. 456–7).

1   (Thurs) Attends Rossini's *William Tell* at Covent Garden with Herbert Spencer.

2   Attends Haydn's *Creation* at Exeter Hall with Bessie Parkes.

3   Visits Cara Bray at Rosehill. Reports that she has been made joint trustee of fund for publication of Harriet Martineau's translation of Comte.

15   Returns to London. Attends GHL's *The Chain of Events* with Spencer, reporting to Bray, 'It is a very long chain and drags rather heavily' (*Letters*, II, 18).

17   James Martineau agrees to write for the *Westminster*.

21   Herbert Spencer alarmed by GE's affection for him. Assures Sara Hennell of her lasting friendship: 'I love you more than ever, not less' (I, 275).

24   Attends Donizetti's *I Martiri* at Covent Garden with Spencer, telling the Brays, 'We have agreed that we are not in love with each other, and that there is no reason why we should not

have as much of each other's society as we like' (*Letters*, II, 22).

26 Attends brilliant *soirée* at Chapman's, with F. W. Newman, W. R. Greg, and Louis Blanc among the guests.

May

1 (Sat) Attends Meyerbeer's *Les Huguenots* with a person 'short-sighted enough to like one' [Herbert Spencer?] (I, 278).

4 Dickens chairs meeting of Booksellers' Association at 142 Strand: 'He is not distinguished looking in any way', GE reports to the Brays (I, 279).

5 Attends annual concert given by the pianist Emanuel Aguilar at Hanover Square Rooms. Asks the Brays to forward her copies of Shakespeare, Goethe, Byron and Wordsworth.

12 Gladstone proposes to the House of Commons the abolition of paper and stamp duties; motion defeated.

13 Visits Clementia Taylor at Sydenham.

16 Dines with Andrew Johnson.

20 Attends Halévy's *La Juive* at Covent Garden, probably with Spencer, subsequently telling the Brays that she 'fell in love with Prince Albert, who was unusually animated and promi-nent' (I, 281).

27 Attends Bellini's *Norma* at Covent Garden, probably with Spencer. Tells Cara Bray, 'My brightest spot next to my love of *old* friends, is the deliciously calm *new* friendship that Herbert Spencer gives me. We see each other every day and have a delightful *camaraderie* in everything' (I, 281). Also describes the great impression which Millais's *The Huguenots on St Bartholomew's Day* made on her.

June

Rumours develop that GE and Spencer are engaged. Introduced to Barbara Smith by Bessie Parkes.

2 (Wed) Asks the Brays to send George Sand's works and Jane Austen's *Sense and Sensibility*.

3 Attends Anniversary Meeting of the Charity Schools at St Paul's Cathedral.

8 Attends Meyerbeer's *Robert le Diable* at Covent Garden.

14 Replies to joint invitation to herself and Spencer to visit Rosehill: 'We certainly could not go together, for all the world

is setting us down as engaged' (*Letters*, ɪɪ, 35). Congratulates Bessie Parkes on her twenty-third birthday.

21   Visits Joseph Parkes.
22   Spencer brings his father to visit GE.
27   Visits Kew Gardens with Spencer.
28   Mary Smith visits GE with Florence Nightingale, Hilary Bonham Carter and Mary Mohl.
30   Tells George Combe that she does not wish to employ the critic Ebenezer Syme again.

July
3   (Sat) Travels to Chandos Cottage, Broadstairs, Kent.
4   Tells Cara Bray, 'I am thinking whether it would not be wise to retire from the world and live here for the rest of my days' (ɪ, 285).
8   Sends Spencer her opinion on Tennyson's *In Memoriam*.
13   Tells Charles Bray that she is obliged to write hurriedly, since she is not alone, a possible indication that Spencer was visiting her.
15   Urges Bessie Parkes to publish her poems. Receives note from Florence Nightingale, and remarks that 'There is a loftiness of mind about her' (ɪ, 285).
?16   Asks Spencer, who rejects her love in the course of this month, to give an assurance that he will not forsake her altogether.
21   Reports herself to Charles Bray as 'Picking up shells (not in the Newtonian sense, but literally); reading Aristotle to find out what is the chief good; and eating mutton chops, that I may have strength to pursue it' (ɪ, 286).
24   Writes to Chapman discussing articles and editorial policy for the *Westminster*.
?29   Tells Spencer that she is not unhappy and that he may rely on her to exclude painful emotions from their relationship.

August
3   (Thurs) The Brays join GE at Broadstairs.
5   Charles Bray returns home.
12   Cara Bray leaves Broadstairs.
19   Reading W. J. Fox's *Lectures Addressed Chiefly to the Working Classes*.
28   Returns to London with a violent headache and sickness.

September

11 (Sat) Tells Cara Bray that the articles for the October edition of the *Westminster* are 'on the whole unsatisfactory' (I, 290).

14 Death of the Duke of Wellington.

18 Writes to Charles Bray recounting conversation with GHL on phrenology.

25 Reports herself to Sara Hennell better satisfied with the final appearance of the October *Westminster*.

October

Review, possibly by GE, of Hawthorne's *Blithedale Romance* appears in the *Westminster*. See Pinney, pp. 457–8.

5 (Tues) Travels to Edinburgh to stay with George Combe.

6 Robert Cox, editor of the *Phrenological Journal*, visits GE.

7 Tells the Brays, 'The Combes are all kindness, and I am in clover – an elegant house, glorious fires, and a comfortable carriage' (I, 292).

12 Visits Craigcrook, summer home of Francis Jeffrey.

20 Arrives to stay with Harriet Martineau at Ambleside in the Lake District.

21 Visits workmen's cottages with Harriet Martineau in connection with Martineau's Co-operative Building Society.

23 Visits Borrowdale.

26 Leaves Ambleside for Rosehill.

29 Harriet Martineau tells Chapman of her pleasure at GE's visit.

30 Tells Bessie Parkes that she has had 'a delightful month – nothing but petting and admiration, beautiful scenery and agreeable talks' (*Letters*, II, 64).

November

1 (Mon) Charles Bray writes to George Combe of GE: 'Her manners are much improved since she went into the world: they were tinged with a slight degree of affectation' (Haight, p. 124).

4 Returns to London from Rosehill. Visited by Spencer.

6 Finishes Kingsley's *Phaeton*, with some disapproval. Begins Thackeray's *History of Henry Esmond*.

13 Tells the Brays that *Esmond* is 'the most uncomfortable book you can imagine' (I, 296–7).

20 Describes her day's work to the Brays: 'My task was to read an article of Greg's in the *North British* on Taxation, a heap of

newspaper articles, and all that J. S. Mill says on the same subject' (I, 297). Visited by GHL.

23   Sends birthday greetings to Sara Hennell.

December
 1   (Wed) Attends annual meeting of the Association for the Repeal of the Taxes on Knowledge at Exeter Hall.
11   Travels to Coventry to spend two days with the Brays.
14   Sends autograph letter of Mazzini's to W. F. Watson for his collection.
20   Hears news of her brother-in-law Edward Clarke's serious illness. Clarke dies the same day.
21   Tells George Combe that she is painfully preoccupied by Clarke's death.
23   Travels to Rosehill, to stay with the Brays prior to travelling to Meriden.
24   Attends Edward Clarke's funeral.
25   Spend Christmas with her sister at Meriden, telling the Brays that 'Chrissey bears her trouble much better than I expected' (I, 300).
28   Earl of Aberdeen forms a ministry following resignation of Lord Derby.
30   Returns to London.

1853

January
 8   (Sat) Tells Charles Bray that she is utterly dejected.
10   GE begs Sara Hennell not to 'lay the sins of the article on the Atomic Theory to poor Lewes's charge'. She herself disapproved of the article, which was by Samuel Brown (I, 302).
17   Tells Charles Bray, 'You are a fine fellow to talk of supporting the *Westminster – for my sake* too. . . . The only thing you can do *for my sake* is to prosper' (*Letters*, II, 81).
22   Writes to Charles Bray, 'Heaven help us! – said the old religion; the new one, from its very lack of that faith, will teach us all the more to help one another' (I, 302).
24   Tells Bray that she has determined to leave Chapman's house.
25   Corrects Charles Bray's mistake of supposing that she dictates

Chapman's letters, and praises Chapman's industry. Doctor summoned to treat her rheumatism.

27 Reports herself to the Brays in frightful pain.
28 Rheumatism improved.

February
1 (Tues) Gives Clementia Taylor her opinion on Gaskell's *Ruth*: 'How women have the courage to write and publishers the spirit to buy at a high price the false and feeble representations of life and character that most feminine novels give, is a constant marvel to me. *Ruth*, with all its merits, will not be an enduring or classical fiction. . . . [Gaskell] is not contented with the subdued colouring – the half tints of real life' (I, 304–5).
3 Charles Bray collects GE and takes her to Rosehill to convalesce.
12 Returns from Rosehill to London. Bessie Parkes tells Barbara Smith that GE has made up her mind to love her (i.e. Bessie Parkes).
15 Tells Cara Bray that she has been reading *Villette*, 'a still more wonderful book than *Jane Eyre*. There is something almost preternatural in its power' (I, 306).
16 Tells the Brays that she is dissatisfied with the *Westminster*: 'I should be glad to run away from it altogether' (I, 301).
23 Spends the evening with Huxley and Masson.
27 Dines with Bessie Parkes.

March
Informs Chapman of her intention of leaving the *Westminster* after the next edition.
5 (Sat) Tells the Brays that the next issue of the *Westminster* will be a particularly good one.
12 Tells the Brays of her delight at the news of Harriet Beecher Stowe's wedding.
18 Reports her disappointment with the next issue of the *Westminster*, not least with GHL's contribution, but has clearly postponed her resignation from the *Westminster*.
23 Enjoys a pleasant *soirée* at Chapman's, telling Sara Hennell that GHL 'has quite won my liking, in spite of myself' (I, 307).
26 Spends all day correcting proofs, though satisfied that the issue will be better than she once feared.

April
Deeply concerned about the poor health and conditions of Chrissey and her family, even considering emigration to Australia with them.
11   (Mon) Visits Clementia Taylor at Syndenham. Tells the Brays that GHL 'has been quite a pleasant friend to me lately' (*Letters*, II, 97).
13   Enjoys 'an agreeable *soirée*. . . . I fell in love with Helen Faucit' (I, 308).
15   Sees Marguerite Ancelot's *Loisa*.
16   Sees Rossini's *William Tell*. Tells Cara Bray that GHL 'has quite won my regard. . . . Like a few other people in the world he is much better than he seems. . . . A man of heart and conscience wearing a mask of flippancy' (I, 308).

May
5   (Thurs) Visits the Brays at Rosehill.
13   Tells Chapman that he may add her 'Idea of a Future Life' (never completed) to his list.
23   Returns to London.
28   Forced to decline article by Foxton for the July *Westminster*.
29   Dines with the Combes at the house of Dr Abram Cox in Kingston, Surrey.

June
11   (Sat) Visits Zoological Gardens. Sees *Adrienne Lecouvreur* by Scribe and Legouvé with GHL.
15   Dines with Sir James Clark together with the Combes and Neil Arnott.
17   Meets Caroline Cornwallis, a prodigy of languages.
18   Advertisement appears in the *Leader* anticipating *The Idea of a Future Life* by 'the Translator of Strauss's *Life of Jesus*'.
25   Attends première of Berlioz's *Benvenuto Cellini*.
26   Visits the Combes.
28   Invites Sara Hennell to visit her so that they may both call on Bessie Parkes in Ockley, Surrey.

July
2   (Sat) Visits Bessie Parkes, the party including Chapman, Sara Hennell and Barbara Smith.

9 Declines an invitation from George and Cecilia Combe to spend the summer with them in Switzerland.

12 Writes to Bessie Parkes, expressing distaste at new edition of Mary Hume's *The Bridesmaid, Count Stephen, and Other Poems*, but pleasure at Bessie Parkes's own verse-letters.

15 Continues her holiday by travelling to Tunbridge Wells, Kent.

27 Considers moving on to Hastings or St Leonards.

30 Finishes reading De Quincey's *Autobiographic Sketches*.

August

Possibly visited at St Leonards by GHL.

3 (Wed) Tells Cara Bray: 'I never felt the delight of the thorough change that the coast gives one so much as now' (I, 309).

9 Tells Cara Bray that she is 'being regenerated by baptism and – beer drinking! This latter sacrament I . . . find . . . very efficacious' (*Letters*, II, 113).

18 Reading Goethe, Schiller, and an article on Shakespeare in the *Prospective Review*.

September

?8 (Thurs) Returns to London from St Leonards.

17 Visits Hyde Park to look for new lodgings.

30 Fire destroys the presses and composing room of Savill and Edwards, printers of the *Westminster*.

October

1 (Sat) Decides to take lodgings at 21 Cambridge Street. Her move here almost certainly marks the beginning of her formal relationship with GHL.

8 Begins a fortnight's stay with the Brays at Rosehill.

16 Herbert Spencer arrives at Rosehill.

17 Leaves Rosehill for London, where she commences residence at 21 Cambridge Street.

20 Reports to Cara Bray, 'I like my lodgings . . . and I have not one disagreeable to complain of at present' (*Letters*, II, 119).

21 Sends Combe her comments on his *Relation of Religion to Science*.

22 Reading Leigh Hunt's *The Religion of the Heart*.

28 Visited by Harriet Martineau.

November
1   (Tues) Again visited by Harriet Martineau.
7   Learns of the illness of her sister Fanny.
8   Visited by R. W. Mackay.
16 Meets Neil Arnott and John Elliotson at an evening party at Mackay's.
19 Harriet Martineau's translation of *The Positive Philosophy of Auguste Comte* appears in Chapman's *Quarterly Review*.
24 Tells Chapman that she wishes to give up any connection with the editorship of the *Westminster*.
25 Responds to Sara Hennell's birthday greetings: 'I begin this year more happily than I have done most years of my life' (I, 317).
29 Compliments Bessie Parkes on her *Summer Sketches and Other Poems*. Gives Combe a two-sided estimation of Huxley's reputation.

December
Ceases editorship of the *Westminster*.
2   (Fri) Reports 10 days of stomach complaints. Writes to Chapman requesting a guarantee of texts for, and the publication of, Feuerbach's *Das Wesen der Christentums* (*The Essence of Christianity*).
17 Begs Chapman to withhold Huxley's contemptuous article against GHL from the *Westminster*.
19 Unsuccessfully advises Chapman to drop Huxley's 'Science' article completely.
23 Tells Combe that her reason for withdrawing from the *Westminster* is Chapman's financial difficulties.
25 Spends Christmas Day alone at Cambridge Street.
28 Dines with Arthur Helps at Sir James Clark's: 'very snug – only he and myself' (I, 319).

1854

January
Works at the *Essence*.
2   (Mon) Begins visit to Chrissey at Meriden.
7   Travels to Rosehill to stay with the Brays.
12 Returns to London.

18 Thanks Sara Hennell for agreeing to criticise the *Essence*.
21 Declines invitation to attend a dance organised by Bessie Parkes's mother, fearing 'to appear like a withered cabbage in a flower garden' (*Letters*, II, 138).

February
6 (Mon) Requests Charles Bray to send a copy of an article by Thomas Guthrie on the importance of the Bible in children's moral education.
11 Thanks Sara Hennell for correcting the manuscript of the *Essence*.

March
Continues to work on the *Essence*. Sara Hennell reads the manuscript in successive instalments, GE expressing extreme gratitude: 'Every stroke of the pen you can save me is so much charity.'
2 (Thurs) Thanks Bessie Parkes for bringing a number of Barbara Smith's paintings.
5 Combe tells Chapman that GE had told him that her connection with the *Westminster* had terminated on 1 January.
9 Discusses points of typography for the *Essence* with Sara Hennell, also telling her, 'I like my independent life in lodgings better and better' (*Letters*, II, 145).
28 Declaration of Crimean War.
31 Begins to send manuscript of the *Essence* to printers.

April
4 (Tues) Sees Rossini's *William Tell* with GHL.
6 Declares herself out of 'a labyrinth of headaches and palpitations' but predicts herself 'deep in proof sheets till the end of May' (I, 321, 320).
14 Considers writing the 'Belles Lettres' section in future editions of the *Westminster* to compensate for the poor financial return for the *Essence* translation.
15 GHL taken severely ill. GE takes over his work for the *Leader*.
26 Tells Sara Hennell, 'I have been almost constantly ill for the last ten days . . . I am too entirely without hope about the book' (*Letters*, II, 152).
29 Urgently begs Sara Hennell's criticism of the appendix of the *Essence*.

May
Essence translation completed.
11 (Sun) Complains of exhaustion on completing the *Essence*, and spends the week idly.
15 Views the French exhibition at the Pall Mall Gallery; is much impressed by Scheffer's painting of Francesca da Rimini.
17 Visits the Royal Academy exhibition.
19 Writes to Cara Bray expressing her admiration for Holman Hunt's *The Light of the World* and Ruskin's attendant correspondence in *The Times*.
22 Visited by Charles Bray.
27 'Finally decided not to live with the Chapmans. . . . I may wish to go to the continent. At all events, I like to feel free' (*Letters*, ii, 158).

June
3 (Thurs) Complains to Sara Hennell of slowness and inaccuracies with the *Essence* proofs.
6 Apologises to Cara Bray for being unable to visit Rosehill before Midsummer.
9 Refuses to visit the Combes.
10 Queen Victoria opens the Crystal Palace at Sydenham.
11 Visited by Charles Bray and William Smith. Discusses with Bray her relationship with GHL.
12 Finds further inaccuracies in the *Essence* proofs.
17 Goes to stay with the Brays at Rosehill, her last visit there.
24 Advertisements appear for the *Essence* translation to be ready 'in a few days.'
25 GHL refuses the Brays' invitation to Coventry.
26 Returns to London.
27 Visited by George Combe.

July
Essence translation published, the first and only time GE published under her real name.
2 (Sun) Spends evening at Chapman's.
3 Advises Cara Bray to 'consider the Strauss mss. waste paper' (i, 324).
7 Review in the Coventry *Herald* by Sara Hennell lavishly praises the *Essence* translation.
9 Visits the Crystal Palace at Sydenham.

14 Clears financial arrangements with Chapman prior to going abroad.
19 Writes to the Brays and Sara Hennell, 'I have only time to say good-bye, and God bless you. *Poste restante*, Weimar, for the next six weeks' (I, 325).
20 GE and GHL leave London together for Weimar, travelling via Antwerp, Brussels, Namur, Liège, Cologne, Mainz and Frankfurt.
21 Records in Journal, 'The day was glorious and our passage perfect' (I, 332).
27 Wander round Liège in 'a state of rapture' (Haight, p. 150).
30 Dr Brabant (a chance encounter) brings Strauss ('a man for whom life has lost all charms') to visit GE and GHL for breakfast (Haight, p. 151).
31 Visit the Goethe house in Frankfurt.

August

2 (Wed) Arrive in Weimar. For an extensive list of reading during subsequent months, and GE's comments on this reading, see I, 374–7.
5 Receives letter from Chapman proposing that she write an article on Victor Cousin's *Madame de Sablé*. The *Spectator* reviews the *Essence* translation favourably.
6 Describes her meeting with Strauss in letter to Chapman.
10 Dine with Liszt at the Altenburg. The company includes Raff, Schade, Cornelius and Princess Wittgenstein. Liszt plays: 'For the first time in my life I beheld real inspiration' (I, 347). Acquaintance with German opera partly stimulated by numerous meetings with Liszt at this time.
16 Tells Charles Bray, 'I have had a month of exquisite enjoyment, and seem to have begun life afresh' (*Letters*, II, 170). Dines with Liszt.
29 Arthur Helps passes through Weimar, visiting GHL and GE.
30 Tells Chapman of her extreme happiness.

September

Combe dismayed at his misapprehension of GE's character.
8 (Fri) Sends Chapman her article on Cousin's *Madame de Sablé*.

October

'Woman in France: Madame de Sablé' appears in the *Westminster*.

 4 (Wed) Asks Chapman to forward a copy of the article on
    Madame de Sablé for Liszt to read.
 8 Bray tells Chapman: 'Nothing that I have yet heard or know
    will make any difference in my conduct towards her' [i.e. GE]
    (*Letters*, VIII, 123). Malicious rumours about the GE–GHL
    relationship begin to circulate in London.
11 Notes that a painful letter from London caused both GHL and
    herself a bad night's sleep.
12 GHL writes to Carlyle and Helps defending his position with
    regard to GE and his family in London.
15 Writes to Chapman, 'I have counted the cost of the step that I
    have taken. . . . I am not mistaken in the person to whom I
    have attached myself. He is worthy of the sacrifice I have
    incurred, and my only anxiety is that he should be rightly
    judged' (*Letters*, VIII, 124–5).
16 Chapman tells Robert Chambers that GHL is not alone to
    blame.
19 GHL receives a letter of generous sympathy from Carlyle in
    respect of his elopement with GE.
22 Sees Wagner's *Lohengrin*.
24 Terms GHL's behaviour towards Agnes beyond reproach.
28 Publication in the *Leader* of 'The Romantic School of Music,'
    an abridged translation by GE of an article by Liszt on Wagner
    and Meyerbeer.
31 GE writes to Sara Hennell to attempt to clear up misunder-
    standings caused by the Lewes affair. Relations with
    Rosehill, however, never completely restored.

November
GHL continues work on his *Life of Goethe*, assisted by GE.
 3 (Fri) Leave Weimar for Berlin, where they also encounter
    a large cross-section of the artistic *intelligentsia*. For GE's
    recollections, see I, 349–64, 367–73.
 8 Begins to translate Spinoza's *Ethics*. Read *Wilhelm Meister* and
    The Merchant of Venice to each other in the evenings.
12 Tells Charles Bray that she cannot think two humans could
    be happier than GHL and herself.
15 Combe wonders if there has been insanity in GE's family, and
    tells Charles Bray that GE, GHL and Thornton Hunt have
    inflicted a great injury on the cause of religious freedom.
21 Visit Otto Friedrich Gruppe.

30 Complete sketches 'Three Months in Weimar', subsequently to appear in *Fraser's Magazine*.

December
9   (Sat) Tells Chapman that Berlin life is eminently agreeable, and that they are both reading substantial amounts.
28 Meet Stahr and Fanny Lewald.
29 Visit Fanny Lewald.

1855

January
2   (Tues) Hear Gluck's *Orpheus*.
9   Writes to Chapman with an idea for an article on 'Woman in Germany'. Hear Beethoven's *Fidelio*.
23 Begins article on Vehse's *Court of Austria*.

February
5   (Mon) Palmerston becomes Prime Minister, following the resignation of Aberdeen's government.

March
3   (Sat) Completes 'Memoirs of the Court of Austria', a review of Vehse, for the *Westminster*.
11 Leave Berlin for England, breaking the journey at Cologne and Brussels, and enjoying in the latter a chance encounter with Berlioz.
14 Takes lodgings at 1 Sydney Place, Dover, while GHL continues to London. Resumes work on Spinoza's *Ethics*.
15 Reading Shakespeare's *Venus and Adonis*.
16 Reading Shakespeare's *Two Gentlemen of Verona* and *Sonnets*.
17 GE's article 'The Art of the Ancients' appears in the *Leader*.
20 Writes to Chapman to offer her sympathy over his serious lung disease.
25 Invited by Chapman to undertake the 'Belles Lettres' section of the *Westminster*. Celebrates with a walk over the hills.

April
GE's article 'Memoirs of the Court of Austria' appears in the

Westminster. For reading this month, including much Shakespeare, see i, 382–3.

4   (Wed) Writes to Charles Bray to discuss her financial affairs.
9   Upset by her efforts to ensure that GHL and his wife would never attempt a *rapprochement*.
18 Arrives in London to live with GHL. Move into temporary lodgings at 8 Victoria Grove Terrace, Bayswater.
23 Decide on 7 Clarence Row, East Sheen, Surrey, as a permanent residence.
25 Visits the British Museum.
26 Chapman visits GE to invite GHL to write on teetotalism for the *Westminster.* GE accepts on his behalf.
28 Completes article 'Three Months in Weimar'. Visited by Rufa Hennell.
29 Writes to Chapman discussing future articles on Kingsley and Dr Cumming.
30 Visited by Bessie Parkes.

May
Writes 'several articles' for the *Leader* (i, 382).
2   (Wed) Move to 7 Clarence Row, East Sheen. GE arranges to have correspondence forwarded in GHL's name. They at first attract few visitors.
7   Requests Charles Bray to lend his volumes of Scott for an article for *Fraser's Magazine.* (The article never appeared.)
9   Completes article on Kingsley's *Westward Ho!*
12 Describes her article 'Three Months in Weimar' to Charles Bray.
19 Article on *Westward Ho!* appears in the *Leader.*

June
'Three Months in Weimar' appears in *Fraser's Magazine.*
13 (Wed) Mention of book ii of the *Iliad* is representative of a course of reading in Greek undertaken in this and the following two years. For details of other reading this month see i, 382.
16 Supplement to the *Leader* includes GE's 'Menander and the Greek Comedy' and GHL's 'The Memoirs of Sydney Smith'.
17 Writes to Charles Bray, 'we like East Sheen better and better and are happier every day, walking hard, reading Homer and science and rearing tadpoles' (*Letters*, ii, 202).

24 Chapman comes to lunch bringing his article 'The Position of Woman'.
25 Writes to Chapman offering a detailed critique of his article.
27 Reassures Chapman of the article's worth.

July

Article 'Liszt, Wagner and Weimar' appears in *Fraser's Magazine*. The *Westminster* publishes in its 'Belles Lettres' section her opinion on 23 books, including *Westward Ho!* and Matthew Arnold's *Poems, Second Series*.

7   (Sat) 'Lord Brougham's Literature' appears in the *Leader*.
10 Charles Bray visits and enters into a heated argument on phrenology.
16 Writes to Charles Bray defending GHL's article on J. S. Buckingham in the *Leader*.
21 'The Morality of Wilhelm Meister' appears in the *Leader*. Reading Keightley's *Life* of Milton prior to reviewing it for the *Leader*.
22 GHL ill with toothache. GE reads to him from Scott.
28 'The Future of German Philosophy' appears in the *Leader*.

August

4   (Sat) Review of Keightley's *Life* of Milton (largely concerned with Milton's view of divorce) appears in the *Leader*.
7   Carlyle reads proof of GHL's *Goethe*.
25 'Love in the Drama' published in the *Leader*.

September

Three articles for the *Leader* as well as the October 'Belles Lettres' for the *Westminster* completed this month.

1   (Sat) 'Heine's poems' appears in the *Leader*.
4   Sends Cara Bray an earnest and lengthy defence of her relationship with GHL: 'If there is any one action or relation of my life which is and always has been profoundly serious, it is my relation to Mr Lewes' (i, 327). Correspondence between the pair subsequently resumed.
15 'Michelet on the Reformation' published in the *Leader*.
19 Leave for two weeks in Worthing, Sussex.
22 'German Mythology and Legend' appears in the *Leader*.

October

Her *Westminster* 'Belles Lettres' column concentrates, unfavourably, on Tennyson's *Maud*. The issues also includes 'Evangelical Teaching: Dr Cumming,' an important denunciation of the Evangelicalism of her youth, and the article which convinced GHL that there was genius in her writing.

3   (Wed) Move to 8 Park Shot, Richmond, Surrey.

9   Finishes article on Margaret Fuller and Mary Wollstonecraft.

12 Finishes article on Carlyle for the *Leader*.

15 Working on the 'Belles Lettres' section of the *Westminster*, including Browning's *Men and Women*, Longfellow's *Hiawatha* and Thoreau's *Walden*. Receives two letters from Princess Wittgenstein.

16 Reading Gall's *Anatomie et physiologie du cerveau*, and Carpenter's *Comparative Physiology*.

20 'Translations and Translators' published in the *Leader*.

27 'Thomas Carlyle' appears in the *Leader*.

30 Publication of GHL's *Life of Goethe*.

November

3   (Sat) GE's review of GHL's *Life of Goethe* appears in the *Leader*.

14 Affected by a severe cold.

21 Sufficiently recovered to leave the house for the first time in two weeks.

29 Completes 'German Wit: Heinrich Heine' for the *Westminster*.

December

15 (Sat) Forwards letter sent to her from Herbert Spencer to Sara Hennell.

24 Travels to Attleborough to spend Christmas with Chrissey.

29 Returns to Richmond.

31 At work on review of Meredith's *Shaving of Shagpat*.

1856

January

'German Wit: Heinrich Heine' appears in the *Westminster*, along with her 'Belles Lettres' section.

1   (Tues) Sends New Year greetings to Charles Bray. Continues to work on reviews of books by Meredith and Julia Kavanagh,

and a translation of von Bohlen's *Introduction to the Book of Genesis*.

5 Reviews of *The Shaving of Shagpat* (highly favourable) and of Julia Kavanagh's *Rachel Gray* appear in the *Leader*.

12 'Introduction to Genesis' appears in the *Leader*.

18 Barbara Smith sends GE a petition in favour of rights for women. Records the sale of 1000 copies of GHL's *Goethe*.

28 Gives qualified praise to the proposed legal reforms for women as helping to raise their position and character.

February

9 (Sat) 'History of German Protestantism' appears in the *Leader*.

16 The *Spectator* asserts its view that no woman is fit for the post of clerk to the Master of the Rolls.

19 Completes her translation of Spinoza's *Ethics* – never published, owing to GHL's dispute with the publisher. Declares herself in happy ignorance of the *Spectator*'s views on emancipation. Reading the third volume of Ruskin's *Modern Painters* and Thomas Rymer Jones's *General Outline of the Animal Kingdom*.

23 GHL's damning review of Alison's *History of Europe* appears in the *Saturday Review*.

25 Tells Sara Hennell of her sympathy for Harriet Martineau's heart condition.

26 Reminds Sara Hennell of the importance of being called 'Mrs Lewes' by visitors.

March

1 (Sat) 'The Poets and Poetry of America' appears in the *Leader*.

9 GHL asks Spencer to refer to GE as Mrs Lewes.

26 Tells Charles Bray that her 'pen is not of the true literary order which will run along without the help of brains' (I, 393).

29 'The Antigone and its Moral' appears in the *Leader*.

30 Treaty of peace signed in Paris ending Crimean War.

31 Congratulates Bessie Parkes on her children's story *The History of our Cat Aspasia*. Tells Charles Bray of her plans to take GHL's sons to Germany for the summer.

April

Contributes 'Art' and 'Belles Lettres' sections to the *Westminster*.

1 (Tues) Asks Charles Bray if John Sibree would consider tutoring

GHL's sons. 'A delicious day! We are going to have a holiday at the Zoological Gardens' (i, 395).

5   Chapman accepts GE's idea for an article on Young. 'Church History of the Nineteenth Century' appears in the *Leader*.

6   Resolve to send GHL's sons to school in Switzerland. 'Keeping Sabbath in Mr Bray's fashion – enjoying the sunshine and reading the newspapers' (*Letters*, ii, 237). Cross remarks, 'The next few weeks are, perhaps, the most signally important and interesting of all in George Eliot's development. There are unmistakable signs of the rising of the sap of creative production' (i, 395–6).

12 'The Court of Austria' published in the *Leader*.

15 Visited for the day by Herbert Spencer.

19 'Who Wrote the Waverley Novels?' published in the *Leader*.

22 Commences 'Worldliness and Other-Worldliness: The Poet Young'.

26   'Heine's Book of Songs' appears in the *Saturday Review*, and 'Story of a Blue-Bottle' in the *Leader*.

29 Proclamation of peace with Russia. Begins reading Riehl's *Land und Volk*.

May

8   (Thurs) Set out for Ilfracombe, Devon, staying at Exeter overnight.

9   Visit Exeter Cathedral. Take lodgings at Runnymede Villa, Ilfracombe. For GE's recollections of this holiday, see i, 396–406. Idea of 'Barton' conceived on this trip: 'One morning as I was thinking what should be the subject of my first story, my thoughts merged themselves into a dreamy doze, and I imagined myself writing a story, of which the title was 'The Sad Fortunes of the Reverend Amos Barton' (i, 415). GHL involved with preparation for his *Sea-Side Studies*.

17 'Pictures of Life in French Novels' appears in the *Saturday Review*, and 'Margaret Fuller's Letters from Italy' in the *Leader*.

31 'The Art and Artists of Greece' appears in the *Saturday Review*.

June

Reading includes P. H. Gosse's *Rambles on the Devonshire Coast*, R. C. Trench's *Life is a Dream*, and Masson's *Life of Chatterton*.

6   Tells Charles Bray, 'between work and zoology and bodily ailments my time has been full to overflowing' (i, 406).

7   Bohn expresses to GHL his doubts about publishing GE's translation of Spinoza's *Ethics*.
13 Tells Barbara Smith that she considers Ruskin the finest writer living.
17 Despatches article on Riehl: 'I felt delightfully at liberty, and determined to pay some attention to seaweeds' (I, 400).
26 Take the steamer for Swansea in South Wales, continuing by rail to Tenby.
29 Writes to Sara Hennell with reminiscences of their visit to Tenby 12 years previously.

July

'The Natural History of German Life', a review of Riehl, appears in the *Westminster*, along with her 'Belles Lettres' and 'Art' sections.
5   (Sat) Sends Chapman her favourable comments on the latest issue of the *Westminster*.
12 Joined at Tenby for five days by Barbara Smith.
19 'A Tragic Story' appears in the *Leader*. Discusses an idea for an article on 'Silly Women's Novels' with GHL, intending it to be an article of wholesome truth as well as some humour.
20 Repeats the 'Silly Women's Novels' idea to Chapman. Records in Journal, 'I have done no visible work. But I have absorbed many ideas and much bodily strength; indeed I do not remember ever feeling so strong in mind and body as I feel at this moment' (I, 411).
28 Joined at Tenby by Edward Pigott.

August

2   (Sat) 'The Lover's Seat' appears in the *Leader*.
6   Tells Charles Bray, 'I never think what I write is good for anything till other people tell me so' (I, 412).
8   Leave Tenby, spending the night at Bath.
9   Return to Richmond.
16 'Ferny Combes' published in the *Leader*.
23 'Recollections of Heine' appears in the *Leader*.
25 GHL leaves for Hofwyl, in Switzerland, with his sons Charles and Thornton.
30 'Felice Orsini' appears in the *Leader*. GE 'chloroformed twice, and at last . . . the tooth was got out' (*Letters*, II, 261).

September
'September 1856 made a new era in my life, for it was then I began to write fiction' (I, 414).
4 (Thurs) GHL returns from Hofwyl.
5 Remarks to Sara Hennell how revealing writing may be: 'We mortals have such a knack of shutting up our best selves quite away from each other' (*Letters*, II, 263).
6 'Sight-seeing in Germany and the Tyrol' appears in the *Saturday Review*.
12 Despatches 'Silly Novels by Lady Novelists' to Chapman.
22 Reading Sophocles's *Ajax*.
?23 Commences writing 'Barton'.

October
'Silly Novels by Lady Novelists' and her 'Belles Lettres' section published in the *Westminster*. The article 'George Forster', in the same issue, may also be by GE (see Pinney, p. 458).
9 (Thurs) Offers Sara Hennell her criticisms of the latter's *Christianity and Infidelity*.
18 Congratulates Sara Hennell on her revision of *Christianity and Infidelity*.

November
5 (Wed) Offers GHL's criticisms of *Christianity and Infidelity* to Sara Hennell. Finishes writing 'Barton'.
6 GHL sends Blackwood the manuscript of 'Barton', proposing a series of clerical tales.
8 Discusses the meaning of 'Islam', and natural theology, in letter to Sara Hennell.
12 Blackwood tells GHL, 'I am happy to say that I think your friend's reminiscences of Clerical Life will do. . . . If the author is a new writer, I beg to congratulate him on being worthy of the honours of print and pay' (I, 419–20).
15 GHL tells Blackwood that his 'clerical friend' is 'somewhat discouraged' by Blackwood's previous letter, but will continue the sketches when other work allows (I, 421).
18 Blackwood assures GHL of his admiration for 'Barton' and offers to 'publish it without seeing more' (I, 422).
22 GHL tells Blackwood of the restored confidence of his unusually sensitive friend, who would like to see 'Barton' published in January 1857 as the first of the Scenes of Clerical Life.

24 Writes to Sara Hennell of the difficulty of repenting past errors, and warmly recommending E. B. Browning's *Aurora Leigh*.

December
Reading in this and the subsequent month includes Sophocles, *Ajax*; Harriet Martineau, *History of the Peace*; Macaulay, *History*; Carlyle, *French Revolution*; Burke, *Reflections on the French Revolution*; and Austen, *Mansfield Park*.
 4 (Thurs) 'Worldliness and Other-Worldliness: The Poet Young' sent to Chapman.
 9 Sends Sara Hennell copies of letters by Varnhagen and Ary Scheffer.
16 GHL deflects a challenge from Thornton Leigh Hunt, father of four children by Agnes, GHL's wife.
17 Sends an autograph of Arthur Helps to Sara Hennell and looks forward to having a week of quiet solitude.
18 GHL sends a paper on anemones to Blackwood and receives the proofs of 'Barton'.
24 GHL travels to Vernon Hill, Hampshire, to spend Christmas with Arthur Helps (a traditional visit).
25 Commences 'Mr Gilfil's Love Story'.
29 Blackwood sends GHL the January *Blackwood's* containing 'Barton': 'It is a long time since I have read anything so fresh, so humorous, and so touching' (i, 425). Also encloses a cheque for 50 guineas.

1857

January
Last contributions to the *Westminster* appear: sections on 'History, Biography, Voyages and Travels' and 'Belles Lettres', as well as the article 'Worldliness and Other-Worldliness: the Poet Young'.
 1 (Thurs) First instalment of 'Barton' appears in *Blackwood's*.
 2 Sends Sara Hennell New Year's greetings and suggests Groombridge as a publisher for her work.
 4 Writes to Blackwood as the author of 'Barton' expressing her appreciation of his efforts.
 8 GHL returns to Richmond.

15 Chapman offers GE a more generous rate of pay for her articles.
17 Finishes ch. 2 of 'Gilfil'.
18 Herbert Spencer to dinner.
26 Writes to Sara Hennell offering to make an exception by reviewing her *Christianity and Infidelity* for the *Leader*, or offering GHL as an alternative reviewer.
30 Blackwood sends GE ('My dear Amos') a copy of the February *Blackwood's*, containing the conclusion of 'Barton'. Blackwood notes Thackeray's approval.

February
 4 (Wed) Adopts the pseudonym George Eliot in a letter to Major William Blackwood. Cross remarks, 'I may mention here that my wife told me the reason she fixed on this name was that George was Mr Lewes's Christian name, and Eliot was a good mouth-filling, easily-pronounced word' (I, 431).
10 Blackwood tells GE of 'Barton's' public acclaim.
11 GHL sends Blackwood the first instalment of 'Gilfil'.
13 Blackwood tells GHL that he has read 'Gilfil' with delight.
14 Reading *Oedipus Rex*, part of a continuing course of study of Greek drama.
16 Blackwood sends GE proofs of the first instalment of 'Gilfil', suggesting modifications in Caterina's character.
18 Thanks Blackwood for his suggestions, but remarks, 'I am unable to alter anything in relation to the delineation or development of character, as my stories always grow out of my psychological conception of the *dramatis personae*' (I, 431).
23 Blackwood confides to GHL his suspicion that 'Gilfil' will be even more popular than 'Barton'.
24 Sends Blackwood the second instalment of 'Gilfil', informing him that the story has grown longer than she expected.
27 Blackwood sends a cheque for £21 for the first instalment of 'Gilfil' together with the proofs of the second instalment.
28 Finishes third instalment of 'Gilfil'. GHL's review of Sara Hennell's *Christianity and Infidelity* appears in the *Leader*.

March
Mutinies in the Bengal army mark beginnings of the Indian mutiny.
 1 (Sun) First instalment of 'Gilfil' appears in *Blackwood's*. Sends

Blackwood the proofs of second instalment and manuscript of third instalment.

2 Sends Sara Hennell her full appraisal of *Christianity and Infidelity*.

7 GHL writes to Blackwood to confirm the financial arrangements for second and third instalments of 'Gilfil'.

11 Blackwood expresses his delight with the proof of the third instalment of 'Gilfil', though querying the necessity of Caterina's dagger.

14 Writes to Blackwood refusing to let Caterina only dream of taking the dagger, and insisting on maintaining her pseudonym.

15 Set out for the Scilly Isles to continue research for GHL's *Sea-Side Studies*. Reading on this holiday includes most of Austen, and novels by Gaskell, Charlotte Brontë and Hawthorne. For general recollections of the trip see I, 436–9 and 444–8.

27 GHL tells Blackwood that the Scillys are enchanting, and should be conducive to good writing.

April

5 (Sun) Tells Sara Hennell of the zoological pleasures of the Scillys, also lamenting the recent death of her niece Frances.

8 Finishes 'Gilfil'.

9 Begins reading Gaskell's *Life of Charlotte Brontë*.

15 Tells Gaskell of her pleasure in reading this biography.

16 Informs Sara Hennell of her delight in reading *Oedipus at Colonnus* and Gaskell's *Life of Charlotte Brontë*. GHL despatches the last instalment of 'Gilfil' to Blackwood.

18 Begins writing 'Janet's Repentance'.

20 GHL sends Blackwood his article 'The Scilly Isles' for inclusion in *Blackwood's*.

28 Blackwood informs GHL of the rumour that *Scenes of Clerical Life* is the work of E. G. Bulwer Lytton.

30 Blackwood despatches proofs of the conclusion of 'Gilfil'.

May

1 (Fri) Tells Blackwood of her dissatisfaction with the ending of 'Barton'.

10 Returns final proofs of 'Gilfil' together with an epilogue.

11 Leave the Scillys for Jersey.

16 Take lodgings at Rosa Cottage, Gorey.

26 Tells Isaac, 'I have changed my name, and have someone to take care of me in the world' (*Letters*, ɪɪ, 331).
27 Congratulates Chapman on his medical degree, also telling him that she is now Mrs Lewes to all her family.

June
2 (Tues) Sends Blackwood first instalment of 'Janet's Repentance'.
5 Writes to Sara Hennell defending her relationship with GHL and emphasising the need for a truthful account of her situation.
6 Describes her life to Mary Cash (*née* Sibree) as 'a preparation for some special work that I may do before I die' (ɪ, 456).
8 Blackwood sends – with qualified approval – proof of chs 1–4 of 'Janet's Repentance'.
9 Vincent Holbeche, family solicitor, sends an enquiry about GE's marriage on behalf of the offended Isaac.
11 Writes to Blackwood defending the drama of 'Janet's Repentance' as the clash 'between *ir*religion and religion' and refusing to make any alterations of substance: 'as an artist I should be utterly powerless if I departed from my own conceptions of life and character' (ɪ, 458, 459).
13 Acknowledges to Holbeche that her marriage is not legal, precipitating ostracism by her family.
14 GHL writes to Blackwood expressing his amazement at the latter's criticisms of 'Janet's Repentance'.
16 Assures Blackwood that her characters will become clear as the story proceeds.
23 Finishes reading aloud to GHL Charlotte Brontë's *The Professor*.
26 Reads Samuel Smiles's *Life of George Stephenson* aloud to GHL.
30 Blackwood congratulates GE on the appearance of 'Janet's Repentance' but again expresses reservations about the harshness of some of the characterisation.

July
1 (Wed) First instalment of 'Janet's Repentance' appears in *Blackwood's*.
4 The reviewer of 'Janet's Repentance' in the *Manx Sun* attributes the work to 'Mr Liggins'.
7 Blackwood sends proofs of second instalment of 'Janet's Repentance' with slight reservations.

12   GE returns proofs. GHL requests Blackwood to refrain from criticising GE's work unless absolutely necessary.
14   Tells Sara Hennell that she expects to have forfeited the correspondence of her brother by her marriage.
19   Sends Bessie Parkes good wishes on becoming editor of the *Waverley Journal*. GHL writes satirically to Blackwood concerning the attribution of *Scenes* to Liggins.
24   Leave Jersey for London.
27   See Donizetti's *Lucrezia Borgia*.
31   Visited by Sara Hennell.

August
1   (Sat) Second instalment of 'Janet's Repentance' appears in *Blackwood's*.
2   GHL sends Blackwood the third instalment.
4   Entertain Barbara Bodichon (*née* Smith) and her new husband to dinner.
12   Blackwood sends proofs of third instalment of 'Janet's Repentance' with unqualified praise. GE begins reading Aeschylus's *Agamemnon*, having completed Sophocles's *Electra*.
15   Blackwood forwards a letter from the Revd W. P. Jones, claiming that 'Janet's Repentance' refers to his brother, who died 23 years previously.
18   Assures Blackwood that 'Mr Tryan is not a portrait of any clergyman, living or dead' (I, 462).
19   Tells Sara Hennell, 'writing is part of my religion, and I can write no word that is not prompted from within' (I, 464).
23   GHL returns proofs of third instalment of 'Janet's Repentance'.
24   GHL leaves to visit his sons at Hofwyl.

September
1   (Tues) Expresses to Bessie Parkes her approval of the contents of the *Waverley Journal*.
3   GHL returns from Hofwyl.
4   GHL sends Blackwood the fourth instalment of 'Janet's Repentance'.
5   Sends Blackwood her preliminary ideas for *Adam Bede*: 'I am inclined to take a large canvas for it, and write a novel' (I, 464).
23   Meets Bessie Parkes at the offices of the *Waverley Journal* and is introduced as 'Miss Evans'.

24   Asks Bessie Parkes to refer to her as Mrs Lewes.
27   Requests Chapman to send the books necessary for an article
      on F. W. Newman. Suggests W. M. W. Call to Chapman as a
      contributor.

October
 9   (Fri) Finishes 'Janet's Repentance'.
10   GHL despatches the last instalment of 'Janet's Repentance' to
      Blackwood.
11   Blackwood sends the final proof of 'Janet's Repentance' with
      a copy of each of the *Scenes* to revise for the book reprint.
17   Sends Blackwood a title page for the *Scenes* and proposals for
      Bede: 'My new story haunts me a good deal, and I shall set
      about it without delay. It will be a country story – full of the
      breath of cows and the scent of hay' (i, 465–6).
21   Recommends Monteil's *Histoire des Français des divers états* to
      Sara Hennell as 'one of the most wonderful books in French
      or any other literature' (i, 465).
22   Begins writing *Bede*.
25   Reading Sophocles's *Philoctetes*.
28   Blackwood finalises the publishing and copyright arrange-
      ments for *Scenes*.
29   Final part of 'Janet's Repentance' appears in *Blackwood's*.
30   Confirms her acceptance of £120 for the first edition of *Scenes*.

November
 5   (Thurs) Blackwood sends the first 16 pages of the first edition
      of *Scenes*.
 7   Thanks Blackwood for the proofs, also reporting that *Bede* 'is
      in progress – slow progress at present' (i, 470).
 8   Visited by Chapman and his brother Thomas.
15   Discusses in letter to Charles Bray the content of his *Philosophy
      of Necessity* and the desirability of its republication, remarking,
      'My own experience and development deepen every day my
      conviction that our moral progress may be measured by the
      degree in which we sympathise with individual suffering and
      individual joy' (i, 472).
22   Thirty-eighth birthday. Tells Sara Hennell, 'Anniversaries are
      sad things – to one who has lived long and done little' (i, 474).
      Birth of Gissing.

December

5 (Sat) GHL tells Blackwood that 'GE has come to stay at Richmond and is writing his new story with a fresh influx of confidence' (*Letters*, II, 406).

6 Writes 'How I Came to Write Fiction' in her Journal, detailing the conception and writing of *Scenes* (see I, 414–17, 428–9, 457). Finishes reading the *Agamemnon*.

7 Blackwood tells GHL that GE is too diffident.

8 Learns of Blackwood's decision to extend the first edition of *Scenes* to 1000 copies, and to give her a further £60.

9 Receive a letter from Blackwood's brother, Major William Blackwood, announcing his intention of visiting.

10 Major William Blackwood calls. GE notes, 'It was evident to us . . . that he knew I was George Eliot' (I, 476).

11 Thanks Blackwood for his confidence in *Scenes* and the extension of the first edition.

13 Reading Riehl's *Die Familie*. Tells Sara Hennell, 'I get more hungry for knowledge every day, and less able to satisfy my hunger' (I, 478). GHL proposes *Physiology of Common Life* to Blackwood.

14 Blackwood sends proof of the title page of *Scenes*.

15 Returns the amended proof with a list of the recipients of complimentary copies.

23 Writes to Charles Bray discussing his views on the gold standard and sending good wishes for Christmas.

25 'We ate our turkey together in a happy *solitude à deux*' (I, 480).

26 GHL travels to Vernon Hill for his annual Christmas visit to Helps.

27 Delane, editor of *The Times*, asks Blackwood for a review copy of *Scenes*.

31 Notes in her Journal, 'Few women, I fear, have had such reason as I have to think the long sad years of youth were worth living for the sake of middle age. . . . May I be able to look back on 1858 with an equal consciousness of advancement in worth and heart' (I, 481).

1858

January

2   (Sat) GHL returns from Vernon Hill with a copy of *The Times* containing Samuel Lucas's favourable review of *Scenes*.

4   *Scenes* subscribed in London.

5   First edition of *Scenes* published. Herbert Spencer to dinner.

6   First four chapters of *Bede* completed and read to GHL.

7   Blackwood sends details of the subscriptions to *Scenes*.

8   Subscriptions already total 580. GE notes that she ordered copies to be sent to Froude, Dickens, Thackeray, Tennyson, Ruskin, Faraday, Albert Smith and Jane Carlyle.

12   Writes to Chapman asking to be excused from contributing the article on F. W. Newman to *Westminster*.

17   Reading Aeschylus's *Choephori*. Agrees with Sara Hennell's disappointment with the January *Westminster*. J. A. Froude sends a letter of thanks for his copy of *Scenes*.

18   Dickens expresses his admiration for *Scenes* and his belief that the writer must be a woman.

20   Reads GHL part of ch. 6 of *Bede*.

21   Writes to Blackwood expressing her deep gratitude for Dickens's praise, and regretting that the 'iron mask of my *incognito*' prevents her writing to him (II, 8).

27   Dickens writes to Blackwood insisting that *Scenes* are the product of a female pen.

28   Faraday thanks GE for his copy of *Scenes*.

30   Writes to Bessie Parkes declaring her interest in the latter's new *English Woman's Journal*.

31   Finishes chs 7 and 8 of *Bede*.

February

2   (Tues) GHL writes to Blackwood expressing his disappointment at the sales of *Sea-Side Studies* and outlining his financial difficulties.

3   GE tells Bessie Parkes, 'I have given up writing "articles", having discovered that my vocation lies in other paths' (*Letters*, II, 431). Finishes reading Aeschylus's *Eumenides*.

10   Blackwood sends £120 as the first instalment for *Scenes*. Ch. 9 of *Bede* completed.

16   GHL visits J. W. Parker, publisher and editor of *Fraser's Magazine*, and hears GE spoken of as a writer of great merit.

25 Derby forms his second Ministry.
26 Visit W. M. W. Call and his wife Rufa (formerly Rufa Hennell), and have their photographs taken by Mayall.
28 Visited by Blackwood. GE gives GHL her permission to reveal her identity to Blackwood, who at last has his suspicion confirmed.

March

1 (Mon) Blackwood tells his wife of the revelation of GE's identity.
5 Visited by Blackwood, who reports Thackeray's high opinion of *Scenes*. Manuscript of chs 1–13 of *Bede* passed to Blackwood.
7 Signs her will.
8 Works on ch. 14 of *Bede*.
11 Blackwood sends his approval of the *Bede* manuscript.
13 GHL informs Blackwood that his praise has restored GE's confidence.
27 Authorises Blackwood to make his own decision as to whether *Bede* should appear in instalments, and requests an outstanding payment of £60 for *Scenes*. Sends Cara Bray her photo.
29 Asks Charles Bray not to spread 'false rumours' that she is commencing a novel (*Letters*, II, 443).
31 Blackwood sends a detailed appreciation of the first section of *Bede*, suggesting minor changes, but stressing its great promise.

April

1 (Thurs) Refuses to disclose the story of *Bede* to Blackwood in advance.
7 Leave for Munich, travelling via Lille, Cologne, Frankfurt and Nuremberg. For GE's account of this trip see I, 18–34, 39–61, 63–4.
12 Take lodgings in Munich at 15 Luitpoldstrasse.
18 Commences vol. II of *Bede* manuscript.
30 Blackwood agrees to GE's scheme of publishing *Bede* as a complete work as soon as it is finished.

May

5 (Wed) Call on Liebig in his laboratory. He explains his new method of mirror silvering, and gives GE a mirror as a souvenir.
12 Visit the anatomist von Siebold.

13   GHL visits the Museum of Comparative Anatomy to watch von Siebold at work.
14   GE sees Flemish pictures in the Pinakothek. Study of Flemish art in Munich galleries anticipates the concerns of ch. 17 of *Bede*.
26   Reads ch. 20 of *Bede* to GHL.
28   Discusses sources of *Scenes*, both actual and imaginary, in letter to Blackwood. Writing ch. 21 of *Bede*.
29   The *Saturday Review* contains a laudatory notice of *Scenes*.
30   See Rossini's *William Tell*. Conceives the fight in the wood between Arthur and Adam during this performance.

June
10   (Thurs) Finishes ch. 21 of *Bede*.
14   Sends condolences to Sara Hennell following the death of her mother.
17   Spends the next eight days working on chs 23–4 of *Bede*.
18   GHL leaves Munich to visit his sons at Hofwyl.
24   GHL returns.

July
 6   (Tues) Visited by Strauss at her lodgings: 'I had a quarter of an hour's chat with him alone, and was very agreeably impressed' (II, 63). *Bede* now completed to ch. 26.
 7   Leave Munich for Dresden, Vienna, Prague and the Tyrol, encountering scenes to be used in 'The Lifted Veil' and *Deronda*.
18   Take lodgings at 5B Waisenhausstrasse in Dresden. GE views, and is deeply impressed by, Raphael's *Madonna di San Sisto*.
23   GHL sends Chapman news of his almost completed article 'Realism in Art: Recent German Fiction'.

August
16   (Mon) GHL sends Blackwood publication details of *Physiology of Common Life* and confirms the good progress of *Bede*.
30   Visit Tauchnitz in Leipzig.
31   Shown around Carus's anatomical museum.

September
Ch. 36 of *Bede* completed at Richmond during the first week of this month, completing vol. II of the manuscript.

2 (Thurs) Return to Richmond.
3 GHL receives an offer from Major William Blackwood for the German publication of *Scenes*, and prepares to negotiate a fee.
4 Passes on Strauss's greetings to Rufa Call. Sends Sara Hennell a Liebig autograph.
5 Discusses Spurgeon, and Ruskin's high opinion of him, in letter to Sara Hennell.
8 Despatches vol. II of the *Bede* manuscript to Blackwood.
11 GHL confirms that GE requires £50 from Brockhaus for the German edition of *Scenes*.
26 J. A. Froude writes a second time requesting that he might know more of the author of *Scenes*.
30 Asks Blackwood to reply to Froude on her behalf stressing her admiration for him, but also the necessity of remaining incognito.

October
GHL's 'Realism in Art: Recent German Fiction' appears in the *Westminster*.
4 (Mon) Blackwood writes of his admiration for the second manuscript volume of *Bede*.
6 Discusses October's *Westminster* in letter to Sara Hennell.
7 Blackwood tells GHL that he had not praised vol. II of *Bede* sufficiently.
10 Chapman visits, expressing dissatisfaction with certain aspects of the *Westminster*.
13 Invites Charles Bray to visit Richmond.
29 Vol. III of the *Bede* manuscript sent to Blackwood.
31 Visited by Bessie Parkes and Barbara Bodichon.

November
1 (Mon) Reading Carlyle's *Life of Frederick the Great*.
3 Blackwood praises vol. III of the *Bede* manuscript and offers £800 for the copyright for four years.
5 Accepts Blackwood's offer. At dinner Herbert Spencer reveals that Chapman had referred casually to GE's authorship of *Scenes*. GE writes to Chapman insisting that he respect her incognito.
6 Sends Sara Hennell autographs, including Thierry, De Tocqueville and Comte.
10 Visited by Wilkie Collins: 'there is a sturdy uprightness about

him that makes all opinion and all occupation respectable' (II, 65).

15 Blackwood agrees to pay the first instalment for *Bede* immediately upon publication.

16 'Wrote the last word of *Adam Bede* . . . *Jubilate*' (II, 65).

17 GHL accepts Blackwood's offer for the publication of the *Physiology of Common Life*.

23 Blackwood sends congratulations on the conclusion of *Bede* and forwards Williams and Norgate's offer of £30 for the continental reprint of *Scenes*, together with the first proof sheets of *Bede*.

25 Accepts Williams and Norgate's offer. Visited by Charles Bray.

26 Sends Cara Bray her advice for the Brays' projected stay abroad.

30 GE writes the 'History of Adam Bede' in her Journal, detailing the conception and progress of the novel (see II, 65–71). Formally concludes her friendship with Chapman following his indiscretion over her incognito.

December

1 (Wed) Requests Blackwood not to delay the publication of *Bede* unduly lest her identity be discovered before the novel's appearance.

2 GHL stresses to Blackwood the necessity of concealing GE's identity if *Bede* is to be received impartially.

9 Blackwood sends £30 for the German edition of *Scenes* and suggests a sum of £50 for the initial offer of American publication.

10 GE suggests not more than £30 for the American publication, and expresses her approval of the typeface for *Bede*.

22 Sends Blackwood a prefatory 'Demonstrance' to *Bede*, written at GHL's insistence.

25 Blackwood advises omission of this preface.

27 GHL suggests a briefer advertisement to replace the *Bede* preface.

28 Writes to Blackwood agreeing that the *Bede* preface is unsuitable, and anticipating renewed writing in the new year: 'I have not yet made up my mind what my new story is to be, but I must not lie fallow any longer' (II, 75).

31 Records in Journal, 'Our double life is more and more blessed – more and more complete' (II, 75).

1859

January

1 (Sat) Tells Chapman that further letter-writing is unlikely to advance their mutual understanding.

3 Publication of part I of GHL's *Physiology of Common Life*.

12 First mention of research for *The Mill on the Floss* – searching *Annual Register* for examples of inundation. Reading Scott's *Life* and Michelet's *De l'amour*.

15 Last proofs of *Bede* read. GHL reports previous two to three weeks almost entirely taken up by house-hunting.

28 GHL records in his Journal his debt to Spencer for introducing him to GE: 'to know her was to love her, – and since then my life has been a new birth' (II, 76).

29 Visit St Paul's Cathedral. Blackwood sends £400 as a first instalment for *Bede*.

31 Asks Blackwood to send presentation copies of *Bede* to John Brown, Jane Carlyle, Dickens, J. A. Froude, Kingsley, Owen and Thackeray.

February

1 (Tues) *Bede* published.

5 Take possession of Holly Lodge, Southfields, near Wimbledon.

11 Move from Richmond to Holly Lodge.

12 Reads John Brown's 'Rab and his Friends' and Scott's *Life*. On GE's behalf, GHL writes to Chapman denying her authorship of *Bede*.

19 Tells Sara Hennell, 'We have met a pleasant-faced, bright-glancing young man, whom we set down to be worthy of the name, Richard Congreve. I am curious to see if our *Ahnung* will be verified' (II, 84).

20 Jane Carlyle expresses her delight at her presentation copy.

22 Begin enquiries for a new servant.

24 Much upset by receiving letter from consumptive Chrissey, and tells Cara Bray: 'It has ploughed up my heart' (II, 85).

26 Enthusiastic reviews of *Bede* appear in the *Athenaeum* and *Leader*, symptomatic of its generally favourable reception.

27 Pay their first call on their neighbours Richard and Maria Congreve.

March

7   (Mon) Blackwood reports *Bede* 'coming in a winner at a slapping pace' (*Letters*, III, 29). New servant begins work.

9   Elizabeth Gaskell admires GE's fiction in a letter to Blackwood.

10 Spend evening with the Congreves.

13 Meet the Positivist J. H. Bridges.

15 Death of Chrissey, before *rapprochement* could be effected.

16 Blackwood announces second edition of *Bede* now a certainty – the edition appears this month. Journal remarks, 'I happened this morning to be reading the 30th Ode, B. III of Horace – "Non omnis moriar"' (II, 93).

21 Tells Sara Hennell: 'Chrissey's death has taken from me the possibility of many things towards which I looked with some hope and yearning in the future' (II, 95).

23 Gives GHL the inscribed manuscript of *Bede*.

24 Unsuccessful visit from Spencer, with whom cordial relationships begin to decline.

26 A. E. Housman born.

31 Offers Blackwood 'The Lifted Veil', 'not a *jeu d'esprit*, but a *jeu de mélancolie*' (*Letters*, III, 41).

April

5   (Tues) Invited by Samuel Lucas to contribute to *Once a Week*.

6   Spend four days in the Isle of Wight in attempt to improve GHL's health.

11 *The Times* declares of *Bede* that 'its author takes rank at once among the masters of the art'.

13 Henry Smith Anders writes to *The Times* asserting that Joseph Liggins is the author of *Scenes* and *Bede*.

15 GHL writes to *The Times* denying Liggins's authorship. Barbara Bodichon sure that *Bede* is by GE.

17 Records success of *Bede* in her Journal, remarking, 'Shall I ever write another book as true as *Adam Bede*? The weight of the future presses on me, and makes itself felt even more than the deep satisfaction of the past and present' (II, 101).

19 Informs Sara Hennell of the pleasure derived from the company of the Congreves.

20 GHL tells Blackwood that the Liggins myth must be refuted.

24 E. G. Bulwer-Lytton praises *Bede* as 'one of the very ablest works of fiction I have read for years' (II, 102).

26 Barbara Bodichon reveals her intuition that GE is the author of *Bede*. GE finishes 'The Lifted Veil'.

27 Blackwood proposes a third edition of *Bede*. GHL suffers unpleasant fall.

29 Decides to rewrite first two chapters of *Mill*. Informs Blackwood of desire to add a sentence to third edition of *Bede* – the only alteration proposed.

May

5 (Thurs) Acknowledges the authorship of *Bede* to Barbara Bodichon but asks her to keep the secret. GHL tells Barbara Bodichon not to address GE as Marian Evans. Blackwood reports the 'third' edition of *Bede* (actually a new impression of the second edition) almost sold.

6 Tells Major William Blackwood it seems impossible to write anything so good and true as *Bede* again.

18 Blackwood sends proof of 'The Lifted Veil', suggesting the deletion of the final blood transfusion (advice ignored), and offering to make an extra payment of £400 for *Bede*.

21 Tells Sara Hennell that she and GHL take it in turns to nurse each other – symptomatic of their variable health in these years. Returns corrected proof of 'The Lifted Veil'.

25 First concert outing since returning from abroad – Handel's *Acis and Galatea*, arranged by Mozart, at St James's Hall.

27 Entertain Blackwood to dinner.

29 Visited by George Meredith – one of several contacts with the novelist during this period.

30 The editor of *The Times* hears news of 'George Eliot's' identity.

June

3 (Fri) Elizabeth Gaskell writes to say that being suspected as the author of *Bede* was the greatest compliment she had yet received.

5 Visited by Blackwood, who reports that GE 'gave me more the idea of the creator of her humorous characters than I have yet seen' (*Letters*, III, 75).

13 The Revd John Gwyther writes to Blackwood claiming that he is sure that he has been depicted as 'Amos Barton', and also identifying other 'originals'.

18 Second Ministry of Parlmerston begins.

20 Attend *Messiah* at the Crystal Palace. Afterwards dine with the

Brays, GE revealing her *nom de plume*. Blackwood delighted with the opening of *Mill*. Third edition of *Bede* published.

25   Blackwood visits Holly Lodge and discusses terms for *Mill*, subsequently telling his brother that it is impossible not to like GE excessively. GHL prepares a denunciation of Liggins for *The Times*.

26   Sara Hennell reports Isaac Evans's remark that no one but his sister could have written *Bede*.

27   Tells the Brays and Sara Hennell that she does not enjoy discussing her books. Editor of *The Times* tells Blackwood that he feels GHL's denunciation is too severe.

29   GHL tells John and Major William Blackwood that the secret of authorship is to be revealed.

30   GHL requests Barbara Bodichon not to pass on any adverse criticism to GE. He tells Bray that the secrecy of the pseudonym is to be abandoned.

July

'The Lifted Veil' appears in *Blackwood's*. Fourth edition of *Bede* published.

2   (Sat) *Athenaeum* attacks 'George Eliot' for mystification over the authorship of her books. Visit from John and Major William Blackwood.

9   Leave to visit GHL's children in Switzerland, having heard that the fourth edition of *Bede* is already sold out. For details of journey, see II, 119.

10   Dickens writes to GE that *Bede* has taken its place among the actual experiences and endurances of his life, and invites her to contribute to his periodical.

13   GHL tells his children of his relationship with GE, about which they are delighted.

19   Leave Lucerne for London.

29   Second edition of *Scenes* published.

30   Langford brings a pug as a present from Blackwood, and also the second edition of *Scenes*. GE tells Charles Lewes: 'I look forward to playing duets with you as one of my future pleasures' (II, 125).

August

6   (Sat) Dickens regrets that he is unable to visit GE and GHL until he comes up to town.

15 Declines invitation to write story for the *New York Century* for fee of £1200.

17 Sends Blackwood progress report on *Mill*: 'my stories grow in me like plants, and this is only in the leaf-bud. I have faith that the flower will come' (II, 129).

18 First letter from Thornton Lewes to his new 'mother'.

25 Travel to North Wales.

31 Abandon North Wales for Weymouth, Dorset, meeting two nieces at Lichfield, Staffordshire, *en route*, and gathering detail for *Mill* in Dorset.

September

5 (Mon) Study mills in Dorset. Read aloud A. H. Layard, *Nineveh and its Remains*.

6 GHL tells Blackwood, 'GE is in high spirits, having found a mill and mill-stream to his heart's content' (*Letters*, III, 145).

13 Suggests to Blackwood that *Mill* should not receive serial publication.

16 Return from Dorset to Holly Lodge.

18 'In much anxiety and doubt about my new novel' (II,133).

19 Writes to Charles Bray about her extreme annoyance with Bracebridge. GHL writes directly and vehemently to Bracebridge.

21 Blackwood offers £3000 for *Mill*, and suggests retaining serial publication. Bracebridge renounces Liggins.

26 Depart for the Trent to gather more material for *Mill*.

28 Return to Holly Lodge.

30 Annoyed by Bracebridge's description of her father as a 'farmer'. GHL asks Charles Bray to move GE's photograph to a private position in his house. Gratified by Spencer's praise of *Bede*.

October

Newby advertises *Adam Bede, Junior: A Sequel*.

7 (Fri) Records in Journal, 'Certain "new" ideas have occurred to me in relation to my novel, and I am in better hope of it' (II, 133). Sends Sara Hennell a detailed description of her aunt, Elizabeth Evans, who suggested characters and incidents in *Bede*.

11 Tolstoy reads *Bede*, a representative instance of its remarkable reputation and market.

16   Vol. I of *Mill* finished. Draws Blackwood's attention to printer's errors in the third edition of *Bede*.
18   Writes to D'Albert, announcing that she has at last found out her new vocation. Major William Blackwood perturbed to find GE's change of signature (from 'George Eliot' to 'Marian Evans Lewes').
23   Spencer dines at Holly Lodge, better relationships having been restored with him. GE resolves to allow no more talk in her house with visitors on the subject of her books.
24   GHL attempts to get Blackwood to instigate legal proceedings against the *Bede* sequel.
25   Finish reading Balzac's *Père Goriot*: 'a hateful book' (II, 139).
27   Blackwood sends the final £400 for *Bede*, and promises a bonus of £800 in the new year.
28   Acknowledges Blackwood's gesture, but in terms the firm considered cold and insensitive.

November
2   (Wed) Reading *Tom Brown at Oxford*.
10   Entertains Dickens to dinner at Holly Lodge, afterwards visiting the Congreves to discuss Positivism. GE pronounces Dickens 'a man one can thoroughly enjoy talking to' (II, 140). Elizabeth Gaskell renounces Liggins.
11   GE acknowledges Gaskell's letter, offering her own generous assessment of Gaskell's work.
14   Invited by Dickens to write a new novel for *All the Year Round*. Asks Sara Hennell never to pass on to her comments made by others about GE's characters and writings.
15   Bradbury and Evans offer to outbid Blackwood's for *Mill*.
18   Declines Dickens's invitation. Reading Thomas à Kempis. Blackwood tells Langford of his disappointment at the tone of GE's reply to his offer. GHL informs Blackwood that 'Maggie goes on gloriously' (*Letters*, III, 208).
21   Sign their wills, their solicitor, Henry Sheard, simultaneously offering advice on the legal background in *Mill*.
22   Fortieth birthday. Records in Journal her annoyance at Blackwood's failure to suppress *Adam Bede, Junior*.
23   Begin reading (on the day before its publication) Darwin's *On the Origin of Species* – 'not impressive' (II, 143).
25   Tells the Brays Darwin's book 'makes an epoch' (II, 144). Rereads Bunyan with pleasure.

26 Writes desiring to know if Blackwoods' wish to remain her publishers.
28 Blackwood explains his conduct, and on the 30th GE sends a lengthy explanation of her own. Also writes to *The Times* emphatically dissociating herself from *Adam Bede, Junior*.

December
1 (Thurs) Major William Blackwood tells his brother that he is chiefly perturbed by GE's determination to drop her incognito. GHL asks Emile Montégut to suggest a translator for *Bede*.
3 Book III of *Mill* finished.
5 Writes at length to Barbara Bodichon, discussing Darwin, and remarking that recent difficulties have taught 'how entirely the rewards of the artist lie apart from everything that is narrow and personal' (II, 147).
6 Writes at length to D'Albert, detailing the changes in her character since he knew her.
7 Long visit from Blackwood, discussing terms for *Mill*.
9 Visited by Tauchnitz.
12 Blackwood finds the first volume and a half of *Mill* wonderfully clever.
14 Blackwood offers £2000 for first edition of *Mill*.
15 Blackwood visits, and tells his brother his former good opinion of GE is restored.
20 Accepts Blackwood's offer.
25 Spend Christmas Day with the Congreves. Bridges also present.
27 GHL sends light-hearted New Year greetings to Blackwood.
28 Death of Macaulay.

1860

January
1 (Sun) Given a set of Waverley novels by GHL.
2 Blackwood pays additional royalty on *Bede* and returns copyright.
3 Acknowledges Blackwood's generosity, and asks his advice on possible titles for *Mill*.
4 GHL offers Blackwood five possible titles for *Mill*.
6 Blackwood makes his own title suggestion: *The Mill on the Floss*.

11   Records in Journal: 'Our New Year opens with happy omens' (II, 154).
12   *The Mill on the Floss* chosen as title.
16   Vol. II of *Mill* manuscript completed. GHL tells Blackwood that the Queen has commissioned two watercolours of scenes from *Bede*. Reading *Humphry Clinker* – 'much disappointed' (II, 156). Chapman asks permission to reprint GE's articles (refused).
26   Entertain Pigott, Redford, and Frederic Chapman to dinner. Maria Congreve and her sister arrive for musical entertainment.
28   Tells Blackwood, 'I have been invalided for the last week, and, of course, am a prisoner in the castle of Giant Despair, who growls in my ear that *The Mill on the Floss* is detestable' (II, 156).

February
 7   (Tues) GHL remarks to Blackwood, 'There never *was* so diffident and desponding an author, since the craft first began' (*Letters*, III, 258).
10   Blackwood receives manuscript of vol. II of *Mill*.
19   GHL requests proof to be sent to Sheard, to prevent legal solecisms.
23   E. G. Bulwer-Lytton calls. GE reports to Blackwood that Lytton 'thinks the two defects of *Adam Bede* are the dialect and Adam's marriage with Dinah; but of course, I would have my teeth drawn rather than give up either' (II, 157).
29   GHL secures £300 for *Mill* from Harpers.

March
 1   (Thurs) Terms for American and German editions of *Mill* arranged.
 3   Informed of death of niece Katie.
 4   Samuel Laurence requests permission to paint GE's portrait – sittings given in August.
?5   GHL tells Blackwood, 'Mrs Lewes is getting her eyes redder and *swollener* every morning as she lives through her tragic story' (*Letters*, III, 269).
17   GHL forbids the confirmation of his two eldest boys.
21   Completes *Mill*.
22   Tells Blackwood, 'I am grateful and yet rather sad to have finished' (II, 160), and sends three corrections. Also remarks,

'It is time that I should go and absorb some new life, and gather fresh ideas' (II, 160).

23 Receives, corrects, and returns, proof of *Mill* conclusion. GHL asks Bray to abstain from biographical statements about GE.
24 Depart for Italy, via Paris. For GE's detailed account of this European trip see II, 164–252.
25 Visit Notre Dame, Sainte Chapelle and Louvre, and see Rossini's *Otello*.

April

1 (Sun) Arrive in Rome. GE at first disappointed.
3 Visit cemetery containing grave of Keats and ashes of Shelley – 'a spot that touched me deeply' (II, 193).
4 *Mill* published.
5 Kneels to receive the Pope's blessing in St Peter's.
7 Third edition of *Scenes* published.
29 Leave Rome.
30 Arrive in Naples, 'declaring it to surpass all places we had seen before' (II, 199).

May

5 (Sat) Visit Pompeii. 'I hope I shall never forget the solemnity of our entrance into that silent city' (II, 204).
6 GHL sends his sons details of the holiday so far.
13 Second visit to Pompeii.
15 Leave Naples.
17 Arrive in Florence.
19 *The Times* reviews *Mill* favourably.
21 Savonarola strikes GHL as a good subject for a novel. GE immediately enthusiastic.
22 Sara Hennell sends signed copy of her *Thoughts in Aid of Faith*. Buy Savonarola's *Poems* and visit his monastery of San Marco.
27 Writes to Major William Blackwood discussing deficiencies in the *Times* review of *Mill*.
30 Spend evening with Theodosia Trollope at Florence.

June

1 (Fri) Leave Florence for Bologna.
4 Arrive in Venice: 'Venice was more beautiful than romances had feigned' (II, 237).

7   Asks D'Albert never to let her know the substance of French criticism of her work.

12   Leave Venice.

23   Tells Blackwood their journey has left them 'immensely enriched with new ideas and new veins of interest' and that she is keen to begin a new and secret 'great project' (II, 252).

25   Visit Hofwyl, taking away Charles Lewes, GHL's eldest son.

26   Introduces GHL to D'Albert at Geneva.

July

1   (Sun) Return to Holly Lodge 'after three months of delightful travel' (II, 25), with Charles, 'the most entirely lovable human animal of seventeen and a half that I ever met with or heard of' (II, 266).

7   Thanks Sara Hennell for her *Thoughts in Aid of Faith*, though also expressing guarded reservations.

9   Sends Blackwood her comments on E. G. Bulwer-Lytton's criticism of *Mill*. GHL writes with blunt criticism of Sara Hennell's *Thoughts*.

18   Offers to lend Charles Bray £100.

20   Trollope announces that Charles Lewes has been nominated as a supplementary clerk in the Post Office.

August

Writes 'Brother Jacob'. Sits for Laurence portrait.

6   (Mon) GHL asks Blackwood to suggest a suitable Edinburgh establishment for his second son, Thornton, to board at.

15   Charles Lewes enters the Civil Service.

?21   Advises Barbara Bodichon on wording for a memorial to her father.

27   Regrets distressing Sara Hennell. Reading Emerson, 'Man the Reformer'.

28   Tells Blackwood of the Savonarola idea, but wishes to write another novel first. Eighth sitting for Laurence. Succeed in letting Holly Lodge.

September

4   (Tues) Make offer for 10, Harewood Square, Marylebone.

11   Thornton Lewes leaves Hofwyl for Edinburgh.

24   Move to Harewood Square.

26   Blackwood sends £1000 as first instalment for *Mill*.

30 GHL delivers Thornton to a schoolmaster in Edinburgh. GE begins *Silas Marner*.

October
17 (Wed) Begin to attend course of chemistry lectures by A. W. Hofmann.

November
13 (Tues) Rereading Sara Hennell's *Thoughts*.
20 Trollope to dinner: 'made me like him very much by his straightforward wholesome *Wesen*' (II, 280). Hears from Arthur Helps of Queen Victoria's admiration for her work.
24 Second edition of *Mill* published.
26 GHL tells Blackwood that GE, recovered from illness, is now writing magnificently.
28 Reports herself suffering from depression: 'the loss of the country has seemed very bitter to me, and my want of health and strength has prevented me from working much' (II, 279–80). Work proceeding slowly on *Marner*, 'the idea of which came to me after our arrival in this house' (II, 280–1).

December
7 (Fri) Tells Maria Congreve of pleasure given by Monday Pops Concerts at St James's Hall, at which GE and GHL become regular attenders.
17 Move to 16 Blandford Square.
20 Records admiration for part II of Spencer's *First Principles*.
26 Tells Barbara Bodichon, 'Everything I do seems poor and trivial in the doing, and when it is quite gone from me, and seems no longer my own, then I rejoice in it and think it fine. That is the history of my life' (II, 284).
29 Blackwood sends £1000 for *Mill*, and £150 each for *Bede* and *Scenes*.
31 Records in Journal, 'this year has been marked by many blessings, and above all, by the comfort we have found in having Charles with us. Since we set out on our journey to Italy on 25th March, the time has not been fruitful in work: distractions about our change of residence have run away with many days; and since I have been in London my state of health has been depressing to all effort.
    'May the next year be more fruitful!' (II, 284).

1861

January

12 (Sat) Tells Blackwood she is writing *Marner*, a 'sudden inspiration' (II, 285).

16 Invites Sara Hennell to call.

22 Warmly thanks Richard Owen for sending a copy of his *Memoir on the Megatherium*.

29 Gives D'Albert a comparative assessment of *Bede* and *Mill*.

February

1 (Fri) 'The first month of the New Year has been passed in much bodily discomfort' (II, 285).

2 Begin four-day trip to Surrey – 'I suppose we must keep soul and body together by occasional flights of this sort' (II, 286).

6 Thanks Maria Congreve for the gift of a basket of eggs.

15 First 13 chapters of *Marner* sent to Blackwood. Reading Carlyle's *Memoirs*.

16 Tells Maria Congreve, 'I have not been working much lately – indeed this year has been a comparatively idle one. I think my *malaise* is chiefly owing to the depressing influence of town air and town scenes' (II, 288).

19 Blackwood congratulates GE on opening of *Marner*, whilst expressing reservations about a 'want of brighter lights' and more likeable characters (*Letters*, III, 380).

20 Remarks to Sara Hennell, 'I am unequal to the least exertion or irregularity. My only pleasure away from our own health is going to the Zoological Gardens' (II, 288).

24 Informs Blackwood of the inspiration for *Marner*, and of its intention of setting 'in a strong light the remedial influences of pure, natural human relations' (II, 290).

27 Blackwood offers £800 for the first edition of *Marner*.

28 Accepts this offer.

March

4 (Mon) Sends Blackwood a motto from Wordsworth's 'Michael' for *Marner*.

6 GHL tells Blackwood that he is reassured by his approval of *Marner*.

10 Last pages of *Marner* sent to Blackwood.

11 Sends a lengthy letter of personal news to Barbara Bodichon.

13 Tells Blackwood that, against his advice, she has decided to retain the carol sung by Aaron Winthorp in ch. 10 of *Marner* and thanks him for his prompt printing of the novel.

18 Set off for a week in Hastings, reading there book v of Macaulay's *History of England*.

19 Sends duplicate corrections (from memory) for end of *Marner*, the corrected proofs having been lost in the post. Writes affectionately to Charles Bray.

23 GHL, having dissected a starfish, reports GE reading Macaulay. GE tells Blackwood that she and GHL are considering a second visit to Florence.

25 Receive first copy of *Marner*.

27 Asks Langford to send a presentation copy of *Marner* to GHL's mother.

28 Blackwood buys portrait of GE by Laurence. GE tells Cara Bray of her gratitude to her: 'I suppose I must lose my memory altogether before I could forget all the tenderness, forbearance, and generous belief that made the unvarying character of your friendship towards me when we used to be a great deal together' (*Letters*, viii, 276).

April

1 (Mon) Blackwood sends cheque for £1350 for *Mill*.

2 Publication of *Marner*. Langford reports 5500 copies already bespoken.

6 Explains to Clementia Taylor her rule of never paying visits.

8 Death of Major William Blackwood. Declines permission for Laurence portrait to be exhibited.

9 Tells Barbara Bodichon of their projected Italian visit.

12 Hear Beethoven's Mass in D at the Exeter Hall, but GE comments the next day to Sara Hennell, 'The enjoyment of such things is much diminished by the gas and bad air. Indeed our long addiction to a quiet life, in which our daily walk among the still grass and trees was a *fête* to us, has unfitted us for the sacrifices that London demands' (ii, 297).

19 Set out for Italy, GE intending to do further research on Savonarola.

21 Send Charles Lewes details of their brief stay in Paris.

May

4 (Sat) Arrive in Florence, but soon plagued by illness. Learn

from Blackwood that he expects to sell the complete print run of *Marner* (7500 copies).

5   GHL sends Charles Lewes further details of their travels.
16 Hear Bottesini, the legendary double-bass virtuoso.
17 Tell Charles Lewes about the Bottesini performance, and describe their working day.
19 Reports to Blackwood, 'We have been industriously foraging in old streets and old books. I feel very grave just now, and enjoy the thought of work' (II, 303).
28 GHL tells Blackwood of the pleasure he derives from GE's affection for his children, shown in several affectionate letters of this period.

June
Discusses fine details of *Romola* with Tom Trollope.
3   (Mon) Set off in company of Tom Trollope to visit monasteries of Camaldoli and La Vernia. For details see *Letters*, III, 422–5.
7   Leave Florence for Berne.
12 See Bertie Lewes at Hofwyl.
14 Return to England.
15 Talks to Blackwood at lunch about progress with *Romola*.
16 Reports in Journal, 'This morning, for the first time, I feel myself quietly settled at home. I am in excellent health, and long to work steadily and effectively' (II, 306).
17 Entertained by Blackwood at Greenwich.
19 Finishes the first volume of her Journal: 'This is the last entry I mean to make in my old book in which I wrote for the first time at Geneva in 1849. What moments of despair I passed through after that – despair that life would ever be made precious to me by the consciousness that I lived to some good purpose. . . . The same demon tries to get hold of me again whenever an old work is dismissed and a new one is being meditated' (II, 306–7). Tells Sara Hennell, 'We have had a perfect journey except as regards health – a large, large exception' (II, 307).
22 GHL writes reprovingly to Edward Walford about inaccurate statements concerning GE's biography in his *Men of the Time*.
30 Death of E. B. Browning.

July
For a detailed account of reading in the second part of this year, see II, 325–6.

2   (Tues) Tells Sara Hennell of disappointment at failure to gain a glimpse of a conspicuous comet.
4   Anthony Trollope and W. G. Clark to dinner.
5   Having finished Tom Trollope's *La Beata*, (which may have suggested some details of Tessa in *Romola*), writes to Trollope to express her appreciation of it.
12 Tells Sara Hennell she has been reading Pierre Helyot, *L'Histoire des ordres monastiques*, Montalembert, *Monks of the West*, and Comte, *Philosophie positive*, vol. v.
26 See Fechter in *Hamlet*.
30 'My mind dwelling with much depression on probability or improbability of my achieving the work I wish to do. I struck out two or three thoughts towards an English novel' (II, 311).

August
Reads E. G. Bulwer-Lytton's *Rienzi* to help with difficulties of historical novels.

1   (Thurs) 'Struggling constantly with depression' (II, 313).
2   Reading Boccaccio.
12 Depressed by inability to construct story of *Romola*: 'I became desperate, and suddenly burst my bonds, saying, I will not think of writing' (II, 313).
17 Musical entertainment with Pigott and Redford – one of several such relaxations this month.
20 GHL reports progress with planning of *Romola* – it is 'slowly crystallising into what will be a magnificent programme' (*Letters*, III, 446).

September
5   (Thurs) Begin fortnight at Malvern to take waters. Reading Anna Jameson, *Legends of the Monastic Orders*, and Marchesi, *Storia di San Marco*.
12 Tells Blackwood, 'I can desire nothing more satisfactory to myself than that our relations should continue as long as my writing life' (*Letters*, VIII, 289).
18 Begins to correct her four books for Cheap edition.
23 Blackwood sends £1000 as second instalment for *Marner*.
25 Sends Blackwood corrections for *Bede* and *Mill*: 'It has moved

me a good deal – reading the books again after a long interval, but it has done me good, for I can say a full Amen to everything I have written' (*Letters*, VIII, 291).

27 Buy new grand piano 'which tempts me to play more than I have done for years before' (II, 319).

29 Finishes correcting proofs for Cheap edition of novels – 'feel my mind free for other work' (II, 317).

October

4 (Fri) 'My mind still worried about my plot – and without any confidence in my ability to do what I want' (II, 317).

7 Begins ch. 1 of *Romola*.

11 Blackwood offers £3000 for copyright of novels. Reading Nardi's *History of Florence*.

12 'In the evening we had our usual Saturday mixture of visitors, talk, and music' (II, 318).

30 'Utterly desponding' about *Romola* (II, 319).

November

Reads Scott's *The Pirate* to help with *Romola*.

5 (Tues) Reading Cicero, *De officiis* and Petrarch's *Letters*. Records in Journal that she is 'dreadfully depressed' about *Romola*.

6 Tempted to abandon *Romola*.

11 See Fechter in *Othello* – 'lamentably bad' (II, 320).

13 Death of A. H. Clough.

14 Visits British Museum reading room for first time, to research costumes for *Romola*.

18 Tells Blackwood she declines to sell her copyrights, also mentioning that 'that journalistic whirlwind,' Dumas *père*, has pronounced *Bede* 'the greatest novel of the age' (*Letters*, VIII, 293).

30 Visited by Wilkie Collins, a frequent caller at this time.

December

Second edition of *Marner* published.

8 (Sun) Tells GHL her scheme for *Romola*.

12 Completes scheme for *Romola*, and determines to revise it.

14 GHL reports GE 'still deep in her researches . . . her distressing diffidence paralyses her' (*Letters*, III, 473–4). Death of Prince Albert.

17 Studying topography of Florence.

23 Speaks of beginning (i.e. re-beginning) *Romola* on New Year's
    Day.

1862

January

 1 (Wed) Tells Blackwood, 'The year opens with good auguries.
    I have begun [i.e. re-begun] my novel [i.e. *Romola*] this
    morning' (*Letters*, IV, 3).
 2 Sends D'Albert her recent news.
 7 Implores Maria Congreve to visit them.
12 Encourages Blackwood to contemplate issuing the Cheap
    edition of *Marner* and *Scenes* at Easter.
13 Tells Cara Bray: 'The year is opening happily for us, except –
    alas! the exception is a great one – in the way of health. Mr
    Lewes is constantly ailing, like a delicate headachy woman'
    (II, 330).
14 Reading Trollope's *Orley Farm*, commenting to Sara Hennell,
    'Anthony Trollope is admirable in the presentation of even
    average life and character, and he is so thoroughly wholesome-
    minded that one delights in seeing his books lie about to be
    read' (II, 331).
23 George Smith calls to ask if GE will be open to a magnificent
    offer for *Romola*.
26 Records in Journal, 'Detained from writing by the necessity of
    gaining particulars: 1st, about Lorenzo de Medici's death; 2d,
    about the possible retardation of Easter; 3d, about Corpus
    Christi day; 4th, about Savonarola's preaching in the Quare-
    sima of 1492. Finished "La Mandragola" – second time reading
    for the sake of Florentine expressions – and began "La
    Calandra"' (II, 332).
31 Reads Proem and opening scene of *Romola* to admiring GHL.
    Records in Journal, 'It is impossible to me to believe that I
    have ever been in so unpromising and despairing a state as I
    now feel' (II, 332).

February

 7 (Fri) Finishes rewriting ch. 1 of *Romola*.
11 Begin three-day stay at Dorking, Surrey.
15 Cheap edition of *Bede* published. Tells Barbara Bodichon, 'We

have had no troubles but the public troubles – anxiety about the war with America, and sympathy with the poor Queen' (II, 335).

17 Reports completion of Proem and first two chapters of *Romola*. Records in Journal, 'I have an oppressive sense of the far-stretching task before me' (II, 336).

19 Visits British Museum for *Romola* research. Finishes reading E. B. Browning's *Casa Guidi Windows*, remarking, 'It contains amongst other admirable things a very noble expression of what I believe to be the true relation of the religious mind to the past' (II, 336).

22 Complains to Blackwood about poor publicity for Cheap edition of her works.

23 Pleased to note the affectionate respect of the obituary notices of A. H. Clough.

26 Considerably depressed by slow progress of *Romola*. Confides to Journal, 'I have a distrust in myself, in my work, in others' loving acceptance of it, which robs my otherwise happy life of all joy. . . . I have written now about sixty pages of my romance. Will it ever be finished? Ever be worth anything?' (II, 336).

27 Smith offers £10,000 for *Romola*, which GHL swiftly recognises as 'the most magnificent offer ever yet made for a novel' (*Letters*, IV, 17–18). Send their servants to the theatre.

28 Finishes reading David Wingate's *Poems and Songs*.

March
 1 (Sat) Idea for swift *Cornhill* appearance of *Romola* – with correspondingly high fee – temporarily abandoned.
 5 Begin week's stay at Englefield Green, Surrey.
24 Reports in Journal having begun ch. 4 of *Romola*.
29 Finishes Christopher Wordsworth's *Greece*.
31 Hear Joachim play at St James's Hall.

April
 2 (Wed) Records in Journal, 'Writing with enjoyment', but progress with *Romola* still slow (II, 338).
16 Begin three weeks at Dorking in attempt to revive GE's health and spirits.
23 Assures Sara Hennell that she is not the author of *Chronicles of Carlingford* (actually by Margaret Oliphant).

May

8   (Thurs) GHL accepts consultant editorship of the *Cornhill*.
9   Sends domestic news, and details of a recent concert visit, to Charles Lewes.
10 Reading Collins's *No Name*. Thanks Cara Bray for printing a correction of the rumour that GE is the author of *Chronicles of Carlingford*.
12 Reads Smith several chapters of *Romola*.
15 Trollope reports that Charles Lewes is not doing well at the Post Office.
17 See Verdi's *Rigoletto*.
19 Accepts £7000 for *Romola* in *Cornhill*. Leighton chosen as illustrator. Informs Blackwood of plans to publish *Romola* elsewhere.
20 Blackwood gracefully acknowledges GE's decision. View Leighton's pictures at the Academy.
21 GE signs agreement with Smith for *Romola*.
22 Smith and Leighton call to discuss the *Romola* illustrations.
23 Visited by Tom Trollope.
27 Entertain Anthony and Tom Trollope and others to dinner.
?31 Completes book II of *Romola*.

June

?4 (Wed) Suggests revisions of Leighton's first illustration; considerable exchange of information, especially on Florentine costume, follows.
?5 Congratulates Leighton on his representation of Nello.
10 Still frustrated by slow progress with *Romola*.
13 GHL informs Charles Bolton that he is at liberty to dramatise *Marner* (never accomplished).
17 Visited by Blackwood.
22 Reads the third book of *Romola* to GHL.
25 Begins fourth book of *Romola*.
26 Visits recently opened International Exhibition at South Kensington with Bara Bodichon.
30 Receives congratulatory letter about *Romola* from Trollope.

July

Publication of *Romola* begins in Cornhill.
5   (Sat) Tells D'Albert that she hopes he will be the official translator of *Romola*.

10   Thanks George Smith for sending a copy of D. G. Rossetti's
     Early Italian Poets.
14   Thanks Sara Hennell for her congratulatory remarks about
     Romola.
31   Finishes book IV of *Romola*.

August
 4   (Mon) Thornton Lewes passes first examination for Indian
     Civil Service.

September
 4   (Thurs) Begins three-week stay at Littlehampton, Sussex,
     writing *Romola* (chs 27–32) and reading Beaumont and Fletcher.
12   GHL writes severely to Sara Hennell asking her never to pass
     on any comments on GE's work.

October
21   (Tues) Blackwood sends details of sales of the Cheap edition
     of GE's works.
22   GE replies, and recommends Trollope's *Orley Farm*.
31   Finishes book VII of *Romola*.

November
14   (Fri) Finishes reading Boccaccio for second time.
25   Much impressed by hearing Joachim play Bach at a Monday
     Pops concert.
26   Tells Barbara Bodichon, 'Pray don't ever ask me again not to
     rob a man of his religious belief, as if you thought my mind
     tended to such robbery. . . . I have very little sympathy with
     Freethinkers as a class, and have lost all interest in mere
     antagonism to religious doctrines' (II, 343).
28   Thanks D'Albert for sending two copies of his translation of
     Marner.
30   Book VIII of *Romola* finished.

December
 8   (Mon) Cheap edition of *Mill* published.
16   First visit from Browning.
17   Records in Journal, 'At p. 22 only. I am extremely spiritless,
     dead, and hopeless about my writings. . . . I am inwardly
     irritable, and unvisited by good thoughts. . . . After this

record, I read aloud what I had written of book ix to George, and he, to my surprise, entirely approved of it' (ii, 345).

21 Thornton Lewes knocks down his tutor, but is reinstated in the tutor's house.

24 Tells Clementia Taylor, 'We go nowhere except to concerts' (ii, 345) and attends *Messiah* that evening.

26 Tells Sara Hennell of her enjoyment of *Messiah*, remarking, 'What pitiable people those who feel no poetry in Christianity. Surely the acme of poetry hitherto is the conception of the suffering Messiah, and the final triumph. . . . The Prometheus is a very imperfect foreshadowing of that symbol wrought out in the long history of the Jewish and Christian ages' (ii, 347).

31 Reflects in her Journal on the many blessings experienced in the passing year, not least 'opportunities which have enabled us to acquire an abundant independence' (ii, 348).

1863

January

1 (Thurs) Thanks Sara Hennell for sending a book mark for her Bible.

17 Blackwood requests corrected copy for the Cheap edition of *Scenes* and *Marner*, and gives a disappointing report of recent sales of GE's novels.

23 Begins four-day visit to Dorking. Subsequently reports to Sara Hennell, 'the quiet and fresh air seemed to make a new creature of me' (ii, 349).

February

2 (Mon) Thanks Sara Hennell for her generous appreciation of *Romola*: 'I have had a great deal of pretty encouragement from immense big-wigs, some of them saying *Romola* is the finest book they ever read; but the opinion of big-wigs has one sort of value, and the fellow-feeling of a long-known friend has another. One can't do quite well without both' (ii, 349).

4 Finishes book x of *Romola*.

6 Instructs Blackwood to reprint the existing text of *Marner* (i.e. the second edition).

22 Visits the Congreves at Wimbledon.

March

1   (Sun) Declines Emily Faithfull's invitation to write a story for the *Victoria Magazine*.

10   Thanks Smith for a gift of Thackeray's *Henry Esmond*, and reports herself impressed by the progress of Gaskell's *Sylvia's Lovers*.

21   Records in Journal, 'making no progress in writing' (*Letters*, IV, 79).

23   Leave for Dorking.

30   Return to Blandford Square.

April

Cheap edition of *Scenes* and *Marner* (in one volume) published.

5   (Sun) Finishes *Romola* book XII. Thanks D'Albert for sending his translation of *Mill*, entitled *La Famille Tulliver*.

16   Discusses Anthony and Tom Trollope, and the latter's views on spiritualism, in letter to Charles Bray.

18   Regrets that she will be in Dorking when Maria Congreve calls, though reporting, 'at present I am rather like a shell-less lobster, and inclined to creep out of sight' (II, 350).

28   Recommends Thackeray's *Lectures on the English Humourists* to Charles Lewes.

May

12   (Tues) Thanks Bessie Rayner Parkes for gift of her *Ballads and Songs*. Looks forward to seeing Barbara Bodichon in June: 'You will come to me like the morning sunlight, and make me a little less of a flaccid cabbage-plant' (II, 354).

16   Finishes book XIII of *Romola*: 'Killed Tito in great excitement' (II, 353). Inspect The Priory with a view to purchase.

18   Begins book XIV of *Romola*.

24   Hear a sermon by Wiseman.

June

1   (Mon) Reaches the end of ch. 70.

6   Small party to celebrate (prematurely) the completion of *Romola*.

9   Completes *Romola*. 'The writing of *Romola* ploughed into her more than any of her other books. . . . In her own words, "I began it a young woman, – I finished it an old woman"' (II, 352).

10 Sends Sara Hennell an autograph of Montalembert.
16 Begin fortnight's holiday on the Isle of Wight.
21 Tells Charles Lewes, 'I am very happy in my holiday, finding quite a fresh charm in the hedgerow grasses and flowers after my long banishment from them' (II, 355).

July
6 (Mon) *Romola* published. Second edition appears later this month.
10 Trollope thanks GE for the gift of a copy of *Romola*: 'You will know what I mean when I say that *Romola* will live after you. It will be given to very few latter day novels to have any such life' (*Letters*, VIII, 311).
11 Sends Sara Hennell details of her opera- and theatre-going, and of the decision to purchase The Priory (see 22 Aug).
17 Hear Gounod's *Faust* for the second time.
18 Discusses Renan's *Vie de Jésus* in letter to D'Albert.
23 Reading Mommsen *History of Rome* – 'I count all minds graceless who read it without the deepest of stirrings' (II, 365).
29 Hear *Faust* for a third time. Receives from F. D. Maurice 'the greatest, most generous tribute ever given to me in my life' (II, 358).
30 Tells Clementia Taylor she does not intend to read all of Renan's *Vie de Jésus*: 'We can never have a satisfactory basis for the history of the man Jesus, but that negation does not affect the idea of the Christ either in its historical influence or its great symbolic meanings' (II, 360).

August
Last instalment of *Romola* appears in *Cornhill*.
2 (Sun) Browning writes to congratulate GE on *Romola*, an opinion subsequently modified.
8 Sends R. H. Hutton a lengthy and important letter discussing *Romola*: 'certain chief elements of my intention have impressed themselves so strongly on your mind, notwithstanding the imperfect degree in which I have been able to give form to my ideas' (II, 360).
10 Begin week's visit to Worthing.
18 Records in Journal, 'Returned home, much invigorated by the week of change; but my spirits seem to droop as usual, now I am in London again' (II, 363).

19 Thanks Barbara Bodichon for writing to her, and sends domestic news.

22 Buy The Priory, 21 North Bank, Regent's Park. GHL records in Journal recent difficulties with his son Thornton, following his failure in the second examination for the Indian Civil Service.

23 Discusses *Romola* in letter to Sara Hennell, declaring also her impatience with the public outcry over the Colenso affair and Renan's *Vie de Jésus*.

September

1 (Tues) Tells Cara Bray and Sara Hennell, 'We are still in a nightmare of uncertainty about our boys' – a reflection of an anxiety which had lasted through much of the summer (II, 364).

15 Begin 12 days in Richmond.

October

10 (Sat) Thanks Mary Cash for sending a portrait of her mother.

16 Thornton Lewes embarks for South Africa. Tells Sara Hennell she is 'taking a deep bath of other people's thoughts' (II, 366).

18 Trollope sends a gift of his newly published novel, *Rachel Ray*.

23 Congratulates Trollope on *Rachel Ray*, and on his writing in general.

November

5 (Thurs) Move to The Priory.

10 Blackwood reports disappointing sales of the Cheap edition of the novels.

14 Complains to Journal, 'I long very much to have done thinking of upholstery, and to get again a consciousness that there are better things than that to reconcile one with life' (II, 367).

19 Invites Bessie Parkes to bring Isa Craig to call.

24 Housewarming at The Priory, also the occasion of Charles Lewes's twenty-first birthday.

28 Sends Maria Congreve an account of the move to The Priory and of the housewarming party, and brings D'Albert up to date with family news.

December

4 (Fri) Acknowledges gift of Cara Bray's *Physiology for Schools*: 'I

thank you, dear Cara, not simply for giving me the book, but
for having put so much faithful labour in a worthy direction'
(II, 370).
24 Death of Thackeray. Visited, and impressed, by Robert
Buchanan.
26 Tells Sara Hennell that reading Renan's *Vie de Jésus* has
lessened her opinion of his mind.
28 Tells Clementia Taylor, 'I am wonderfully well in body, but
rather in a self-indulgent state mentally, saying "Soul, take
thine ease", after a dangerous example' (II, 373).

1864

January
1   (Fri) GHL retrospectively records in his Journal, 'In a domestic
sense it has been a checquered (sic) year', mentioning problems
with his children and with The Priory (*Letters*, IV, 126).
19 Sends good wishes to Maria Congreve, who is visiting Italy
in an effort to improve her husband's health: 'I please myself
that you will all come back with stores of strength and
delightful memories' (II, 374).
22 Tells Sara Hennell of her recent interest in the personality and
writings of Robert Buchanan, and reports the high opinion of
Cara Bray's *British Empire* entertained by Herbert Spencer's
father. Writes to Hedwig Sauppe, an old Weimar acquaintance,
stating that permission to translate *Romola* should be obtained
from the publisher.
29 Death of half-brother Robert Evans.

February
2   (Tues) Thanks her nephew Robert Evans for news of the death
of his father.
4   Entertain Theodore Martin and Anthony Trollope.
6   Sympathises with Bessie Parkes on the death of her friend
Adelaide Proctor.
7   Watches Kate Bateman in Augustin Daly's *Leah the Forsaken*.
11 GHL suggests GE should write a play for Helen Faucit, and
sketches a plot himself. This is perhaps *Savello*, for details of
which see *Letters*, IV, 132–3.
12 Writes a letter of sympathy to Robert Evans's widow, Jane.

14   F. W. Burton asks to take her portrait.

March
  3   (Thurs) Pleased to hear of Clementia Taylor's interest in 'David Gray' by Robert Buchanan: 'It is good for us all that these true stories should be well told' (II, 378).
  7   Asks Cara Bray to call when she visits Sydenham. Blackwood sends a cheque for £150, again reporting poor sales of the Cheap edition.
 15   Thanked by widow of Robert Evans for her letter of sympathy, and told that *Bede* was the last book he read.
 20   Sends Sara Hennell an autograph of Sir John Herschel.
 25   Shares Clementia Taylor's delight at Northern successes in the American Civil War, also remarking, 'I wish an immortal drama could be got out of *my* sorrows, that people might be the better for them two thousand years hence. But fog, east wind, and headache are not great dramatic motives' (II, 380–1).
 27   Spend a week in Glasgow, seeing Helen Faucit act.

April
  4   (Mon) Delighted to receive animated first letter from Thornton in South Africa, and reports selected details of it to Barbara Bodichon. Visit Leighton's studio.
  6   Visited by Herbert Spencer, discussing his relation to Comte.
  9   See Mulready's pictures at the South Kensington Museum.
 15   Thanks Mary Marshall for sending news of the death of her mother (also Mary Marshall), an aunt of Cara Bray and Sara Hennell.
 18   Attend working-class deputation to Garibaldi at Crystal Palace, meeting F. D. Maurice.
 25   First meeting, at a Covent Garden performance of Rossini's *William Tell*, with the Lehmanns, soon to become close friends.
 30   Informs Sara Hennell of her impending departure for Italy. Tells Nina Lehmann that she hopes to be able to accept her invitation to dinner.

May
  3   (Tues) Thanked by Smith for 'Brother Jacob', which had been given to the *Cornhill gratis* as a result of the comparative failure of *Romola*.

4   Set out for Italy with Frederic Burton, the holiday lasting seven
    weeks. On their visit to Venice the idea for *The Spanish Gypsy*
    occurs to GE.
15 Asks Theodosia Trollope if it will be possible to visit her on
    their journey from Venice to the Alps.
18 GHL sends Charles Lewes details of the pleasures of the stay
    in Venice.

June
20 (Wed) Return to London. Charles Lewes becomes engaged.
24 Writes to D'Albert with details of their Italian holiday, and of
    Charles Lewes's engagement.
25 First meeting with Richard Monckton Milnes.
29 First sitting for a portrait by Burton. Begins a Spanish drama –
    later to become *The Spanish Gypsy*.

July
'Brother Jacob' appears in the *Cornhill*.
13 (Wed) Reading Newman's *Apologia* with 'absorbing interest'
    (*Letters*, iv, 158). Also sends Sara Hennell her views on Holman
    Hunt's *Afterglow in Egypt*.
17 Writes in Journal, 'Horrible scepticism about all things para-
    lysing my mind. Shall I ever be good for anything again? Ever
    do anything again?' (ii, 386).
19 Reading Gibbon.

August
28 (Sun) Envies Sara Hennell her opportunities of seeing and
    hearing J. H. Newman: 'I . . . should like to make an expedi-
    tion to Birmingham for that sole end' (ii, 387).

September
6   (Tues) At work on Spanish drama.
13 Begin two-and-a-half-week stay at Scarborough and Harrogate,
    taking the waters to improve GHL's health. GE begins to study
    Spanish. Reading includes Tennyson's *Idylls*.
26 Sends Sara Hennell details of their early experiences in York-
    shire.

October
GHL resigns as consulting editor of the *Cornhill*.
1   (Sat) Return to The Priory, GE much gratified by the improve-

ment in GHL's health, though this is not finally restored until November.

3   Invites Maria Congreve to stay the following weekend.
5   Finishes first draft of Act I of Spanish drama.
10 Tells Maria Congreve that her visit was 'pure delight' (II, 390).
12 Begins Act II of Spanish drama.
15 Sits for her portrait by Burton.
20 GHL begins a fortnight's water cure at Malvern.

November

4   (Fri) Reads Act II of Spanish drama to GHL.
10 'Sticking in the mud continually in the construction of the 3d, 4th, and 5th Act'(II, 391).
23 Belatedly sends birthday greetings to Sara Hennell.

December

15 (Thurs) 'Much malaise and feebleness' (*Letters*, IV, 169). Sends Charles Bray a cheque for unemployed weavers.
25 GHL records his appointment as an adviser to the *Pall Mall Gazette*. GE finishes Act III of Spanish drama.

1865

January

1   (Sun) Records in Journal, 'The last year has been unmarked by any trouble except health. . . . The last quarter has made an epoch for me, by the fact that, for the first time in my serious authorship, I have written verse' (II, 394).
2   Begins 'My Vegetarian Friend', published as 'A Minor Prophet' in *Jubal*.
8   Visited for two nights by Maria Congreve. Thanks George Smith for the gift of an oyster dish.
9   GHL invites Nina Lehmann to call.
12 Sends D'Albert her family news.
13 GHL sends lengthy outline of his conception of the *Fortnightly Review* to Henry Seymour.
15 Begin 11 day holiday in Paris, spending six evenings at various theatres, and visiting Comte's house, subsequently telling Maria Congreve, 'Such places, that knew the great dead,

always move me deeply; and I had an unexpected sight of interest in the photograph taken at the very last' (II, 395).

28   Finishes 'A Minor Prophet'.

February

6   (Mon) Sends her recent news to Sarah Hennell.
7   Appearance of first number of *Pall Mall Gazette*.
15   Death of Wiseman.
17   Visited by Maria Congreve.
18   Host their first evening party since the previous winter. Sunday afternoon At Homes now begin to replace Saturday evening parties.
19   Sends Maria Congreve a report of the party: 'If the severest sense of fulfilling a duty could make one's parties pleasant, who so deserving as I? I turn my inward shudders into outward smiles, and talk fast with a sense of lead on my tongue' (II, 397).
21   Notes in Journal, 'George has taken my drama away from me,' an action caused by GE's prolonged depression (II, 397).
27   Sends Barbara Bodichon the date of Charles's wedding: 'We have loved Gertrude better and better as we have seen more of her, and we both feel that we could have desired no better lot for Charlie' (*Letters*, VIII, 333).

March

(?) Reads Aeschylus, and works on drama by Klein in unsuccessful effort to stimulate composition of *Gypsy*.
1   (Wed) Writes 'A Word for the Germans' for the *Pall Mall Gazette*.
7   'A Word for the Germans' published.
9   Much impressed by Helen Faucit's performance of Rosalind in *As You Like It*.
10   Visited by Sara Hennell. Writes to congratulate Helen Faucit on her performance.
12   Begins two-day stay with the Congreves.
17   'Servants' Logic' published in the *Pall Mall Gazette*.
18   Commiserates with Cara Bray on the death of the Brays' adopted daughter Nelly: 'I don't know whether you strongly share, as I do, the old belief that made men say the gods loved those who died young. It seems to me truer than ever, now

life has become more complex, and more problems have to be worked out' (II, 400).

20   Attend marriage of Charles Lewes to Gertrude Hill.

21   GHL persuaded at a meeting of the stockholders to become editor of the *Fortnightly Review*.

25   Notes in Journal, 'I am in deep depression, feeling powerless. I have written nothing but beginnings since I finished a little article for the *Pall Mall*' (II, 401).

29   Sends letter on 'Futile Falsehoods' to *Pall Mall Gazette*. Begins *Felix Holt*.

April

3   (Mon) 'Futile Falsehoods' published.

May

4   (Thurs) Sends article on Lecky's *History of Rationalism* to *Fortnightly*.

13   'Modern Housekeeping' appears in the *Pall Mall Gazette*.

14   Herbert Spencer to lunch.

15   Appearance of first number of *Fortnightly*, to which GE contributes two articles: 'The Influence of Rationalism' and 'The Grammar of Ornament'. Begin five-day stay in Eastbourne, Sussex.

18   Explains to Sara Hennell both her own involvement and that of GHL in the *Fortnightly*.

28   Finishes Bamford's *Passages from the Life of a Radical*. Begins to reread J. S. Mill's *Political Economy*.

June

7   (Wed) Finishes reading the *Annual Register* for 1832.

13   Spends two hours discussing *Holt* with GHL.

15   Records in Journal: 'Read again Aristotle's *Poetics* with fresh admiration' (II, 404).

19   Notes in Journal, 'Walked together on Wimbledon Common, in outer and inner sunshine, as of old; then dined with Mr and Mrs Congreve, and had much pleasant talk.'

20   Reads opening of *Holt* to GHL.

25   Reading Shakespeare's *King John*.

July

3   (Mon) Again attends *Faust* at Covent Garden.

10 Writes to Clementia Taylor about J. S. Mill, whose work she has been reading in recent weeks.
22 Last sitting for Burton portrait.
23 Records in Journal that she is working 'doggedly' at *Holt*, 'seeing what determination can do in the face of despair' (II, 406). Reading Daniel Neal's *History of the Puritans*.
29 Maria Congreve to lunch.
31 Sends a lengthy letter of news to Cara Bray.

August
1 (Tues) Declines to contribute to fund for Mazzini under the present terms.
2 Finishes reading Aeschylus's *Agamemnon* for the second time.
10 Leave for month in Normandy and Brittany, GE keeping a Journal of their travels.

September
1 (Fri) Illustrated edition of *Romola* printed. Probably published later this month.
7 Return from a month's holiday in Normandy and Brittany. For itinerary, see II, 409. Subsequently reports to Sara Hennell: 'Our travelling in Brittany was a good deal marred and obstructed by the Emperor's fête. . . . But the Norman churches, the great cathedrals at Le Mans, Tours, and Chartres, with their marvellous painted glass, were worth much scrambling to see' (II, 412).
14 Sympathises with Sara Hennell following the death of her friend Joanna Bonham Carter, and reaffirms their friendship: 'the delight I had in you, and in the hours we spent together, is really part of my life, and can never die out of me' (II, 410).
16 Helps Sara Hennell with the title of *Present Religion*.

October
14 (Sat) Reaches p. 74 in manuscript of *Holt*.
15 Shown several memorabilia of E. B. Browning by Robert Browning, a developing admirer.
18 Death of Palmerston.
28 Discusses David Masson's *Recent British Philosophy* in letter to Sara Hennell.

November

6   Earl Russell forms Ministry.

12   Death of Elizabeth Gaskell.

15   Reading includes Henry Fawcett, *The Economic Position of the English Labourer*; J. S. Mill, *On Liberty*; Daniel Neal, *History of the Puritans* (vol. IV now reached); and Strauss's second *Life of Jesus*.

16   Writes Mr Lyon's story (ch. 6 of *Holt*). Reads the Bible.

22   Reaches end of ch. 7 of *Holt*.

24   Finishes Neal's *History*. Begins Hallam's *View of the State of Europe during the Middle Ages*.

December

4   (Mon) Sends Maria Congreve Trollope's *Orley Farm* and *The Small House at Allington*, also telling her, 'I think more of you than you are likely to imagine, and I believe we talk of you all more than of any other mortals' (II, 414).

8   Hear Handel's *Israel in Egypt* at the Exeter Hall.

11   Finishes ch. 10 of *Holt*.

17   Sends a lengthy letter of personal news to D'Albert.

21   Clarifies her views of Dissent and Establishment in letter to Gertrude Lewes: *'as a system of thought* . . . the Church of England is the least morally dignified of all forms of Christianity . . . but as a portion of my earliest associations and most poetic memories, it would be more likely to tempt me into partiality than any other form of dissent' (*Letters*, IV, 214).

24   Records in Journal, 'For two days I have been sticking in the mud from doubt about my construction . . .' (II, 415).

1866

January

5   (Fri) Invites Harrison to visit, subsequently seeking his advice on legal problems in *Holt*, which give rise to a considerable correspondence during this month,

9   Entertain Huxley, Beesly, Burton, Spencer and Harrison.

15   Discusses Proudhon and Courbet in letter to Barbara Bodichon.

23   Begin fortnight in Tunbridge Wells.

28   Reports to Maria Congreve an improvement in GHL's health.

February

12 (Mon) Sends Sarah Hennell an account of the stay at Tunbridge:
    'Alas! we had chiefly bad weather. . . George was a little
    benefited, but only a little. . . After the notion I have given
    you of my health, you will not wonder if I say that I don't
    know when anything of mine will appear. I can never reckon
    on myself' (II, 424).

March

7   (Wed) Reading Theocritus, Mill's *Logic*, and books on English
    history and law.
8   Anthony Trollope to lunch.
17 Hear Joachim, Piatti and Hallé in music by Beethoven at St
    James's Hall.
26 Reads the existing manuscript of *Holt* to GHL.
31 Records sickness hindering progress in previous fortnight.
    Now working on chs 30–1 of *Holt*.

April

9   (Mon) Writes to Sara Hennell, 'I torment myself less with
    fruitless regrets that my particular life has not been more
    perfect. The young things are growing, and to me it is not
    melancholy but joyous that the world will be brighter after I
    am gone than it has been in the brief time of my existence' (II,
    425).
10 Notes the poor progress of Gladstone's Reform Bill in the
    Commons. Again seeks Harrison's advice.
12 Manuscript of *Holt* vol. II completed.
16 Begins vol. III of *Holt* manuscript.
18 GHL tells Blackwood that *Holt* should be ready for publication
    by the end of May, and invites him to make an offer for the
    copyright.
20 Blackwood expresses his satisfaction that GE should be contem-
    plating a return to his firm, but declines to make a definite
    offer until he has been able to see the manuscript.
21 Manuscript of vols I and II sent for Blackwood's opinion.
22 Blackwood describes his delight with the opening of *Holt*.
24 Blackwood offers £5000 for five-year copyright of *Holt*, and
    expresses himself 'lost in wonder and admiration of Mrs
    Lewes's powers' (*Letters*, IV, 243).
25 GHL accepts Blackwood's offer: 'It is a great pleasure to me to

be writing to you again, as in the old days. After your kind letters, I am chiefly anxious that the publication of *Felix Holt* may be a satisfaction to you from beginning to end' (ii, 427).

26 Blackwood sends a lengthier encomium.

27 Describes to Blackwood some of the research for, and depression caused by, *Holt*, and thanks him for his enthusiasm: 'Your letter has made me feel, more strongly than any other testimony, that it would have been a pity if I had listened to the tempter Despondency' (ii, 428).

?30 Asks Blackwood to suggest historical adviser for two points in *Holt*.

May

1 (Tues) Begin a week's stay near Dorking to improve GHL's health. GHL requests Blackwood to offer the right of translation of *Holt* into German to Frederick Lehmann.

2 Harrison answers queries on transportation, and non-combatants being made prisoners of war.

7 Tells William Blackwood of her satisfaction in returning to the firm, and that there is now no need to print epistolary sections of *Holt* in italic.

?23 Asks Harrison to comment on the trial scene in *Holt*.

26 Harrison offers four legal comments on the trial scene. GE writes to Harrison agreeing to alter the scene so that Esther will become the last witness.

31 Finishes *Holt*, subsequently remarking to Maria Congreve, 'As soon as I had finished I felt well' (ii, 430).

June

1 (Fri) Harrison concludes his legal examination of the proofs, and congratulates GE on the accuracy of her researches.

2 Final proof of *Holt* handed over to Blackwood and his nephew, who call to express their delight in the novel's conclusion.

3 Visit GHL's mother.

5 Blackwood and his nephew to lunch. Writes to Cara Bray regretting the impossibility of a meeting before she and GHL begin their holiday. See Donizetti's *L'Elisir d'amore*.

7 Leave for Holland, Belgium and Germany.

10 See the Oberammergau passion play presented in Antwerp.

14 *Holt* published, and soon accorded excellent reviews.

20   E. G. Bulwer-Lytton sends Blackwood a two-sided response to *Holt*.
23   Thanks Blackwood for sending details of the favourable reception of *Holt*, and sends him news of their holiday.
25   Sends Maria Congreve an account of the progress of their holiday: 'Already we feel great benefit from our quiet journeying and repose' (ii, 433).
26   Blackwood again enlarges on the reception of *Holt*, dismissing *The Times*'s claim that the trial scene had been suggested by a recent novel of Charles Reade's.

July
Derby forms his first Ministry.
19   (Thurs) Harrison writes of *Holt*'s excellent reception, and hopes that GE may be able to produce a Positivist work of art.
21   Blackwood tells GHL, 'I do not know that I ever saw a Novel received with a more universal acclaim than *Felix*' (*Letters*, iv, 289).

August
 2   (Thurs) Return home from continental tour. Invites the Congreves to dine in the course of the coming week.
 3   Trollope thanks GE for *Holt*: 'To me the great glory of *Felix Holt* is the fulness of thought which has been bestowed on it. . . . I think its success is unrivalled' (*Letters*, viii, 381).
 4   Asks Harrison to visit soon. Expresses to Blackwood her approval of the physical appearance of the three volumes of *Holt*.
 5   Thanks Trollope for his praise of *Holt*.
10   Sends Sara Hennell an account of their travels, including the Oberammergau passion play: 'All the rest was inferior, and might even have had a painful approach to the ludicrous; but both the person and the action of the Jesus were fine enough to overpower all meaner impressions. Mr Lewes . . . felt what I am saying quite as much as I did, and was much moved' (ii, 438).
14   Regrets having to decline an invitation to visit her nephew Robert Evans and his wife because of the pressures of preparing for Bertie's departure for South Africa.
15   Replies to Harrison's request with a lengthy letter on aesthetic and novelistic problems, promising to bear 'the great possibility

(or impossibility)' of his suggestion in mind. Also reveals that she is going to rework *Gypsy* (II, 442).

30   Notes in Journal, 'I have taken up the idea of my drama, *The Spanish Gypsy*, again, and am reading on Spanish subjects – Bouterwek, Sismondi, Depping, Llorente, &c.' (II, 439).

September

6   (Thurs) Tells Blackwood that she is 'swimming in Spanish history and literature' (II, 444).

8   Give farewell dinner party for Bertie Lewes, who sets out the next day to join Thornton in South Africa.

10   Blackwood, slightly disappointed at the sale of *Holt* in three volumes, suggests reprinting the novel in two.

11   Agrees to Blackwood's proposal.

14   Sends an unusually semi-confessional letter of sympathy to the American journalist Harriet Peirce.

15   Journal recalls, 'Finished Depping's *Juifs au Moyen Age*. Reading Chaucer, to study English. Also reading on Acoustics, Musical Instruments, &c.' (II, 445).

21   Sends D'Albert her domestic news.

24   Gertrude Lewes's first child dies as a result of an accident during birth.

29   Thanks Sara Hennell for her sympathy over the loss of Gertrude's baby.

October

15   (Mon) Decides on new form for *Gypsy*.

November

2   (Fri) Encourages Blackwood's scheme for an illustrated edition of the novels.

9   GHL resigns editorship of the *Fortnightly*. Trollope writes regretting the resignation, and asking GHL's opinion of John Morley as a possible successor.

22   Reading Renan, *Histoire des langues sémitiques*, and Ticknor, *Spanish Literature*. Thanks Sara Hennell for her birthday greetings: 'I am very well now, and able to enjoy my happiness. One has happiness sometimes without being able to enjoy it' (II, 446).

December

6 (Thurs) Finish a week at Tunbridge Wells, where reading
   includes works on astronomy and history, and Spanish ballads
   on Bernardo del Carpio.

7 Tells Sara Hennell, 'No, I don't feel as if my faculties were
   failing me. On the contrary, I enjoy all subjects – all study –
   more than I ever did in my life before. But that very fact makes
   me more in need of resignation to the certain approach of age
   and death. Science, history, poetry – I don't know which
   draws me most, and there is little time left me for any of them'
   (II, 446–7).

9 Thornton writes to say he has bought a farm at Wakkerstroom
   in the Transvaal.

11 Publication of the (two-volume) edition of *Holt*. Thanks Jane
    Senior for the offer of the use of a house in Spain, but declines,
    chiefly on the grounds of GHL's ill health.

13 Blackwood, though noting that sales have been disappointing,
    sends first instalment of £1666 for *Holt*.

15 Regrets having been out when Eliza Linton called, and hopes
    her visit will soon be repeated.

21 Blackwood formally suggests a stereotyped (and illustrated)
    edition of GE's works and offers terms: £5000 for five novels
    for five years.

22 GE accepts.

23 Thanks George Smith for the gift of a travelling bag.

27 Set out for France and Spain, chiefly to improve GHL's health.

31 Meet Renan in Paris.

1867

January

4 (Fri) Sends Barbara Bodichon a description of their journey so
   far, including their encounter with Renan.

10 Again studying Spanish.

16 Reading Comte. GE tells Maria Congreve, 'My gratitude
    increases continually for the illumination Comte has contribu-
    ted to my life' (III, 3–4), and also sends her an account of their
    travels.

23 See Nina Lehmann at Pau.

26 Reports to George Smith the usefulness of the travelling bag.

February

2   (Sat) Gives Barbara Bodichon details of their travels, and mentions their proposed itinerary.

5   Harrison, in the *Pall Mall Gazette*, proves the folly of a legal criticism of *Holt* in the *Edinburgh Review*.

18 Thanks Harrison for his *Pall Mall* article, also telling him, 'Just now we read nothing but Spanish novels – and not much of those. We said good-bye to philosophy and science when we packed up our trunks at Biarritz' (III, 10).

21 Informs Blackwood of her literary purpose in visiting Spain, and of the success of the trip.

March

10 (Sun) Tells Maria Congreve, 'Mr Lewes says he thinks he never enjoyed a journey so much' (III, 12).

16 Return to London from Spain. GE resumes work on *Gypsy*.

20 Blackwood sends £2166, but reports a scant sale for the second edition of *Holt*.

21 Tells Blackwood of her Spanish poem, written and then put by in 1864, of which GHL is now hopeful, and of 'private projects about an English novel' (III, 16).

25 Sends Cara Bray details of their holiday, likening Renan's manner to that of an amiable Dissenting minister.

April

5   (Fri) Receives first number of *Bede*, which commences the Stereotyped edition of the novels.

6   Urges Cara Bray to call on her when in town.

8   Blackwood announces that his nephew William's marriage has been broken off.

12 Sends news of their holiday to D'Albert.

18 GHL's fiftieth birthday.

May

5   (Sun) Attends the first of Congreve's Positivist lectures.

9   Writes to Barbara Bodichon, discussing the death of a neighbour, Joseph Neuberg, and a visit to the historical-portrait collection at South Kensington.

11 The Calls to dinner.

12 Attends Congreve's lecture again, noting decreased attendance.

13   Writes to Sara Hennell about the Congreve lectures.
14   Discusses female enfranchisement in letter to Morley, telling him that her attitude is very nearly his own.
19   Attends Congreve.
22   Thanks Jane Senior for advice on millinery.
26   Attends Congreve.
27   See Academy exhibition.
30   Agrees with Clementia Taylor's desire 'to see women socially elevated – educated equally with men, and secured as far as possible along with every breathing creature from suffering the exercise of any unrighteous power' (III, 18). Tells Blackwood of her delight with the Stereotyped edition of *Bede*, and especially with the title-page vignette.

June
1   (Sat) Reaches the point of Fedalma's appearance in the Plaça in *Gypsy*.
5   Blackwood to dinner. Reads him, to his pleasure, the first 56 pages of *Gypsy* manuscript.
20   Spend day at Eton with Oscar Browning.
26   Begin fortnight on the Isle of Wight.

July
10   (Wed) Return from Isle of Wight.
15   Blackwood sends cheque for £2166, but reports the near-failure of the Stereotyped edition of the novels.
16   Replies to a letter from Cara Bray, mentioning Arthur Helps's unsuccessful china-clay speculation, and giving details of the two portraits of her by Burton and Laurence.
26   Thanks Oscar Browning for sending her a chair. Tells Smith her new production (i.e. *Gypsy*) will not be suitable for the *Cornhill*.
27   Read Congreve's 'Mr Broadhead and the Anonymous Press', a defence of the instigator of the Sheffield trade-union outrages.
28   Tells Maria Congreve of her cordial satisfaction with Congreve's pamphlet.
29   Leave for Germany, meeting Edmund Benson and his wife on the Channel crossing. Much reading of Tennyson on this tour.

August
'O May I Join the Choir Invisible' written during this month.
8   (Thurs) Reading Shakespeare's *Pericles* and *Venus and Adonis*

(which GHL finds 'wretched stuff' – *Letters*, IV, 386). Send news of their travels to Charles Lewes.

13 Advises Emanuel Deutsch to send the proof of his article on the Talmud to her at Dresden.

15 New Reform Bill receives the royal assent, greatly extending the franchise.

23 GHL sends Charles Lewes details of their daily programme during their stay at Ilmenau.

October

1 (Tues) Return to London. Records in Journal, 'We returned home after revisiting the scenes of cherished memories – Ilmenau, Dresden, and Berlin. Of new places we have seen Wetzlar, Cassel, Eisenach, and Hanover. At Ilmenau I wrote Fedelma's soliloquy after her scene with Silva, and the following dialogue between her and Juan. At Dresden I re-wrote the whole scene between her and Zarca' (III, 21).

2 Thanks Blackwood for sending grouse while they were away – the grouse were forwarded to, and eaten by, GHL's mother.

9 Reading Percy's *Reliques*.

10 Begins gypsy-camp scene of *Gypsy*. Finishes reading *Los Judios en España*. Also reading *Iliad* book III.

11 Begins reading Prescott's *Ferdinand and Isabella*.

12 Warmly recommends Deutsch's article 'The Talmud' in the current *Quarterly Review* to Sara Hennell.

16 GHL and Spencer begin brief walking tour in Surrey, Spencer introducing GHL to the Cross family.

18 Writes to Blackwood expressing admiration for Theodore Martin's *Memoir of W. E. Aytoun*.

31 Journal records, 'I have now inserted all that I think of for the first part of *The Spanish Gypsy*. On Monday I wrote three new Lyrics. I have also re-written the first three scenes in the Gypsy camp, to the end of the dialogue between Juan and Fedalma. But I have determined to make the commencement of the second part continue the picture of what goes forward in Bedmar' (III, 23).

November

1 (Fri) Begins book II of *Gypsy*. Stereotyped edition of *Mill* published.

7 Congratulates Harrison on his article 'Culture: A Dialogue' in

the current *Fortnightly*, also discussing her qualified veneration of Browning. Blackwood, singing Disraeli's praises, suggests GE write an address to working men for his magazine, and sign it Felix Holt.

9   Asks Blackwood to put the beginning of *Gypsy* in type, but to keep the poem's existence a secret. Tells him of her disappointment at the lack of success of the Stereotyped edition, especially among young men, 'who are just the class I care most to influence' (III, 25).

10 Writes to Cara Bray to express delight at the promise of a visit from her.

14 Blackwood urges the case for the proposed 'Address to Working Men', reminding GE of the topicality of the Reform issue.

16 Invites Emily Davies to discuss her plans for a college for women (eventually Girton College, Cambridge).

19 Discussion with Emily Davies.

20 Emily Davies tells Barbara Bodichon that GE 'said she thought the higher education of women was *the* thing about which there could be no doubt' (*Letters*, VIII, 409).

22 Begins 'Address to Working Men, by Felix Holt' for *Blackwood's*. Urges Emily Davies to raise funds on a major scale, also telling Sara Hennell of her enthusiasm for the Women's College scheme.

29 Blackwood expresses his enthusiasm for *Gypsy* and satisfaction on hearing of progress with the 'Address'.

December

4   (Wed) Sends manuscript of 'Address' to Blackwood.

5   Hears part of debate on Abyssinia in House of Commons.

7   Returns proof of 'Address' to Blackwood.

12 Thanks Blackwood for the revised proofs of the 'Address', but remarks, 'I feel the danger of not being understood. Perhaps, by a good deal longer consideration and gradual shaping, I might have put the ideas into a more concrete easy form' (III, 27).

16 Consoles Emanuel Deutsch after the attacks made on his article.

21 Reading Herbert Spencer's *First Principles*.

25 'George and I dined happily alone: he better for weeks than he has been all the summer before, – I more ailing than usual,

but with much mental consolation, part of it being the delight he expresses in my poem' (III, 28).

26 Reports herself depressed by the troubled state of European affairs and threat of war.

27 GHL leaves for Germany for research on his *Problems of Life and Mind*.

28 Blackwood sends payment of £25 for 'Address'.

1868

Stereotyped edition of *Marner* appears in first half of this year.

January
During this month, 'Address to Working Men, by Felix Holt' appears in *Blackwood's*, and GE writes book III of *Gypsy*.

8 (Wed) GHL returns to London, having 'had a brilliant time, gained great instruction, and seen some admirable men who received him warmly' (III, 33).

9 Thanks Maria Congreve for gift of mittens.

12 Tells Arthur Helps of her enjoyment in reading Queen Victoria's *Leaves from the Journal of our Life in the Highlands*.

27 Begin three-day visit to Tunbridge Wells to improve their health. Some proofs of *Gypsy* corrected there.

30 Writes to D'Albert with family news and distress at national and international affairs.

February
'A wretched month of malaise' sees little accomplished (III, 34).

7 (Fri) Finishes book III of *Gypsy*.

9 Helps Charles Lewes with his translation of Lessing's *Emilia Galotti*.

25 Begin two-day visit to Cambridge. Lord Derby resigns as Prime Minister on grounds of ill health.

29 Disraeli forms his first Ministry.

March
4 (Wed) Gives £50 to Emily Davies's scheme.

14 Writes affectionately to Jane Senior, promising to communicate again on their return from Torquay.

18 Begin month at Torquay, Devon, where GE finishes *Gypsy* book IV, and GHL works at articles on Darwin.
22 Deplores spoilt nature of Torquay in letter to Sara Hennell: 'Our selfishness does not adapt itself well to these oncomings of the millennium' (III, 35).
?28 Writes to Barbara Bodichon about the role of women: 'the deepest disgrace is to insist on doing work for which we are unfit' (*Letters*, IV, 425).
31 Discusses technical details of *Gypsy* edition, including the poem's length, in letter to Blackwood.

April
 1 (Wed) Blackwood sends favourable comments on books II and III of *Gypsy*.
 3 Requests Blackwood to change spelling of Fidalma to Fedelma in proof *passim*.
?4 Suggests that *Gypsy* be now announced, explaining that she chose the title 'because it is a little in the fashion of the elder dramatists, with whom perhaps I have more cousinship than with recent poets' (III, 36).
16 Return to London from Torquay.
17 Thanks Maria Congreve for the gift of her husband's pamphlet on Ireland on which she gives an opinion, and offering to contribute towards the expenses of publishing his translation of Comte's *Positive Polity*.
18 Goes to see Holman Hunt's *Isabella and the Pot of Basil*.
21 Sends Blackwood the manuscript of book IV of *Gypsy*, and reports that she has been persuaded by GHL to return to the original ending. Gives permission for Carl Buchheim to include extracts from her works in his *Materials for German Prose Composition*.
22 Blackwood expresses his enthusiasm for what he has seen of *Gypsy*.
29 *Gypsy* completed.

May
 2 (Sat) Blackwood offers £300 for first edition of *Gypsy*.
 5 Queries the terms for *Gypsy*. Thanks Mary Cash for the gift of her *Credentials of Conscience*.
 7 Tells Cara Bray that she is apprehensive of what the public will think of her turning to poetry.

15   Attends lecture by Deutsch on the Talmud.
17   Blackwood refuses to revise his offer for *Gypsy*.
20   Accepts Blackwood's offer.
25   *Gypsy* published. Harrison sends thanks in advance for his presentation copy, and reminds GE of his Positivist suggestion of 19 July 1866. GE gracefully sidesteps Harrison's request: 'It would be better for you to encourage the growth towards a realisation in your own mind, rather than trust in transplantation' (III, 51).
26   Leave for two months in Germany and Switzerland (for itinerary see III, 52). Reading whilst there includes Morris's *Earthly Paradise*.

June
 4   (Thurs) *The Times* praises *Gypsy*.
 6   The *Spectator* follows suit.
23   GHL declines permission for dramatisation of *Gypsy*.
27   Sends Charles Lewes an account of their stay in Petersthal.

July
13   (Mon) Visit peasant's cottage at St Märgen (partly the inspiration for 'Agatha').
23   Return to London.
24   Reports to Blackwood on their holiday: 'I think we were hardly ever, except in Spain, so long ignorant of home sayings and doings' (III, 54).
27   Blackwood reports reasonable sale of *Gypsy*, but generally poor reviews: 'The reviewers have looked perseveringly for faults and shut their eyes to the beauties' (*Letters*, IV, 460–1).
28   GE replies, 'I am serene, because I only expected the unfavourable' (III, 55). Darwin suggests that he and GHL exchange photographs.
30   Thanks the Revd William MacIlwaine for pointing out *errata* in *Gypsy*.

August
Reading this month includes Lucretius, *De rerum natura* book I, *Iliad* book IV, Milton's *Samson Agonistes*, Grote, Marcus Aurelius and Comte. On an unknown date, writes at length to a new acquaintance, Clifford Allbutt, chiefly in clarification of her religious views.

7 (Fri) Darwin writes to tell GHL that his recent articles on Darwin's work have been excellent.

8 Writes to Emily Davies on the physical and spiritual differences between the sexes.

30 Thanks F. D. Maurice for the gift of his *The Conscience: Lectures on Casuistry*.

September

Second editon of *Gypsy* published.

14 (Mon) Begin three-day visit to Allbutt at Leeds, visiting a large art exhibition held in aid of the Leeds Infirmary. For details see III, 75–8.

20 Warmly invites the Congreves to attend a meal of their choice.

24 Corrects *Gypsy* for third edition. Reading A. W. Kinglake, *The Invasion of the Crimea*. Visited by the Congreves, with whom they go to the Zoo.

October

10 (Sat) Reads article on Ostrovsky by W. R. Shedden-Ralston in the July issue of *Edinburgh Review*.

13 Requests piano arrangements of Verdi's best operas.

20 Blackwood reports sescond edition of *Gypsy* nearly sold out.

21 Tells Blackwood that she is brooding on many subjects and hopes that the coming months will not be barren.

November

Third edition of *Gypsy* printed during this month, though sales of the poem generally moderate. Stereotyped edition of *Scenes* published.

3 (Tues) Spends the night with the Congreves, Richard Congreve commenting on Positivist strains in *Gypsy*.

4 Begin week at Sheffield and Matlock, touring an iron works at the former, and at the latter revisiting places previously seen in the company of her father.

11 Harrison congratulates GE on *Gypsy*, and gives his developing views on its meaning.

12 Invites Maria Congreve to stay. Returns proofs for third edition of *Gypsy*. GHL asks Darwin if he may be allowed to call on him.

14 Called on by Darwin, who thoroughly enjoys an hour of talk.

16 Writes to Barbara Bodichon about the visit to Matlock, reflecting

that 'I am one of those perhaps exceptional people whose early childish dreams were much less happy than the real outcome of life' (III, 65).

18   Darwin proposes GHL for the Linnean Society.
20   Tells Sara Hennell about her Northern holiday, and sends news of Herbert Spencer.
22   Records in Journal, 'The return of this St Cecilia's Day finds me in better health than has been usual with me in these last six months. But I am not yet engaged in any work that makes a higher life for me – a life that is young and grows, though in my other life I am meditating the subject of Timoleon' (III, 67).

December

2   (Wed) Resignation of Disraeli's Ministry.
9   Gladstone forms his first Ministry.
12   Suggests Blackwood advertises third edition of *Gypsy* more prominently.
14   Blackwood apologises and reports over 700 copies of the edition sold.
16   Tells Maria Congreve with pleasure of the speed with which that 'mass of Positivism', *Gypsy*, has sold (III, 68).
19   Congratulates Charles Bray on his arguments against the ballot: 'It has been a source of amazement to me that men acquainted with practical life can believe in the suppression of bribery by the ballot, as if bribery in all its protean forms could ever disappear by means of a single external arrangement' (III, 68–9).
29   Blackwood sends cheque for £333 for first two editions of *Gypsy*, and criticises Browning's *The Ring and the Book*.
30   Records in Journal considerable satisfaction with the passing year, desiring that in the next year 'I may do some good lasting work, and make both my outward and inward habits less imperfect – that is, more directly leading to the best uses of life' (III, 70).
31   Tells Blackwood that she deeply regrets that Browning has spent his powers on a subject unworthy of his talent, and hopes that she may finish some new work in the coming year.

1869

Ideas in GE's notebook for this year include *Middlemarch*, Timoleon, The Congress of Rivers, Vision of Jubal, Death of Pan, Agatha, a passage from Marcus Aurelius, Libanius, Stradivarius, 'Ex oriente lux', Der arme Heinrich, Homeric hymn to Ceres, the burning of the Crucifix, Daphnis, Theocritean idyll on the killing of the bull, death of d'Aubigné, and Arion.

January
Stereotyped edition of *Holt* published.
1   (Fri) First mention of *Middlemarch*, though thought of since completion of *Holt*. Again considers Timoleon as subject for a poem.
5   Reminds Barbara Bodichon of loan of a shilling from one of GE's servants.
6   GHL learns of Thornton's illness, believed to be kidney stone.
9   GHL tells Blackwood of his instruction to Thornton to return to England: 'The vision of him haunts me incessantly' (*Letters*, v, 4).
11 Probable first visit to The Priory of Emilia Pattison, a disputed model for certain features of Dorothea.
14 GHL writes to invite Charles Eliot Norton and wife to lunch. (For a full account of their visit, see Norton's letter to G. W. Curtis, *Letters*, v, 7–9).
21 GE, in thanking Oscar Browning for greetings on his birthday, refers to 'the growth of a maternal feeling towards both men and women who are much younger than myself' (*Letters*, v, 5).
22 Thanks Susan Norton for gift of James Russell Lowell's *Under the Willows and Other Poems*.
23 Poem 'Agatha' completed. Complains in Journal of ill-health since the New Year, and records characteristically wide reading, including Byron, Clough, Jonson and Spenser.
25 Begins 'How Lisa Loved the King'. Reading Bright's speeches, Manzoni's *I Promessi sposi*, and Mommsen's *Rome*.
31 Company at the by now much-frequented Sunday afternoon At Homes includes Emilia Pattison, Eliza Lynn Linton, Burton, Palgrave, and Holland.

February

5   (Fri) Writes the song of Minuccio in 'How Lisa Loved the King'.

6   Hear Clara Schumann play at a Pops Concert. GE reading *inter alia* Arnold's poetry, and a speech by Bright on the Irish question. Reads a 'deservedly high' appreciation of Lowell's poems in the *Spectator* (III, 77).

7   Visited by D. G. Rossetti.

8   Susan Norton and her daughters lunch at The Priory.

11 Entertain Spencer and Sara Hennell to dinner, the latter also staying the night.

14 Poem 'How Lisa Loved the King' finished. Invites J. B. Payne to discuss *Gypsy*. Sunday afternoon guests include Browning, Harrison, the Pattisons and Barbara Bodichon.

15 'How Lisa Loved the King' sent off to Blackwood. Writes to Sara Hennell elucidating the mention of Elisha in Browning's *The Ring and the Book*.

18 Blackwood expresses his admiration for 'How Lisa Loved the King' and offers £50 for it.

19 Tells Blackwood of her intention of commencing *Middlemarch* immediately, the various elements of the story having been 'soliciting my mind for years', and the plan being sketched already: 'But between the beginning and the middle of a book I am like the lazy Scheldt; between the middle and the end I am like the arrowy Rhône' (*Letters*, v, 16).

21 Emanuel Deutsch and Emilia Pattison to lunch.

22 Apologises to Blackwood over difficulties caused by corrections in 'How Lisa Loved the King'.

26 Goes to see Michelangelo's *Entombment* with Barbara Bodichon. Blackwood explains reasons for declining permission for 'How Lisa Loved the King' to appear in the *Atlantic Monthly*.

March

3   (Wed) Set out for Italy, staying in Florence (20–5 Mar, 23–7 Apr), Naples (26 Mar–4 Apr), and Rome (4–21 Apr), travelling out via Paris, Lyon and Marseille, and returning via Munich.

20 Arrive for a six-day stay in Florence with the Tom Trollopes.

29 Visit Pompeii.

April

6 (Sun) Notifies Blackwood of errors in revise of 'How Lisa Loved the King'.

18 GHL's fifty-second birthday – forgotten by both him and GE. Visited at Rome by Anna Cross and her son John Walter – their first encounter.

May

4 (Tues) Tells Maria Congreve, 'Our long journey . . . has been a history of ailments' (III, 79).

5 Return to London. 'How Lisa Loved the King' published in *Blackwood's*.

7 GE sends a lengthy and personal letter to Harriet Beecher Stowe, acknowledging gratefully the warrant to call her friend; and thanks Robert Lytton for drawing attention to linguistic errors in *Gypsy*: 'For in authorship I hold carelessness to be a mortal sin' (*Letters*, v, 33).

8 Thornton returns from South Africa suffering from tuberculosis of the spine, the preface to five months of suffering.

9 Visited for the first time by Henry James. He comments, 'Yes, behold me literally in love with this great horse-faced blue-stocking' (Haight, p. 417). Thornton, as James soon discovers, in very considerable pain.

11 Acknowledges Blackwood's payment of £50 for 'How Lisa Loved the King', and expresses anxiety over Thornton's condition.

12 Asks Barbara Bodichon to visit Thornton.

13 Visited by American publisher James T. Fields, who proposes uniform American edition of GE's works.

18 Thornton visited in GE's absence by his mother, Agnes Lewes, Paget having pronounced the illness very serious.

20 Authorises Fields Osgood's uniform American edition of the novels.

24 'Agatha' sold to Fields Osgood for the *Atlantic Monthly* for £300. Writes to invite Emanuel Deutsch to lunch.

26 Writes to Maria Congreve, giving her details of Thornton's illness.

30 Tells Browning of Frances Julia Wedgwood's admiration for his work.

June

6 (Sun) Congratulates Harrison on his engagement and hopes that he will call.

13 Tells Cara Bray of Thornton's illness, and asks her to send her own news.

14 Writes to Barbara Bodichon to correct any impression of irreverence or flippancy in a discussion of Mark Pattison.

July

2 (Fri) Sends Barbara Bodichon an account of Thornton's condition.

3 Journal records the completion of five 'Brother and Sister' sonnets, partly the result of the contemplation of childhood involved in preparing for *Middlemarch*. Reading includes Lucretius; Hugo, *L'Homme qui rit*; and von Hillern, *Ein Arzt der Seele*.

9 Visited by Cara Bray.

11 Apologises to Cara Bray for behaviour at their recent meeting, and to Harriet Beecher Stowe for the break in their correspondence necessitated by Thornton's illness: 'We have both been absorbed in our new duties to this poor child, and have felt our own health and nervous energy insufficient for our needful activity of body and mind' (III, 91). Has enjoyed Stowe's *Oldtown Folks*.

14 Return from a two-day stay in Hatfield, Hertfordshire.

15 Begins Nisard's *History of French Literature*.

18 Journal records discussion of women's suffrage at Sunday afternoon At Home.

19 Writing introduction to *Middlemarch*. Three further 'Brother and Sister' sonnets completed.

22 Tells Cara Bray of an improvement in Thornton's condition. Reading Reybaud, *Les Réformateurs modernes*.

24 'I read aloud Fourier and Owen, and thought of writing something about Utopists' (III, 96).

25 Reading Plato's *Republic* selectively.

26 Irish Church disestablished.

31 Reads Shakespeare's sonnets. 'Brother and Sister' sonnets finished.

August

'Agatha' published in the *Atlantic Monthly*.

2   (Mon) Begins writing Vincy–Featherstone part of *Middlemarch*.
5   First chapter of *Middlemarch* completed. Reading Renouard's *History of Medicine*.
8   Thornton becomes paraplegic.
10 Apologises to Emilia Pattison for unmannerly outburst of motherly affection.
17 GHL forced to engage new nurse for Thornton, Charlotte Lee's health having broken down.
21 Tells Cara Bray of fluctuations in Thornton's condition. Discusses *Mill* with Emily Davies.
23 Comments to Cara Bray on new revelations in Byron's biography, admitting that his poetry has fallen greatly from her favour.
29 Reaches p. 40 of *Middlemarch* manuscript.
30 Thanks Barbara Bodichon for sending flowers to Thornton, but reports, 'He is strangely indifferent about everything now' (*Letters*, VIII, 467).
31 Lunch with the Crosses at Weybridge, Surrey. Cross, detailing the visit, records, 'Our visitors had come to the house as acquaintances, they left it as lifelong friends' (III, 98).

September

1   (Wed) More planning of *Middlemarch*, now written up to the beginning of ch. 3.
2   Spend the morning at Hatfield Park.
9   Thanks Jane Senior for enquiry as to Thornton's (improving) health.
10 Journal records, 'I have achieved little during the last week, except reading on medieval subjects – Encyclopaedia about the Medical Colleges, Cullen's *Life*, Russell's *Heroes of Medicine*, &c, I have also read Aristophanes' *Ecclesiazusae* and *Macbeth*' (III, 99).
11 Despondent about the prospects for *Middlemarch*.
21 Records further difficulties in work on *Middlemarch*. Visited by Maria Congreve, and asks her to supply information about provincial hospitals. Counsels Sara Hennell to take regular holidays, and discusses Byron, who 'seems to me the most *vulgar-minded* genius that ever produced a great effect in literature' (III, 100).
22 Begin three-day visit to Watford, Hertfordshire.

24   Records 'great depression' (III, 100).

October
Girton College (later at Cambridge) opens at Hitchin, Hertford-shire.
  4   (Mon) Tells Jane Senior, 'There is no subject on which I am more inclined to hold my peace and learn, than on the "Women Question"', at the same time expressing her steadfast belief in the necessity of equal educational opportunities for women (*Letters*, v, 58).
  5   'Ever since the 28th I have been good for little, ailing in body and disabled in mind. . . . I have begun a long-meditated poem, "The Legend of Jubal", but have not written more than twenty or thirty verses' (III, 101).
 12   W. G. Clark announces at lunch his intention of resigning holy orders.
 13   Reading Lecky's *History of Morals*, having recently finished Müller's *History of Sanskrit Literature*, and Spencer's *Psychology*. Approximately 100 verses of 'Jubal' completed. Thornton increasingly weak.
 14   Sends greetings to Oscar Browning on his return from Russia.
 19   Thornton dies with GE at his side. Confides to Journal, 'This death seems to me the beginning of our own' (III, 19).
 20   Writes to Cara Bray about Thornton's death.
 22   Thanks Barbara Bodichon for her letter of sympathy. 'Just now all else seems trivial compared with the powers of delighting and soothing a heart that is in need' (*Letters*, v, 60–1).
 23   Travel to Limpsfield, Surrey, for three-week stay, GHL giving orders that no letters should be forwarded from London.

November
  6   (Sat) Thanks Oscar Browning belatedly for the gift of a pair of Russian slippers, and apologises to Emilia Pattison for delay in writing to her.
 13   Return to The Priory from Limpsfield.
 14   GHL describes the previous months of suffering to Blackwood, and reports GE now reflecting more calmly on their loss.
 15   Tells Sara Hennell, 'We both of us felt, more than ever before, the blessedness of being in the country, and we are come back much restored' (III, 102).
 19   Give copies of their books to Girton College.

22 Fiftieth birthday.
25 Tells Barbara Bodichon: 'I have a deep sense of change within, and of a permanently closer relationship with death' (*Letters*, v, 70).
28 Last mention of *Middlemarch* until 7 March 1870.

December
10 (Fri) Informs Harriet Beecher Stowe of Thornton's death in a lengthy letter.
25 Attend Rosslyn Unitarian Chapel, and visit Thornton's grave. Dine with Charles and Gertrude Lewes.
28 Enquires after Emilia Pattison.

1870

Reading this year includes Carlyle, *French Revolution*; Fielding, *Tom Jones*; and essays by Hume and Macaulay.

January
 3 (Mon) Maria Congreve dines and stays the night.
 9 Entertains D. G. Rossetti to lunch.
13 'Jubal', growing partly out of the experience of Thornton's sufferings, completed.
15 Sends Harrison qualified praise of his article 'The Positivist Problem'.
31 Thanks Oscar Browning in fulsome terms for his recent letter.

February
 1 (Tues) GHL spends three days alone at Hastings in poor spirits as a result of Thornton's death.
 5 Listen to Neruda at St James's Hall.
 6 Called on by Neruda.
11 Writes to invite Barbara Bodichon to Sunday lunch.
17 Thanks William Morris for an autographed copy of *The Earthly Paradise*.
21 Writes to Emilia Pattison.

March
 6 (Mon) Dickens, entertained to lunch, looks exhausted, but tells anecdotes dramatically.

7   Tells Blackwood that her novel proceeds very slowly (the first mention of *Middlemarch* since 28 November 1869) and that GHL's health alarms her.
14 Leave for Germany and Austria in hope of improving GHL's health, badly affected by Thornton's death,
28 GHL tells his mother of his enthusiastic reception in Berlin.
29 GHL informs Charles Lewes, 'The Mutter and I have come to the conclusion that the Music of the future is not for us' (*Letters*, v, 85).

April
3   (Sun) Sends Maria Congreve a report on their holiday so far.
17 Leave Vienna, where GE had suffered a badly ulcerated throat, for Salzburg.

May
'Jubal' published in *Macmillan's Magazine*.
6   (Fri) Return to The Priory.
8   Commends Emerson's *Society and Solitude* in a letter to Oscar Browning; and thanks D. G. Rossetti for an inscribed copy of his *Poems*: 'I have a gret deal to be acquainted with and to like better and better' (*Letters*, v, 93).
9   Barbara Bodichon to dinner.
10 Accepts invitation to visit the Pattisons. Herbert Spencer to lunch.
13 Cara Bray to dinner.
15 Tells Sara Hennell how much she approves of plans to republish Charles Hennell's *Inquiry*: 'When I remember my own obligation to the book, I must believe that among the many new readers a cheap edition will reach, there must be minds to whom it will bring welcome light in studying the New Testament, – sober, serious help towards a conception of the past instead of stage-lights and make-ups' (III, 105). Dine with distinguished company at Lord Houghton's.
18 Gratefully accepts portrait of Charles Hennell, and thanks Sara Hennell for her appreciation of 'Jubal'.
20 Recalls in her Journal her chief activities since Thornton's death, concluding, 'I am not hopeful about future work. I am languid, and my novel languishes too' (III, 110).
23 John Blackwood, after an hour's talk with GE, tells his nephew

William that GE's new novel 'promises to be something wonderful' (*Letters*, v, 99).

25 Begin four-day stay with the Pattisons, GE's first visit to Oxford, meeting Mary Augusta Arnold (later Mrs Humphry Ward), Jowett and Pater. For GE's recollections, see III, 110.

29 Gives C. V. Stanford permission to publish musical settings of songs in *Gypsy*. Reading Dickens's *Edwin Drood*.

June

9 (Thurs) Death of Dickens – 'a great shock to us' (III, 113).

13 Acknowledges the gift of a copy of the new edition of Frederick Locker's *London Lyrics*.

14 Invites Georgiana Burne-Jones and her children to join GE and GHL on a stay in Whitby.

15 Set out for East Coast holiday, again aimed at improving GHL's health, staying at Cromer, Harrogate and Whitby. Reading includes Trollope, *Vicar of Bullhampton*; Balzac, *Illusions perdues*; Mendelssohn's *Letters*; Rossetti's *Poems*; and the latest volume of *The Earthly Paradise*.

July

8 (Fri) Writes to commiserate with Edith Bulwer-Lytton on the death of her uncle, the Earl of Clarendon: 'for nearly a year death seems to me my most intimate daily companion' (III, 115).

10 Urges Georgiana Burne-Jones to join them, delighting in the effect of Harrogate on GHL's health. Reading at Harrogate includes *Edwin Drood*, and poems by Milton and Rossetti.

15 GHL sends E. R. Bulwer-Lytton details of their routine at Harrogate, remarking that to be with GE 'is a perpetual Banquet to which that of Plato would present but a flat rival' (*Letters*, VIII, 482). Start of Franco-Prussian War, in which GE much interested, and by which much distressed.

21 Sympathises with Charles and Gertrude Lewes on the death of the latter's aunt, Mary Gillies: 'I think too much, too continually of death' (*Letters*, v, 110).

August

During this month welcome news arrives of the engagement of Bertie Lewes to Eliza Harrison.

1 (Mon) Return from East Coast to London.

4   Records in Journal that the results of the previous two months have not been rich. Begins to write 'Armgart'.
8   Leave for three weeks at Limpsfield, where most of 'Armgart' is written. Reading includes Lockhart's *Life* of Walter Scott, J. A. Froude's *History of England*, and *Lettres d'Auguste Comte à M. Valat.* 'The weather was perfect, and the place seemed more lovely to us than before' (III, 120).
9   Elementary Education Act approved.
12   Writes at length to Sara Hennell, with details of East Coast holiday, reading, and family matters.
21   Declines to write short stories for Scribners.
25   Comments to Barbara Bodichon on the French defeats.
29   Return from Limpsfield.

September
'Armgart' finished.
12   (Mon) Tells Cara Bray; 'We think of hardly anything but the War, and spend a great portion of our day reading about it' (*Letters*, v, 114).
14   Commiserates with Emanuel Deutsch on the onset of illness.

November
Begins a story called 'Miss Brooke'.
17   (Sat) Hear Spurgeon preach for the first time: 'my impressions fell below the lowest judgement I ever heard passed upon him' (III, 121).
22   Fifty-first birthday. GHL presents GE with a lockable book for her autobiography.

December
2   (Sun) Records in Journal, 'I am experimenting in a story ("Miss Brooke") which I began without any very serious intention of carrying it out lengthily. It is a subject which has been recorded among my possible themes ever since I began to write fiction, but will probably take new shapes in the development. I am today at p. 44' (III, 126). Reading Wolf's *Prolegomena to Homer*, and rereading Goethe's *Wilhelm Meister*. Indicates willingness to increase financial support for Octavia Hill's Walmer Street Industrial Experiment.
4   Blackwood lunches with GE and GHL, and reports decision to combine 'Miss Brooke' with *Middlemarch*.

10   Death of GHL's mother, aged 83.
20   Begin nine-day visit to Barbara Bodichon at Swanmore, Isle of
      Wight.
24   GHL plays practical joke with scourge from the Tractarian
      Swanmore Parsonage.
25   Attends Tractarian service at Swanmore with Barbara
      Bodichon.
31   'Here is the last day of 1870. I have written only 100 pages –
      good printed pages – of a story which I began about the
      opening of November, and at present mean to call "Miss
      Brooke". Poetry halts just now' (III, 127).
        'In my private lot I am unspeakably happy, loving, and
      beloved. But I am doing little for others' (*Letters*, v, 127).

1871

'New' edition of *Romola* published by Smith.

January
 1   (Sun) GHL resumes work on *Problems of Life and Mind*.
 2   GE tentatively (and unsuccessfully) recommends Nassau
      Senior for Educational Board. Sends New Year greetings to
      Sara Hennell.
 8   First of several visits to The Priory by Turgenev.
17   Acknowledges gift of photographs from Julia Margaret
      Cameron.
24   Congratulates E. B. Hamley on letter to *The Times* criticising
      the ruthlessness of the Prussians in the Franco-Prussian War.
27   GE sympathises with the French in the war, and tells D'Albert,
      'physically I feel old, and Death seems to me very near' (*Letters*,
      IX, 10).

February
Begin this month to search for a country house. The search
continues through March.
11   (Sat) Turgenev present at one of their parties: 'To see him is
      to like him,' GHL remarks (*Letters*, IX, 21).
16   Offers money for Gertrude Lewes to be taken out in a pony
      carriage.
27   Thanks Cara Bray for sending review of Edward Noel's *Letters*.

March
14 (Wed) Inspect cottage at Weybridge.
19 Confesses in Journal her fear that she has 'too much matter –
too many "moments" ' in *Middlemarch*. Records having completed about 236 printed pages of the novel (III, 129).
31 GHL inspects Brookbank, a cottage at Shottermill, near
Petersfield, Hampshire.

April
3 (Mon) Tells Cara Bray of the enthusiasm of Anna Maria Bridges
for Cara Bray's *Duty to Animals*.
4 Congratulates George Howard on arrival of baby.
5 GHL offers Osgood Ticknor the early sheets of 'Armgart' and
invites them to make an offer for *Middlemarch*.
6 GHL and GE inspect Shottermill and engage servant there.
19 Thanks Anne Gilchrist for her help in accommodating them
at Shottermill.
21 Fourth edition of GHL's *History of Philosophy* published.
23 Enquiries after Mark Pattison's health, and reproaches his wife
for failing to inform her of it.
25 Writes to D'Albert.

May
1 (Mon) Take up residence at Shottermill. GHL remarks, 'There
I shall dig, and dig, and dig at the foundations of philosophy,
and she will create' (*Letters*, IX, 14).
6 Herbert Lewes sends news of opposition to his engagement
from his fiancée's parents.
7 GHL invites Blackwood to visit Shottermill and proposes that
Middlemarch be in four volumes.
25 Marriage of Herbert Lewes.
31 Blackwood visits, and takes away book I of *Middlemarch*.

June
2 (Fri) Blackwood expresses intense delight with the opening of
Middlemarch.
6 GHL takes GE to London in attempt to ease the neuralgic pain
of the previous months. Quinine prescribed.
17 Writes to Barbara Bodicon, expressing delight with their stay
at Shottermill.
23 GHL inspects alterations at the Priory.

26 Cancel acceptance of invitation to attend Scott Festival at Edinburgh in August, on grounds of ill health.
31 Finishes book II of *Middlemarch*.

July
'Armgart' appears in this month's editions of *Macmillan's* and *Atlantic Monthly*. Reading includes Turgenev's *Dmitri Rudin*.
10 (Mon) Writes to Charles Lewes regretting the necessity of vacating Shottermill, where health had improved and work proceeded satisfactorily.
14 Book II of *Middlemarch* sent to Blackwood. First meeting with Tennyson: 'Tennyson, who is one of the "hill-folk" about here, has found us out, so that we have lost the utmost perfection of our solitude – the impossibility of a caller' (*Letters*, v, 169).
15 GHL accepts Osgood Ticknor's offer for the American publication of *Middlemarch*.
17 Read Keller's 'Romeo und Julia auf dem Dorfe'.
18 Ballot Act passed.
20 Blackwood expresses delight with book II of *Middlemarch*.
24 Agrees with Blackwood that *Middlemarch* will be long, but remarks, 'I don't see how I can leave anything out, because I hope there is nothing that will be seen to be irrelevant to my design, which is to show the gradual action of ordinary causes rather than exceptional, and to show this in some directions which have not been from time immemorial the beaten path' (III, 137).
25 Commiserates with Edith Bulwer-Lytton on the death of her son Rowland.
31 Congratulates Mary Finlay Cross on her story 'Marie of Villefranche'.

August
3 (Thurs) Thanks Cara Bray for sending news of herself. Confirms Alexander Main in his accentuation *Romŏla*, and regrets general misunderstanding of meaning as well as pronunciation.
9 Forcibly expresses her enthusiasm for Scott in a letter to Main.
14 Describes routine of days at Shottermill in letter to Maria Congreve.

21   GHL suggests £6000 for the four-year English copyright of *Middlemarch*, or a two-shilling royalty.
22   Two-day visit from Barbara Bodichon begins.
26   Tennyson calls, and reads *Maud* and 'Northern Farmer' aloud.
31   Again visited by Tennyson, who reads 'Boadicea', 'Tears, Idle Tears', 'Northern Farmer New Style' and 'Guinevere', GE weeping at the latter.

September
1   (Fri) Return to The Priory. GE's health soon deteriorates.
6   GHL attempts to reassure Blackwood about recently negotiated arrangements for the American publication of *Middlemarch*.
7   GHL again reassures Blackwood over the American publication of *Middlemarch*, and reports, 'Mrs Lewes is not at all well – depressed in spirits and in liver . . . but perhaps gestation is more favourable when so much emotion accompanies it' (*Letters*, v, 184).
11   Learn of Herbert Lewes's marriage. GE expresses herself moved by quality of Main's criticism of *Gypsy*.
13   Sends greetings to D'Albert.
16   Seriously ill for five days with gastric fever.
18   Blackwood sends a specimen page for *Middlemarch*.
26   GHL encourages Alexander Main's proposal for a common-place-style selection from GE's work.
30   GHL expresses disappointment at Blackwood's cautious response to the Main proposal.

October
5   (Thurs) GHL reports an improvement in GE's health to William Blackwood, and requests last-minute alterations to the title page and binding of *Middlemarch*.
6   GE reports improvement in her condition to Cara Bray.
9   Blackwood records his delight in reading the proof of *Middlemarch*: 'she who can administer to the world such tonics as *Middlemarch* must speedily cure herself of all ailments' (*Letters*, v, 199).
11   Blackwood decides to accept the Main proposal.
12   GHL advises Main on further dealings with Blackwood.
13   Servants Grace and Amelia resign after 10 years' service.
20   Sends letter of sympathy to the Blackwoods on the death of

John Blackwood's only surviving brother, James. Reads GHL
book III of Middlemarch.

24 Begin four-day visit to Anna Cross at Weybridge.
31 Expresses support for Elizabeth Garret Anderson's Hospital
    for Women.

November

1   (Wed) Purchase of army commissions abolished.
6   Printing of book I of *Middlemarch* completed.
9   Expresses approval of Main's draft.
10 Osgood Ticknor announce that they have transferred *Middle-
    march* to Harpers.
19 Promises Sara Hennell an author's copy of *Middlemarch*.
24 Barbara Bodichon to dinner.
26 Blackwood and son to lunch.

December

Wise, Witty, and Tender Sayings in Prose and Verse, an anthology of
GE's writings by Alexander Main, published. GHL writes on
Dickens for the *Fortnightly*.

1   (Fri) Book I of *Middlemarch* published.
7   GHL proposes transpositions in *Middlemarch* books II and III.
12 See Irving in Chatrian's *The Bells*.
15 Sends Sara Hennell a two-sided appreciation of Forster's *Life
    of Dickens*, the first volume of which has recently appeared.
16 First US instalment of *Middlemarch*, in *Harper's Weekly*. GE,
    now writing more steadily, tells GHL of future developments
    in the novel.
20 Records in Journal, 'My health has become very troublesome
    during the last three weeks, and I can get on but tardily. Even
    now I am only at p. 227 of my fourth part. But I have been
    also retarded by construction, which, once done, serves as
    good wheels for progress' (III, 145).
28 Thanks Main enthusiastically, both for his *Sayings*, and for his
    friendship.
31 Blackwood, sending New Year greetings, reports good sales
    for *Middlemarch* and a good reception for the *Sayings*.

1872

January
Discusses use of dialect in her novels in letter to W. W. Skeat.
1   (Mon) Four-day stay with Anna Cross begins. Sends Black-
    wood an account of their 'rather doleful Christmas' (III, 146).
4   Sends New Year greetings to Sarah Hennell.
5   GHL tells Blackwood of the difficulty of obtaining copies of
    Middlemarch at two London railway termini.
17 Attends the Tichborne trial. Blackwood sends belated con-
    gratulations on the third book of *Middlemarch*.
18 Tells Blackwood that 'there remains the terror about the
    *un*written,' but that GHL is much satisfied with book IV.
22 Reading Johnson's *Lives of the Poets* 'with a delicious revival of
    girlish impressions' (III, 150).
26 Writes to congratulate Main notwithstanding some lukewarm-
    ness in the critical reception of his work. Blackwood sends
    good news of *Middlemarch* sales.
27 Large dinner-party and musical entertainment at The Priory,
    with Spencer and Harrison present, the first of such a size for
    four years.
29 Describes *Middlemarch* to D'Albert, and the Tichborne trial to
    Sara Hennell.

February
GHL's 'Dickens in Relation to Criticism' appears in the *Fortnightly*.
Book II of *Middlemarch* published. Begins corresponding with Elma
Stuart.
3   (Sat) Blackwood confident of the commercial success of *Middle-
    march*, and again praises its artistic merits.
5   Recommends Emilia Pattison to visit the Burne-Jones studio.
27 Trollope writes of his dislike for vol. I of Forster's *Life of
    Dickens*.

March
4   (Mon) Expresses distrust of spiritualists in letter to Harriet
    Beecher Stowe.
12 GHL solicits approval of *Middlemarch* book IV from Blackwood.
17 Commiserates with Clementia Taylor on the death of Mazzini.
20 Writes affectionately to E. R. and Edith Bulwer-Lytton.

27 GHL thanks E. R. Bulwer-Lytton for remarks on his Dickens article.
29 Gives her own estimation of *Middlemarch* in replying to that of Alexander Main.

April

1 (Mon) Book iii of *Middlemarch* published.
2 Blackwood sends his first cheque (of £500) for *Middlemarch*.
3 Encourages Ethel Harrison to call more frequently.
?10 GHL regrets that sales of *Middlemarch* have not been larger.
15 Writes to Cara Bray, asking her to forward news to Rufa Call.
16 GHL sends Main a photograph of Charles Lewes.

May

8 (Wed) Journal records *Middlemarch* book v complete.
23 Begin three-month stay at Elversley, Park Road, Redhill, Surrey. Severe tooth trouble at this time.
29 Writes to Sara Hennell, though keeping Redhill address secret.
31 GHL, regretting the social pressures of London life, tells Main that he and GE propose to continue a hermit-like existence at Redhill, where *Middlemarch* will, he hopes, be finished.

June

Book iv of *Middlemarch* published.
4 (Tues) Sends Barbara Bodichon an account of their Redhill life. Receives from an affable barrister a legal cavil regarding *Middlemarch*.
15 GHL pays an unsatisfactory visit to the Crystal Palace.
18 *Daily Telegraph* praises *Middlemarch*, declaring it 'almost profane to speak of ordinary novels in the same breath with George Eliot's'. Other reviews share this enthusiasm.
24 Writes at length to Harriet Beecher Stowe, again discussing spiritualism.
25 GHL delightedly reports to Anna Cross an improvement in GE's health, and suggests to Main that he might attempt an anthology of Augustus de Morgan's mathematical writings.
30 Sends good wishes to Emily Southwood Hill for her forthcoming marriage.

July
1 (Mon) Commiserates with Jane Senior on the death of her elder brother.
2 Book VI of *Middlemarch* despatched to Blackwood.
3 Thanks Charles Ritter for sending a volume of Strauss's *Select Essays*.
4 Tells Maria Congreve 'Our days go by in delicious peace, unbroken except by my little anxieties about all unfinished work' (III, 164).
19 Birth of Blanche Southwood Lewes, daughter to Charles.
29 Blackwood sends an admiring appraisal of Book VI of *Middlemarch*.

August
Book V of *Middlemarch* published.
4 (Sun) Sends Blackwood a report on progress with *Middlemarch*.
8 Blackwood sends a cheque and a statement of the *Middlemarch* account.
9 Book VII of *Middlemarch* completed and sent off.
17 GHL thanks Edward Dowden for the generosity of his article on GE in the *Contemporary Review*.
18 Congratulates George Robertson on his engagement to Caroline Crompton.
28 GHL suggests Main write up his recent Scottish walking-tour as a magazine article.

September
2 (Mon) First 90 pages of *Middlemarch* book VIII despatched to Blackwood.
7 Blackwood sends his approval of *Middlemarch* book VII.
8 Blackwood expresses his delight with *Middlemarch* book VIII: 'Dorothea is better than any sermon that ever was preached by man' (*Letters*, v, 307).
10 GHL thanks Blackwood for his praise: '[Dorothea] is more like her creator than any one else and more so than any other of her creations' (*Letters*, v, 308).
13 Arrive to stay with Henry Bullock-Hall, J. W. Cross's brother-in-law, at Six Mile Bottom, Cambridgeshire.
16 Leave Six Mile Bottom.
17 Corrects proofs of *Middlemarch* book VIII.
18 Set out for Homburg.

25 Sends Anna Cross an account of their foreign experiences so
    far.
26 Gambling scene at the Kursaal provides germ for *Daniel
    Deronda*.

October
Book VI of *Middlemarch* published.
 2 (Wed) 'Finale' of *Middlemarch* sent to Blackwood.
 4 Sends Blackwood details of Homburg life.
 8 Proof of *Middlemarch* 'Finale' returned to Blackwood.
13 Leave Homburg for Stuttgart and Karlsruhe.
27 Writes to Anna Cross, regretting that Bullock-Hall was unable
    to join them in Paris.
31 Return to England. GE writes to D'Albert.

November
 1 (Fri) Book VII of *Middlemarch* published. Writes to Lucy Smith,
    having read an obituary of her husband in *Blackwood's*.
 2 Birth of Herbert Lewes's daughter Marian Evans Lewes.
 4 Sends 'an egotistic note' to Main, describing her reaction to
    the completion of *Middlemarch* (*Letters*, v, 325).
 5 Defends two 'errors' in *Middlemarch* pointed out by Courtney
    Kenny.
 7 Visit Hertford Gallery of Pictures in Bethnal Green Museum,
    East London.
 8 GHL, on GE's behalf, advises a young correspondent against
    throwing himself on literature as a living.
11 Spencer writes to GHL in praise of the most recent part of
    Middlemarch: 'I cannot conceive anything more perfectly done'
    (*Letters*, IX 63).
14 Tells Main of the intense comfort which his response to her
    work has afforded her.
19 Writes to Sara Hennell in advance of her birthday.
22 Tells Sara Hennell to expect to be disappointed in the 'Finale'
    of *Middlemarch* but to look back to the 'Prelude'.

December
 1 (Sun) Publication of eighth and final book of *Middlemarch*.
    GE expresses approval of the sensitivity of the review of
    Middlemarch in *Blackwood's*.
 2 Sends Bessie Belloc good wishes on moving to a new home,

and regrets that her (i.e. GE's) rules prevent her calling to see it.

5   GHL describes to Main the variety of kinds of admirer of *Middlemarch*.

7   Requests advice of Paget on correction of medical error in *Middlemarch*.

8   F. W. H. Myers sends warm appreciation of *Middlemarch*: 'You know the worst, and one thanks you in that you have not despaired' (*Letters*, IX, 68). GHL discourages an article on a possible model for Dinah by 'Guy Roslyn'. GE defends the accuracy of bright dilated eyes in the description of the opiated Lydgate.

11 Thanks Cross for his interest in a plan for buying a site near Shere, Surrey.

12 Sends news to Maria Congreve.

13 First meeting, at The Priory, with Edith Simcox.

16 Tells Emilia Pattison of her present happiness: 'it is a holiday to sit with one's feet at the fire reading one's husband's writing' (*Letters*, v, 344).

18 Asks Simpson for further news of *Middlemarch* sales. Also writes to Lucy Smith.

19 Sends subscription to the Working Women's College.

21 Attend christening of Blanche Lewes. Blackwood sends a statement of the *Gypsy* and *Middlemarch* accounts.

24 Begin five-day visit to Anna Cross.

1873

January

1   (Wed) Records in Journal, regarding *Middlemarch*, 'No former book of mine has been received with more enthusiasm', also noting that 'Hardly anything could have happened to me which I could regard as a greater blessing, than the growth of my spiritual existence when my bodily existence is decaying' (III, 191). Thanks Main for a year's worth of sympathy.

2   GHL also writes to Main.

4   Thanks Anna Cross for her interest in her illness, which is described at some length.

6   Blackwood proposes a Guinea edition of *Middlemarch*, and presents a further payment.

9 Thanks Main for noting minor error in *Middlemarch*, and asks him to keep a note of others.

13 Begins reading Sterne's *Tristram Shandy* aloud.

16 Expresses her gratification at Alice Wellington's appreciation of her work. GHL decides not to allow James Mackaye to dramatise *Silas Marner*.

17 Blackwood agrees to publish GHL's *Problems of Life and Mind*.

18 Death of E. G. Bulwer-Lytton.

23 Sir James Paget advises removal of troublesome tooth.

24 Congratulates Jane Senior, the first woman to be appointed an inspector of workhouses and pauper schools.

February

11 (Tues) Regrets the poor quality of reviews of *Middlemarch* in letter to Ritter.

16 George Robertson and his bride Caroline, du Maurier and Barbara Bodichon to lunch.

19 Invites Oscar Browning to bring his photographs of Greece to lunch.

25 Expresses approval of the Guinea edition of *Middlemarch* (published around this date) to Blackwood.

26 Blackwood asks permission to include 'The Lifted Veil' in a Blackwood anthology, but on the 28th GE declines.

March

1 (Sat) Asks Lucy Smith for a copy of her Memoir of her husband: 'it is an unforgettable picture of that union which is the ideal of marriage, and which I desire young people to have in their minds as a goal' (III, 197).

2 Thanks Mary Simpson for sending a photograph and explains why a weekday call from her provoked GHL's ire.

8 Supports John Hollingshead in an attempt to change the law of copyright regarding dramatisation of novels.

11 GHL sends vol. I of *Problems* to Blackwood.

13 Visit Burne-Jones's pictures. Blackwood reports the Guinea edition of *Middlemarch* beginning to go out of print.

14 Tells Blackwood, 'I wish there were some solid philosophical Conservative to take the reins' after the resignation of Gladstone (III, 199).

16 The Hon. Mrs Frederick Ponsonby introduced to GE, an indication of GE's social acceptance.

17   Acknowledges receipt of Curtius's *Griechische Geschichte*.
18   Writes guardedly to Elizabeth Stuart Phelps about plans for another novel.
19   Sends two guineas for concert in aid of Elizabeth Garret Anderson's Hospital for Women.
20   Sends Cara Bray £50 in hope that she will produce a further work discouraging children's cruelty to animals. Writes to Burne-Jones in appreciation of his work.
21   Sends a letter of strongly emotional recollections to D'Albert.
22   Approves Cara Bray's outline, and urges her to accept the cheque.
23   Browning, Darwin and Joachim amongst 23 afternoon callers.
26   GHL tells Main that he has arranged with Chapman and Hall for Main to undertake a synthesis of biographies of Johnson, to be called *Life and Conversations of Dr Johnson*.
30   Sends suggested reading to Barbara Bodichon.

April
4   (Fri) GHL warns Main of Chapman's laxity in business matters.
9   Spend all day house-hunting at Tonbridge, Kent, and Reigate, Surrey, one of several such expeditions at this time.
14   Blackwood tells GHL that the Guinea edition of *Middlemarch* has been reprinted, and queries some anti-religious remarks in *Problems of Life and Mind*.
15   GHL reports GE 'deep in the Greek poets' (*Letters*, ix, 88).
21   Lunch with Emerson. GE sends the ailing Blackwood a letter of miscellaneous news.
22   Dissuades Main from including quotations of her work in his new Johnson publication: 'I hate a style speckled with quotations' (*Letters*, v, 404).
25   Encourages Lucy Smith in her plan of going to live with a young female undergraduate at Cambridge.
28   Blackwood sends news of sales, and suggests a cheaper edition of GE's works.

May
8   (Thurs) Death of J. S. Mill.
12   Death in Alexandria of Emanuel Deutsch, whose achievements and sufferings influenced *Deronda*. Recommends Pigott as Secretary of the Royal Academy.
15   Visit the Castellani collection at the British Museum.

18 Guests at a representatively crowded Sunday At Home include Thomas Woolner, Lord Houghton, Frederic Harrison and George du Maurier.

19 Three-day visit to Myers at Cambridge, having a memorable conversation with him. Tells Maria Congreve, 'We were invited ostensibly to see the boat-race, but the real pleasure of the visit consisted in talking with a hopeful group of Trinity young men' (III, 205). (The group included Gurney, Jebb and Sidgwick.)

22 Finishes rereading Aristotle's *Poetics*.

24 Blackwood reveals he would be happier if GHL could find another publisher for *Problems*.

25 GHL defends his views to Blackwood, but is happy to seek another publisher.

27 *Problems* passed to Trübner. Visited by Blackwood and his nephew William.

28 C. V. Stanford requests permission to publish settings of poems from *Gypsy*.

June
Increasing study of books on Judaism in preparation for *Deronda*.

2 (Mon) Much taken with a house called Blackbrook, near Bickley, Kent. Thanks Cara Bray for sending news of the death of Rebecca Franklin, 'a friend whom one once looked up to with reverence' (*Letters*, v, 419). 'She was always particularly good and affectionate to me, and I had much happiness in her as my teacher' (III, 206).

7 Two-day visit to Jowett, GHL recording 'one continuous excitement of talk' (*Letters*, IX, 100). Blackwood writes to defend the terms for the Guinea edition of *Middlemarch*.

9 Stay the night with the Crosses.

20 Writes to congratulate Frederic Harrison on his criticism of James Stephen's *Liberty, Equality, Fraternity*.

24 Leave for two months in France and Germany. For a brief account of this trip, see III, 211.

25 Death of Thornton Hunt.

29 Discusses new plans for novel and play *Deronda* with GHL at Fontainebleau.

July
30 (Wed) GHL buys Jewish books to help with GE's new novel.

August
9   (Sat) Apologises for being unable to visit D'Albert.
23 Return to The Priory. GE invites Emily Faithfull, proprietor of the Victoria Printing Press, to call.
24 Grants permission for an expanded edition of Main's *Sayings* to include extracts from *Middlemarch*.

September
2   (Tues) Asks Cara Bray to let her see the manuscript of *Paul Bradley*.
5   Considerably disappointed on arrival to take over Blackbrook, and agree to curtail lease, though staying there for September and October.
11 Recommends *Paul Bradley* to Macmillan.
17 Sends Anna Cross an account of their holiday, and of their disappointment with Blackbrook. Blackwood proposes a one-volume edition of *Middlemarch*.
18 Sends manuscript of Cara Bray's *Paul Bradley* to Macmillan with letter of recommendation.
19 Agrees to a one-volume *Middlemarch*, expressing wish to make corrections.

October
1   (Wed) Death of Landseer.
3   First meeting with Elma Stuart, GE's 'spiritual daughter'.
4   Sends Elma Stuart a lock of hair. GHL tells Main that both GHL and GE have read the sheets of his *Life and Conversations of Dr Samuel Johnson* and approve of it.
10 Passes to Cara Bray Macmillan's advice that she should approach the Society for Promoting Christian Knowledge with the *Paul Bradley* manuscript.
19 Sends Cross a clarification of her attitude to religions: 'I have no antagonism towards any religious belief, but a strong outflow of sympathy' (III, 216).
22 Considering a new drama.
28 Lunch with Darwin.

November
GHL asks John Fiske to refrain from sending visitors to the Priory with letters of introduction.
1   (Sat) Writes warmly to T. C. Allbutt.

5   Tells Blackwood she is 'slowly simmering towards another big
    book' (III, 218).
11 Blackwood sends details of the sale of the Guinea edition of
    Middlemarch. GE tells Barbara Bodichon of her disappointment
    with Blackbrook, and comments on J. S. Mill's *Autobiography*.
12 Agrees with Blackwood's doubts about Main's new Preface,
    wishing to avoid any suggestion of a preaching tendency in
    her work.
17 Letter to Emilia Pattison reveals that reading currently includes
    Max Müller's *Lectures on the Science of Religion* and Herbert
    Spencer's *Study of Sociology*, as well as the study of works of
    Jewish history.
19 Visit Emily Clarke in Brighton.
20 Vol. I of GHL's *Problems* published.
21 GE returns proof of opening of one-volume edition of *Middle-
    march*.
23 Visited by John Fiske. (For his account see *Letters*, v, 463–5.)

December

5   (Fri) Regrets missing Harriet Stephen and invites her to call
    again.
6   Accepts invitation to join the Crosses for Christmas.
9   Finally obtain their own carriage.
22 Congratulates Cara Bray on the SPCK's interest in *Paul Bradley*,
    also giving some suggestions for the improvement of the tale.
24 Begin four-day visit to the Crosses.
28 Thanks Clementia Taylor for her greetings.

1874

'Sketches towards Daniel Deronda' made in the first two months
of this year.

January

1   (Thurs) Confides to Journal, 'The happy old year in which we
    have had constant enjoyment of life, notwithstanding much
    bodily malaise, is gone from us for ever. More than in any
    former year of my life, love has been poured forth to me from
    distant hearts. . . . Nothing is wanting to my blessings but the

uninterrupted power of work. For as to all my unchangeable imperfections I have resigned myself' (III, 221–2).

5   Helps C. E. Appleton find a Parisian correspondent for the *Academy*.

7   Congratulates Appleton on the first number of the *Academy*.

11 GHL told by Trübner that a further edition of *Problems* will be required.

14 Congratulates Main on the penetrating choice of quotations from *Middlemarch* added to the new edition of *Sayings*.

16 Attend a *séance* at the house of Erasmus Darwin, also attended by Charles Darwin. Unimpressed.

17 Blackwood sends further settlement of *Middlemarch* and *Gypsy* accounts. GHL asks Blackwood to send a letter of encouragement to GE: 'I am hard at work and wish she were; but she simmers and simmers, despairs and despairs, believes she can never do anything again worth doing, etc, etc' (*Letters*, VI, 11).

18 Entertain F. W. H. Myers, Sir Henry Maine, and Cross and his sister Emily to lunch.

25 Sunday-afternoon callers include Edith Simcox, Mark and Emilia Pattison, Cross, and Robert Browning.

26 Parliament dissolved.

30 Requests Page's *Advanced Text Book of Geology* from Blackwood.

February

1   (Wed) Serious kidney pain, the first of a series of attacks which continue until GE's death.

5   Recurrence of kidney pain.

8   Only recorded visit to The Priory by Ruskin.

9   Tells Barbara Bodichon that she does not mind about the Conservative majority in Parliament (the first since 1841).

10 Discusses recent attacks on Herbert Spencer in letter to Sara Hennell.

12 Deeply congratulates Lucy Smith on the private publication of her husband's *Knowing and Feeling*, and hopes it will be made public.

17 Comforts Cara Bray on the rejection of *Paul Bradley* by the SPCK. Resignation of Gladstone's first Ministry.

19 GHL sends Main a frank appraisal of *Life and Conversations*.

20 Writes to Blackwood about the election result, criticising Gladstone's literary output, and remarking, 'I, who am no believer in salvation by ballot, am rather tickled that the first

experiment with it has turned against its adherents' (III, 224). Also suggests cheap edition of her novels. Disraeli forms his second Ministry.

March
2   (Mon) Attend performance of Sheridan's *School for Scandal*.
3   Writes to congratulate Helena Faucit, the Lady Teazle of this production.
6   Manuscript of *The Legend of Jubal and Other Poems*, gathered together this month, despatched to Blackwood.
8   Barbara Bodichon to lunch.
10 Hear Joachim and Piatti at a party given by Sir James and Lady Frances Colville.
11 Invites Anna Cross to lunch.
19 Enquires of E. A. Bond the progress made with a fund to support Octavia Hill, to which GE and GHL had contributed £200.
20 Asks Alice Helps to order her a new cloak.
21 Commiserates with Lady Lytton on death of her second son.
25 Further commiserates with Cara Bray on her failure to find a publisher for *Paul Bradley*.
26 Congratulates William Allingham on his *Laurence Bloomfield*, considering it superior to Crabbe.
28 Asks Alice Helps to call to discuss clothing.
29 Thanks Elma Stuart for the gift of a table made by her.
30 Birth of GHL's second grandchild, Maud Southwood Lewes.

April
1   (Wed) Blackwood sends remainder of revise for *Jubal*, and expresses his (slightly lukewarm) appreciation of the volume.
2   GE suggests price of six shillings for this volume, and requests royalty terms.
15 Visited by niece Edith Griffiths (the eldest daughter of Isaac Evans) and her husband.
16 Look at two houses at Earlswood Common, Redhill.
23 Sends letter of miscellaneous news to Sara Hennell.
24 Visit the Crosses at Weybridge and inspect a house, one of several such inspections in the Home Counties this summer.
25 Disappointed with choice of paper for *Jubal*.

May

Jubal published. One-volume edition of *Middlemarch* printed. Congratulates Jane Senior on her report on the education of girls in pauper schools, and expresses her dissatisfaction with the Poor Law.

1 (Fri) Blackwood apologises for the *Jubal* paper.

9 Thanks her niece Edith for sending photographs of Griff.

11 Writes affectionately to Mary Cross, thanking her for the gift of a specially painted vase.

13 Invites the over-admiring Main to visit them in the country.

26 Asks Anna Cross and her son to Sunday lunch.

30 Thanks James Thomson for the gift of his 'City of Dreadful Night', which she finds admirable.

31 F. T. Palgrave calls at The Priory.

June

Reading in this and the following month includes Austen's *Mansfield Park* and Trollope's *The Way We Live Now*.

2 (Tues) Start a four-month stay at Earlswood Common, Redhill, where GE makes considerable progress with *Deronda*, and GHL continues work on *Problems*.

5 Thanks Annie Fields for a letter of appreciation.

11 GHL reads beginning of *Deronda*.

14 Tells Anna Cross of their happiness in their new house, and hopes that J. W. Cross will find them a permanent dwelling of this kind.

16 Expresses satisfaction with swift sale of *Jubal*, and disappointment at the impending threat of the restoration of the Empire in France.

18 James Thomson writes of his considerable admiration for GE's writings.

23 GHL reports GE hard at work on *Deronda* and asks Blackwood to advertise *Jubal* more prominently.

July

1 (Wed) In a letter of continued sympathy to Lucy Smith, reports herself 'revelling in the sweet peace of the country' (III, 237). Approves Clementia Taylor's interest in the condition of workhouse girls: 'You see my only social work is to rejoice in the labours of others, while I live in luxurious remoteness from all turmoil' (III, 235).

15 Explains her reluctance to being made a biographical subject in a lengthy letter to George Bancroft.
16 Asks Barbara Bodichon's advice on Holmwood Common as a place of residence.
21 Thanks Roland Stuart, whom she calls an adopted grandson, for sending a photograph of his mother.

August

4 (Tues) Blackwood reports excellent sales of *Gypsy*, *Jubal*, and, most of all, *Middlemarch*.
8 Tells Blackwood of her delight at this good news, but depression when reading her own past work.
11 GHL reports over 5000 of the one-volume edition of *Middlemarch* sold in the previous two months, and the demand not slackening.
18 Finish reading Edward Burnett Taylor's *Researches into the Early History of Mankind*.
21 Entertain Lord Lytton (formerly E. R. Bulwer-Lytton) for two days.
23 Sends tactful note of sympathy to Harriet Beecher Stowe regarding her brother's alleged adultery.
25 GHL invites Elma Stuart to visit them at Redhill.

September

Reading this month includes Austen's *Persuasion*. Learns Maria Lewis's address and sends her £10, the first of several such donations.

8 (Tues) GHL gives Main a confident prediction of the high quality of *Deronda*.
16 Visit Emily Clarke at Brighton. William Blackwood reports continued high sales of *Middlemarch*.
22 Thanks Elma Stuart for gifts of clothing.
23 Sends news to Barbara Bodichon.
25 Return to The Priory.
26 Declines her nephew Robert's suggestion that communication be reopened with his aunt, Fanny Houghton.
28 Begin four-day visit to W. H. Bullock-Hall at Six Mile Bottom.

October

3 (Sat) Begin fortnight's holiday in Paris and Brussels.
19 Return to London.

20   Visit Wiltshire (Salisbury and environs) on brief walking-tour in search of locations for *Deronda*.
26   Asks Barbara Bodichon to recommend a housemaid. Urges Elma Stuart to take better care of herself.
28   Again visit Wiltshire (Devizes and Marlborough) for four-day study of possible *Deronda* locations.

November

 1   (Sun) GHL recommends Matthew Arnold's 'Review of Objections to *Literature and Dogma*' to Elma Stuart. 'Much that he says on Religions we both think very good' (*Letters*, vi, 87).
 9   Cross takes GE to Lord Mayor's Show, one of several outings arranged by him at this time.
10   Thanks Alexander Macmillan for sending a complimentary copy of David Masson's *Life of Milton*, and compliments him on the quality of his publishing list.
11   Belatedly answers a letter from Harriet Beecher Stowe: 'Will you not agree with me that there is one comprehensive Church whose fellowship consists in the desire to purify and ennoble human life, and where the best members of all narrower Churches may call themselves brother and sister in spite of differences?' (iii, 243).
17   Shown round the Bank of England by Cross.
19   Blackwood, with tactful indirectness, encourages progress on *Deronda*.
20   First of two visits to Russian church. Sends 'the gossip of our lives' to Sara Hennell, in anticipation of their adjacent anniversaries (*Letters*, vi, 93).
22   Second visit to Russian church.
23   Asks Cara Bray to send a proof of *Paul Bradley*.
28   GHL obtains from Spencer J. S. Mill's *Three Essays on Religion* for GE to read.

December

 1   (Tues) David Masson acknowledges GE's letter of appreciation of his *Life of Milton*.
10   In reply to Mary Ponsonby's lengthy expressions of her religious difficulties, GE sends an unusually full statement of her own views: 'the fellowship between man and man which has been the principle of development, social and moral, is not dependent on conceptions of what is not man' (iii, 245).

30 Sends a legal query to Harrison, perhaps with *Deronda* in mind. Blackwood sends New Year greetings.
31 Two-thirds of vol. I of the *Deronda* manuscript completed.

1875

January
1 (Fri) Thanks Albert and Anna Druce for the gift of some flowers. Sends further legal query to Harrison.
2 Thanks Main for his New Year greeting, and George Smith for a box of bonbons.
3 Writes to Emilia Pattison arguing against changes in the final chapter of her husband's *Isaac Casaubon*.
7 Asks Harrison for advice on resettlement of estates in tail (such as that of Sir Francis Mallinger in *Deronda*).
8 Invites Harrison to call for further discussions.
10 Writes at length to Elma Stuart, urging her to take better care of herself.
11 Blackwood sends a cheque and a statement of the year's account – sales of *Middlemarch* have been especially pleasing.
13 Confides to Journal, 'The last year has been crowded with proofs of affection for me, and of value for what work I have been able to do. This makes the best motive or encouragement to do more; but, as usual, I am suffering much from doubt as to the worth of what I am doing, and fear lest I may not be able to complete it so as to make it a contribution to literature, and not a mere addition to the heap of books. I am just now beginning the part about "Deronda", at p. 234 [i.e. end of ch. 15]' (III, 250–1). Congratulates Emily Cross and Francis Otter on their engagement.
15 Encourages Clementia Taylor in her philanthropic work.
23 Death of Charles Kingsley.
27 Sympathises with Elma Stuart on the death of her mother.
30 Urges Mary Ponsonby 'to consider your early religious experience as a portion of valid knowledge, and to cherish its emotional results in relation to objects and ideas which are either substitutes or metamorphoses of the earlier' (III, 253).

February
2 (Tues) Visit Kew and Richmond to choose a scene for *Deronda*.

GHL reassures Elma Stuart that she will always be a welcome visitor.

6   Invites Frederick Locker to call with his new wife, but only on a Sunday afternoon.
7   Thanks Blackwood for the gift of A. W. Kinglake's *The Battle of Inkerman*, of which she sends a critique. Expresses disappointment with Margaret Majendie's *Gianetto*, though explaining that she is 'obliged to fast from fiction' (III, 255).
11 Encourages Mary Ponsonby to send papers detailing her religious struggle.
18 Begins reading J. H. Bridges's translation of Comte's *System of Positive Polity*.
19 Seeks further legal advice from Harrison.
21 Vol. II of GHL's *Problems* published.

March

2   (Tues) Further violent kidney attacks. *Deronda* written whilst suffering these continuing pains. Counsels Oscar Browning in his difficulties at Eton.
4   Thanks Elma Stuart for a further parcel of clothes.
8   Further sharp kidney attack.
15 Manning created Cardinal.
18 Visited by Lord and Lady Lytton.
20 Sends news to D'Albert.
24 Apologises to Lucy Crompton for an unfortunate remark made unknowingly by Cross concerning her father, Lord Romilly. Humorous letter about clothing sent to Elma Stuart.

April

7   (Wed) See Salvini in *Othello*.
8   Dine at Lord Lytton's.
19 Again see Salvini in *Othello*.
21 William Blackwood relates to his uncle the details of a recent visit to GHL and GE, informing him that one volume of the *Deronda* manuscript is now ready for inspection.

May

1   (Sat) Begin three-day visit to Jowett at Oxford.
3   Fresh kidney attack, which quickly passes, but the attacks recur until 9 May.

6 Leslie Stephen sends information on the resignation of Cambridge scholarships for *Deronda*.
10 Encourages Lucy Smith to publish her privately circulated memoir of her husband.
12 Drives with Cara Bray.
16 Birth of George Herbert Lewes, son to Bertie.
19 Gives Blackwood the manuscript of *Deronda* chs 1–8.
20 Blackwood expresses his delight with the manuscript, which he stayed up late to read.
25 Blackwood, encouraged by GHL, sends a further, unusually fulsome, appreciation of *Deronda*.
30 See Salvini's *Hamlet*.

June
1 (Tues) Requests Harrison's further legal assistance.
2 Sends details of her requirements to Harrison.
4 Alice Helps to dinner.
9 Thanks Harrison for his advice.
12 Writes to Emily Clarke.
14 Again see Salvini's *Hamlet*.
17 Move for three-and-a-half months to The Elms, at Rickmansworth, Hertfordshire, where work takes place on vols II and III of *Deronda*.
18 Further legal query despatched to Harrison.
24 Give limited assistance to Octavia Hill's campaign to prevent fields near Swiss Cottage being built on.
29 Death of Bertie Lewes at Durban, the news not reaching England until the end of July. Artizans' and Labourers' Dwellings Improvement Act approved.

July
3 (Sat) Publication of GHL's *On Actors and the Art of Acting*.
8 GHL meets Queen of Holland, GE declining the invitation.
16 Asks Emilia Pattison to send news of her health.
28 Has tooth pulled.

August
1 (Sun) GHL tells G. J. Holyoake, 'The uninterrupted peace is very favourable both to health and work. We see no one – absolutely no one' (*Letters*, VI, 160).

9 GE enthuses over her Hertfordshire environs in letter to Clementia Taylor.
13 Tells Barbara Bodichon of Bertie Lewes's death, though circulation of news of this bereavement generally limited in order to avoid letters of condolence. Sends brief details of her biography to Elizabeth Stuart Phelps.
14 Discusses death of Bertie in letter to Cross: 'He was a sweet-natured creature – not clever, but diligent and well-judging about the things of daily life' (*Letters*, VI, 165). Despairs of finishing *Deronda* satisfactorily.
19 Professes herself happy to continue discussing metaphysics with Mary Ponsonby.
21 Visited for the weekend by Charles Lewes and family

September
2 (Thurs) Encourages Elma Stuart to write a detailed story of her self-initiation as a wood-carver.
11 GHL asks Blackwood to send Andrew Wilson's *The Abode of Snow* for GE to read aloud.
19 Asks Anna Cross to send details of a skin ointment.
21 Undertake to help find governess position for Phoebe Marks.
23 Return to The Priory from Rickmansworth.
24 Set off for holiday in Wales, where reading includes Austen, *Emma*; Dickens, *Uncommercial Traveller*; Sterne, *Sentimental Journey*; Turgenev, *Nouvelles moscovites*.

October
9 (Sat) Return from Wales.
10 Records in Journal, 'Our stay at Rickmansworth, though otherwise peaceful, was not marked by any great improvement in health . . . rather the contrary' (III, 263). Tells Blackwood she had a 'bad time' at Rickmansworth, 'and did less of everything than I desired' (III, 263). Suggests February publication for the first part of *Deronda*.
13 Sends D'Albert her news, including her feelings on Bertie's death.
18 Commiserates with Emilia Pattison on being advised to winter out of England because of arthritis. Blackwood agrees to begin publishing *Deronda* in February. Newnham College, Cambridge, opens.

20 First two volumes of *Deronda* sent to Blackwood. Decide to publish the novel in eight monthly parts.

November
3   (Wed) Blackwood reports the opening of *Deronda* ready in proof, and offers the same terms as for *Middlemarch*.
4   GHL accepts this offer.
10 Asks Blackwood whether to rearrange the first four parts of *Deronda*. Blackwood sends the first 256 pages of proof and an encomium of the book's quality.
17 Blackwood sends a further 180 pages of proof, and gives his opinion on the splitting of the parts.
18 GHL sends Blackwood his thoughts on part-division and publication date.
19 Thanks Mrs Ernst Benzon for the gift of a scarf, and reminds Elma Stuart to send news of herself.
20 Sends pre-birthday greetings to Sara Hennell, revealing that she has re-established contact with Maria Lewis.
22 GHL suggests a form of advertisement for *Deronda* to Blackwood.
30 Asks Alice Helps to call. Blackwood remarks, 'You may rest assured that you are writing one of the most remarkable Books that ever was produced by man or woman. I know nothing like it' (*Letters*, vi, 195).

December
25 (Sat) Records in Journal, 'I have finished the fifth book, but am not so far on in the sixth, as I hoped to have been, – the oppression under which I have been labouring having positively suspended my power of writing anything that I could feel satisfaction in' (iii, 201).
27 Read approvingly Mark Pattison's article 'Philosophy at Oxford'.
29 Blackwood sends settlement of the *Middlemarch, Jubal* and *Gypsy* accounts.

1876

January
2   (Sun) GHL sends New Year reflections to Main, and comments on the progress of *Deronda*.

10   Blackwood is requested by GHL to ensure that advertisements
     for *Deronda* appear in the *Contemporary* and *Fortnightly* reviews.
12   GHL asks Blackwood to check that advance proofs of *Deronda*
     have been sent to Harpers, and on the 14th insists that
     publication of *Deronda* may have to be delayed if Harpers wish
     it. Blackwood tells GHL he is troubling too much about the
     matter.
?24 Go to see Frederick Walker's pictures at Deschamps' Gallery.
25   Writes lengthily to J. F. Payne following the death of his
     mother, also discussing her purposes in writing fiction: 'my
     writing is simply a set of experiments in life – an endeavour
     to see what our thought and emotion may be capable of'
     (*Letters*, VI, 216).
28   GHL tells Blackwood that he hopes to send vol. III of the
     Deronda manuscript, though progress is slow.
30   GHL writes to warn William Blackwood not to mention any
     reviews of *Deronda*.
31   William Blackwood to lunch.

February
 1   (Tues) First of eight parts of *Deronda* published. Others follow
     at monthly intervals, ending in September. GHL sends Black-
     wood manuscript of part VI.
 3   Offers to lend Cara Bray £40 in expectation of a publisher's
     advance on her *Elements of Morality*, and discusses vivisection.
 6   Ill again.
12   Attending as usual the Saturday-afternoon Pops Concert at St
     James's Hall, is moved by the music to kiss the violinist
     Neruda.
14   Suffers for five days from lumbago.
24   Attend performance of Liszt's *The Legend of St Elizabeth*.
     Blackwood sends an enthusiastic appreciation of *Deronda*,
     though retaining doubts about Mordecai.
26   Dine with Lord and Lady Lytton before the Lyttons depart for
     India.
27   GHL tells Blackwood that his comments on Mordecai have
     made GE despondent.
29   Blackwood reports that sales of *Deronda* are exceeding those
     for *Middlemarch*.

March

1 (Wed) GHL tells Main that ill health has restricted the writing of both GE and himself.

2 Blackwood expresses unbounded congratulations on part VI of *Deronda*.

3 GHL reports that these congratulations have greatly raised GE's spirits. GE writes to Emilia Pattison, praising the pictures of Burne-Jones and Frederick Walker.

6 Blackwood reports continued good sales of *Deronda*.

13 Begin 12-day stay in the Bullock-Halls' house at Weybridge, though returning to The Priory at the weekend.

18 Writes humorously to Blackwood about corrections to *Deronda* suggested by various correspondents.

28 Acknowledges George Grove's admiration of *Deronda*.

29 Mary Dickens, as requested by GE, sends details of the opening night of Tennyson's *Queen Mary*.

30 Writes to Barbara Bodichon, discussing vivisection *inter alia*.

31 GHL asked to become a member of the council of the Physiological Society.

April

10 (Mon) Part VII of *Deronda* sent to Blackwood.

12 Confesses to Journal that Jewish part of *Deronda* is 'likely to satisfy nobody', though gratified by the novel's good sales, and by her own better health (III, 277).

17 Blackwood sends admiring comments on part VII of *Deronda*.

18 Sees Irving in Tennyson's *Queen Mary*. Tells Blackwood that she regrets including a motto from Whitman at the head of part IV, ch. 29.

May

1 (Mon) Queen Victoria proclaimed Empress of India.

2 Thanks Main for his continued affectionate sympathy.

6 Thanks Harriet Beecher Stowe for her letter – 'one of the best cordials I could have' (III, 280).

10 Asks Elma Stuart's advice on underclothing.

11 Blackwood agrees to let Harpers have proof of *Deronda* more than a month in advance, and sends further good news of sales.

13 Dine with Anton Rubinstein (a model for Klesmer?) at the Lehmanns.

18 John Blackwood to lunch. Dine with Lady Portsmouth. Manuscript of first half of part VIII of *Deronda* sent to William Blackwood.
20 Spend weekend with Jowett in Oxford.
23 GHL tells Blackwood that there is no objection to Edward Dowden making a book-length study of GE.
31 Declines invitation to meet Leopold, King of the Belgians, but GHL presented in her place.

June

3 (Sat) Records in Journal, regarding *Deronda*, 'Growing interest in the public, and growing sale, which has from the beginning exceeded that of *Middlemarch*. The Jewish part apparently creating strong interest' (III, 283).
4 Writes to Elma Stuart regretting inability to give more time to her on her recent visit.
7 Reads GHL penultimate chapter of *Deronda* and sends manuscript to William Blackwood.
8 *Deronda* finished.
10 Set off for two-and-a-half months in France and Switzerland – for detailed itinerary, see III, 285. Blackwood sends his verdict on the conclusion of *Deronda*: 'criticism and eulogism are out of place' (*Letters*, VI, 262).
12 Proof-reading final pages of *Deronda* in Paris.
30 Trade Union Amendment Act approved.

July

6 (Thurs) GE sends Blackwood, and GHL sends Charles Lewes, news of their travels so far.
12 Thanks Jane Senior for the suggestion of a house: 'We *do* desire, above all earthly possessions of a material sort, a house in the country to which we could go, not simply in summer, but from time to time throughout the year' (*Letters*, VI, 269). Also gives an account of their daily timetable in Ragatz. Blackwood sends a still-favourable account of *Deronda* sales.
17 GHL reports GE's health considerably improved.

August

15 (Tues) Elementary Education Act approved.

September

1 (Fri) Return to The Priory from France and Switzerland. Final part of *Deronda* published.
2 Writes to D'Albert telling him of their holiday and of the completion of *Deronda*. Tells Blackwood of her delight at the Chief Rabbi's approval of the Jewish characterisation in *Deronda*.
4 Apologises to Catherine Spence for her infelicitous reception at The Priory. Begin four-day visit to the Bullock-Halls at Six Mile Bottom.
8 Asks Cara Bray to send news.
12 Sends details of the continental holiday to Elma Stuart.
23 Visited by Emily Davies, their talk turning to the necessity of telling the truth, and the education of women. Manuscript of third volume of GHL's *Problems* sent to the printer.
26 Take GE's niece, Emily Clarke, visiting them briefly, to W. S. Gilbert's *Dan'l Druce, Blacksmith*, based on *Marner*. Thanks Haim Guedalla, a Jewish community worker, for his praise of the Jewish elements in *Deronda*.

October

2 (Mon) Explains to Haim Guedalla her reasons for refusing permission for him to publish her letter of 26 September; and regrets in letter to Barbara Bodichon the critical tendency to divide *Deronda* into separate portions: 'I meant everything in the book to be related to everything else there' (III, 291).
5 Visiting Bullock-Hall, they pay a visit to stables at Newmarket, Suffolk, GE noticing a defect in the Derby winner.
7 Return from four-day visit to Bullock-Hall.
8 Cross their only Sunday guest. Writes Blackwood an affectionate appreciation of his services. Blackwood subsequently remarks to his nephew, 'It is the greatest compliment a man in my position could possibly receive, and . . . brought warm tears to my eyes' (*Letters*, VI, 293).
12 Sends Elma Stuart autographs of Shelley and the French executioner Sanson. Blackwood thanks GE for her generous letter.
14 Asks Lucy Smith to send more news of herself.
19 Blackwood offers £4000 for 10-year control of copyright.
20 Gratified, in looking over accounts in consideration of Black-

wood's offer, to find 24,577 copies of *Middlemarch* had been distributed before Christmas 1875.

23 GHL, in amiable tone, seeks clarification of Blackwood's past and future terms.

28 Blackwood explains a blunder in the previous terms of the lease of the copyright.

29 In discussing *Deronda* in a letter to Harriet Beecher Stowe, deplores English misunderstanding of the Jews: 'The best that can be said of it is, that it is a sign of the intellectual narrowness – in plain English, the stupidity – which is still the average mark of our culture' (III, 295). GHL tells Blackwood that a royalty arrangement would be preferable to a down sum for the renewed copyright lease.

November

3 (Fri) GE explains to Blackwood the reasons for preferring a royalty arrangement, discussing also her disappointment with reviews of *Deronda*.

4 Has tooth extracted.

21 Blackwood apologises for being unable to make a more generous offer.

22 Sympathises with Cara Bray's illness, sends items of personal news, and comments, 'It is remarkable to me that I have entirely lost my *personal* melancholy. I often, of course, have melancholy thoughts about the destinies of my fellow creatures; but I am never in that *mood* of sadness which used to be my frequent visitant even in the midst of external happiness. And this, notwithstanding a very vivid sense that life is declining and death close at hand' (III, 296–7). GHL agrees royalty terms for copyright lease, reminding Blackwood not to reveal to GE public disappointment with the Jewish sections of *Deronda*.

29 Taken by Cross to see The Heights at Witley, Surrey.

December

1 (Fri) Records in Journal her disappointment at the critical reception of *Deronda*, but her gratification with its sales and approval by the Jewish community.

6 Buy The Heights at Witley. For GE's description of the house, see II, 298–9.

15 Notes in Journal pleasure at Jewish reception of *Deronda* and a second request to translate *Romola* into Italian.
16 Guinea edition of *Deronda* published. Assures Elizabeth Stuart Phelps that her attitude to Christianity has been consistent throughout her novels.
21 Sympathises with Cara Bray's illness, and indulges in several recollections of their past life.
23 GHL sends Christmas greetings to Elma Stuart, passing on GE's request for a letter from her.
24 Spend five days with Anna Cross.
26 Matthew Arnold present at their Boxing Day dinner.

1877

January
1 (Mon) Journal records anxiety over public affairs but concludes, 'As to our private life, all is happiness, perfect love, and undiminished intellectual interest' (III, 301). Queen Victoria proclaimed Empress of India in Delhi.
10 Call on W. B. Scott.
12 Blackwood sends a cheque for £2215 to settle the previous year's account.
13 Edward Dowden tells Blackwood that he has had to abandon his plans to write a book on GE.
19 In response to a query from James Sully, GE replies that she believes the term 'meliorist' was her own coinage.
21 Edith Simcox inscribes copy of her newly published *Natural Law* for GE.
30 Suggests to Blackwood that *Romola* be included in his stereotyped edition of her works. Recommends Helen Allingham as an illustrator, and remarks that 'there is no book of mine about which I more thoroughly feel that I could swear by every sentence as having been written with my best blood' (III, 302).

February
1 (Thurs) Requests Andrew Clark to give an opinion on GHL's rheumatic gout.
5 Points out to Elma Stuart shortcomings in W. H. Mallock's 'Modern Atheism' in the January issue of the *Contemporary Review*.

8   Blackwood agrees to publish a stereotyped edition of *Romola*, and suggests GE or GHL approach Helen Allingham regarding illustrations, also including an assessment of GE's work by his retired chief proof-reader.

13   Invites Helen Allingham to illustrate stereotyped edition of *Romola* (declined).

19   Has severe renal attack.

23   Further kidney trouble.

27   GHL suggests a uniform edition of the novels to Blackwood – eventually the 'Cabinet' edition. Also agrees to an illustrated edition of *Romola*, and hints that Dowden should be urged to reconsider the possibility of a study of GE.

March

4   (Sun) Go to see pictures by Millais.

8   Gives hints on writing in Midlands dialect to William Allingham.

11   Dinner with Elizabeth Benzon, where Joachim plays for them.

16   Attend music party given by Leighton, hearing Joachim, Petri and Piatti.

19   Blackwood makes further suggestions for the Cabinet edition.

20   Suggests the Cabinet edition comprise eight volumes. Sends strictures on Harriet Martineau's *Autobiography* to Cara Bray.

21   Hear performance of Beethoven's posthumous string quartets.

23   Again asks Elma Stuart to send more detailed news of herself.

24   Morning encounter with Tennyson, one of many meetings at this time. Attend the last Saturday Pops Concert of the season. Death of Bagehot.

27   Further suggestions from Blackwood about the Cabinet edition, to which GHL replies on the 29th with an idea of his own – that the edition be set from existing type but on finer paper.

30   Tennyson reads *Maud* and the two 'Northern Farmer' poems to a group of their friends at The Priory.

April

10   (Tues) Commiserates with Mary Cash on the death of her father, John Sibree.

17   Vol. iii of GHL's *Problems* published.

28   Thanks Mrs Burne-Jones for the offer of tickets to a showing of her husband's pictures, and mentions her problems in contemplating a new morning dress.

30 Blackwood announces that he has finally decided that the Cabinet edition should be in 19 or 20 volumes.

May

3 (Thurs) Liszt writes to introduce the Wagners.

4 Attend private view at the Royal Academy.

6 First meeting with Cosima Wagner, daughter of Liszt. Considerable contact with the Wagners in the ensuing weeks.

8 GE asks Burne-Jones if she may introduce Cosima Wagner to him.

10 Returns to Clementia Taylor her husband's *Some Account of the Taylor Family* and *Auld Lang Syne*.

11 Attend a rehearsal of *Die Walküre* and *Tannhäuser*.

14 Attend rehearsal of *Siegfried* and *Lohengrin*, afterwards taking Cosima Wagner to Burne-Jones's studio.

15 Princess Louise asks to be introduced to GE at a dinner with the Goschens. GE offers £10 towards the education of Joan Grüner, a Girton student. Tells Sara Hennell of her dislike of Harriet Martineau's *Autobiography*: 'the more I think of the book and all connected with it, the more it deepens my repugnance . . . to autobiography' (III, 306–7).

16 Sends Barbara Bodichon a list of the current Italian names for the water-wagtail.

17 Hear Wagner read *Parzival*. GE sends Catherine Paget a copy of her works as a wedding present.

18 Attend rehearsal of *Tristan und Isolde*.

19 Begin three-day visit to Jowett.

21 Thanks William Allingham for a copy of his *Hunterian Oration*.

27 Returns to Trübner the Jewish books consulted for *Deronda*. Expresses her gratitude to Elma Stuart for a gift of embroidery.

31 Warmly thanks David Kaufman for his favourable review of *Deronda*. Servants move in to The Heights, Witley, whilst GE and GHL go to Cambridge for five days, staying with the Sidgwicks.

June

4 (Mon) Arrive at Witley, where reading includes Scott, *Heart of Midlothian*, and *Legend of Montrose*; Richardson, *Sir Charles Grandison*; Dumas, *Les Trois mousquetaires*; Trollope, *The American Senator*; Reade, *A Woman Hater*; Turgenev, *Virgin Soil*;

Zola, *L'Assommoir*; Tennyson, *Idylls of the King*, and plays. Much contact with Sir Henry and Lady Holland at this period.

5   Thanks Charles Ritter for sending translations of extracts from *Deronda*.

10   GHL writes to Cross expressing delight with The Heights.

12   Harrison asks if GE might state the extent of her commitment to Positivism, eventually giving rise to publication of 'A College Breakfast Party'.

14   Promises to bear in mind Harrison's request for some Positivist substitutes for Christian family prayers.

18   GHL tells Tennyson that he and GE have just read *Harold* for the first time, and *Mary* for the fourth. Hope to see him over the summer.

20   GHL invites Blackwood to call at Witley at his convenience.

22   Reading *Life, Letters, and Literary Remains of John Keats*, ed. R. M. Milnes.

24   Birth of Elinor, third daughter of Charles Lewes.

July

Printing details of the Cabinet edition finally decided.

9   (Mon) GHL sends Blackwood a copy of Kaufman's pamphlet on GE and Judaism, advising him to choose a translator carefully.

12   GHL sends to Elma Stuart an anecdotal letter, reporting great delight with the Heights.

23   Thanks Charles Ritter for the gift of his translated anthology of her works, *Fragments et pensées*.

31   Harrison spends the day at Witley.

August

26   (Sun) Asks William Allingham not to forget to send his news.

28   Cross introduces GE to tennis, subsequently a much-enjoyed recreation.

September

17   (Mon) Visit Tennyson.

25   Begin five-day visit to the Bullock-Halls.

29   Return to London.

October
One-volume edition of *Deronda* published.
4 (Thurs) Visited at Witley by Jowett.
5 Introduced by Cross to badminton.
7 GHL tells Lady Holland how GE started to write fiction (*Letters*, IX, 169).
12 Informs David Kaufman that his article on *Deronda* has now been translated.
17 Condemns W. H. Mallock's *New Republic* in letter to Mary Ponsonby: 'I think direct personal portraiture – or caricature – is a bastard kind of satire' (III, 317).
25 Leave Witley, GE much strengthened in health, for five-day visit to the Bullock-Halls at Six Mile Bottom. Blackwood apologises for being unable to offer greater remuneration for the Cabinet edition.
29 Return to The Priory.

November
3 (Sat) Attends christening of grand-daughter Elinor at Rosslyn Hill.
6 Thanks Cross for the gift of a badminton set, and admits to finding 'some smaller wholes among the lyrics' rather than *In Memoriam* or the *Idylls*, 'the works most decisive of Tennyson's high place among the immortals' (II, 318).
9 Edith Simcox disappointed at GE's failure to comment on her *Natural Law*.
10 Declines to contribute a volume on Shakespeare to the 'English Men of Letters' series. Records in Journal, 'We are at last in love with our Surrey house, and mean to keep it. The air and abundant exercise have quite renovated my health, and I am in more bodily comfort than I have known for several years' (III, 319).
11 GE at last refers, somewhat lukewarmly, to Edith Simcox's *Natural Law*.
13 Thanks Elizabeth Stuart Phelps for the gift of her *The Story of Avis*, which she is reading slowly; also repeating her misgivings about the benefits of reading contemporary fiction, and the quality of modern criticism.
16 Outlines her attitude to human misery in response to a *cri de coeur* from Myers: 'I only long, if it were possible to me, to help in satisfying the need of those who want a reason for

living in the absence of what has been called consolatory belief' (*Letters*, ıx, 201). Sends Sara Hennell the customary letter of accumulated news in anticipation of her birthday.

21　Blackwood sends proof of 'A College Breakfast Party', and good news of sales of the one-volume edition of *Deronda*. Also seeks GE's permission for Main's new project, *The George Eliot Birthday Book*.

23　Main compiling his *GE Birthday Book*. Thanks Sara Hennell for her letter, attempting to explain off-handedness in Herbert Spencer's conduct, and attacking Mallock's *New Republic*.

27　Writes affectionately to D'Albert.

December
　3　(Mon) Writes to withdraw from spending Christmas with the Burne-Jones family.
　4　Sends Main suggestions for the *Birthday Book*.
11　Visited by Edith Simcox, a visit recorded in some detail in Simcox's autobiography (see *Letters*, ıx, 206–7).
17　Sends Main criticisms of the draft *Birthday Book*.
24　GHL sends Christmas greetings to Elma Stuart and Anna Cross.
25　Christmas spent quietly at home, Anna Cross being ill.
26　Visited by Charles Lewes and family. Writes to Charlotte Carmichael, regretting her inability to do anything to increase appreciation of the Celts.
31　Ends her Journal with conflicting views about the prospect of further literary achievements, and acknowledging the usefulness of the Journal in the past: 'I have often been helped, in looking back in it, to compare former with actual states of despondency. . . . In this way a past despondency has turned to present hopefulness' (ııı, 324).

1878

January
Cabinet edition begins publication, commencing with vol. ı of *Romola*, and continuing with the publication of one volume of GE's works per month.
　6　(Sun) Leslie Stephen among the Sunday-afternoon callers.
12　Thanks Elma Stuart for the gift of a writing board.

15 Trollope calls, following his return from South Africa.
16 Asks Edith Simcox to obtain for the *The Child's Own Book*, and pays her for a copy of Cobbett's *Rural Rides*, also discussing the moral responsibilities and influence of the writer.
17 Reading includes J. R. Green, *History of the English People*, and W. E. H. Lecky, *A History of England in the Eighteenth Century*. Mentions the phonograph in a letter to Barbara Bodichon, and rejoices at London University opening its degrees to women.
18 Blackwood sends a cheque for £1006 and an account of sales in the past year.
26 Discusses liking for Pascal and La Bruyère in letter to Blackwood.
31 GHL tells Barbara Bodichon of his interest in a patient fitted successfully with a false larynx.

February
Vol. II of *Romola* appears in the Cabinet edition.
13 (Wed) GE indulges in much philosophical conversation during a call on Edith Simcox.
14 Thanks Louise Houlton for the gift of her *Swallow Flights*.
16 GHL presented to Princess Christian.
28 Attend marriage of Elinor Locker to Lionel Tennyson.

March
Marner, 'Brother Jacob' and 'The Lifted Veil' appear in the Cabinet edition.
11 (Mon) Edith Simcox discusses 'The Lifted Veil' with GE and GHL.
15 Asks Barbara Bodichon to write with news of herself.
20 Attend concert at the Royal Academy of Music, performers including Henschel, Joachim, Piatti and Strauss, all of whom GE and GHL hear several times this season.
21 See the telephone demonstrated.
23 Discusses Wagner's setting of Heine's 'The Two Grenadiers' (heard at concert on the 20th) in letter to Georgiana Burne-Jones.
27 Thanks Elma Stuart for sending her violets, discussing – *inter alia* – her recent musical experiences.
29 Attend musical party given by Charlotte Moscheles.
31 Entertain Tennyson to dinner.

April

Vol. i of *Bede* appears in the Cabinet edition.

9 (Tues) Explains to Lord Houghton that she is unable to receive the American poet and journalist Louise Moulton, having a horror of being interviewed or written about.

12 Dine with Tennyson.

15 Lord Acton sends a personal eulogy of her work.

29 Tells Cross, '"Non omnis moriar" is a keen hope with me' (*Letters*, ii, 226). GHL roughs out a stage version of *Deronda*.

May

Vol. ii of *Bede* appears in the Cabinet edition.

2 (Thurs) Take Emily Clarke to see Irving in Boucicault's *Louis XI*.

3 Attend private view at the Royal Academy.

7 Jowett writes, 'The more I think of it the more I agree in what you said that the really great and abiding interest of philosophy is human motive' (*Letters*, ix, 227).

16 Asks Barbara Bodichon to recommend a housekeeper, and also a governess for the Bullock-Halls. William Blackwood sends a highly satisfactory statement of sales of the Cabinet edition.

22 Order furniture for Witley.

26 Edith Simcox finds Shakespeare's generic superiority to other dramatists a topic of Sunday afternoon conversation.

28 Death of Lord John Russell.

31 Attend a dinner given by the Goschens for the Crown Prince and Princess Royal. Many 'swells' present.

June

Vol. i of *Scenes* appears in the Cabinet edition.

7 (Fri) Sends Cara Bray her favourable impression of the Crown Prince and Princess Royal.

8 Begin three-day visit to Jowett. For details see *Letters*, vii, 30–1.

?21 Go to Witley. GHL remarks, 'We were both knocked up by London gaieties and Royalties and have said adieu to all for another five months.' GHL's health – he developed intestinal cancer this month – a continual concern. Cross remarks, 'I think he was himself aware that something was seriously wrong, but the moment the pain ceased, the extraordinary buoyancy of his spirits returned' (III, 333–4).

27 Hopes that Blackwood has enjoyed his travels, and that he continues to appreciate a holiday from business.

July
Vol. II of *Scenes* appears in the Cabinet edition.

1 (Mon) 'A College Breakfast Party' published in *Macmillan's Magazine*.

10 Start reading P. G. Hamilton's *Modern Frenchmen*.

12 Advises Cara Bray on a publication problem with her *Elements of Morality*.

16 William Blackwood sends a half-year statement of sales.

18 Reaffirms, in a letter to Clementia Taylor, her refusal to speak on public topics: 'My function is that of the *aesthetic*, not the doctrinal teacher – the rousing of the nobler emotions, which make mankind desire the social right, not the prescribing of special measures, concerning which the artistic mind, however strongly moved by social sympathy, is often not the best judge' (III, 330).

30 Decide that GHL's health will prevent their visiting Blackwood in Scotland.

August
Vol. I of *Mill* appears in the Cabinet edition.

1 (Thurs) Tells D'Albert: 'You remember me as much less of a conservative than I have now become' (*Letters*, VII, 47).

9 Sends William Blackwood corrections for Cabinet edition of *Jubal* and *Deronda*.

10 Visited by Edith Simcox, who notices GHL's deteriorating health.

11 Sends advice to Charles Ritter on his French translation of 'O May I Join the Choir Invisible'.

12 GHL is read part of Tennyson's unfinished *Becket*, about which GHL records serious reservations.

15 Agrees typeface for Cabinet edition of *Jubal*.

22 Take the Tom Trollopes to visit Tennyson. GE records, 'I saw an expression in his face that always reminds me of a large dog laying down its ears and wagging its tail on being stroked and patted' (*Letters*, IX, 237).

26 Asks Georgiana Burne-Jones to send news of herself: 'We have

been so ailing in the midst of our country joys, that I need to hear of my friends being well, as a ground for cheerfulness' (III, 332). GHL congratulates Alexander Macmillan on the first three volumes of the 'English Men of Letters' series, which GE has read aloud.

September
Vol. II of *Mill* appears in the Cabinet edition.
24 (Tues) Hopes Blackwood may be able to send better news of his own health.

October
Vol. I of *Holt* appears in the Cabinet edition. GHL's illness intensifies during the course of this month.
21 (Mon) Visiting the Bullock-Halls for four days, spends some time with Turgenev, who admires GE's work as she does his.

November
Vol. II of *Holt* appears in the Cabinet edition.
1   (Fri) Henry James, calling at Witley, much upset to find their lack of interest in his *Europeans*. Turgenev sends GHL capsules for pain.
5   Tells Elma Stuart, 'The larger world is so sad, with its wars and rumours of wars, that one is more than ever in need of the small world of specially beloved ones' (*Letters*, VII, 75).
11 Leave The Heights for the Gloucester Hotel, Brighton.
14 Return to London.
16 Reads proof for Cabinet edition of *Deronda*.
18 GHL told by Sir James Paget of thickening of his mucous membrane.
21 Sends Blackwood first section of manuscript of *Impressions of Theophrastus Such*.
22 Blackwood declares himself delighted with the new work.
25 Tells Barbara Bodichon, 'I have a deep sense of change within, and of a permanently closer companionship with death' (*Letters*, VII, 84).
30 Death of GHL following eight days of intense illness.

December
Middlemarch and *Deronda* appear in the Cabinet edition completing the prose fiction of the edition.

4 (Wed) Funeral of GHL. GE not present. Reads *In Memoriam*, Shakespeare and Donne, but is unable to answer any of the many letters of sympathy received.
9 Death of Anna Cross.
31 Receives proofs of *Such*.

1879

January
1 (Wed) Records in diary, 'Here I and sorrow sit' (III, 345). Unable to see the Burne-Jones family.
5 Completes second reading of GHL's unfinished *Problems*.
6 Edith Simcox meets Cross at The Priory.
7 Writes to Barbara Bodichon, her first letter since GHL's death: 'I bless you for all your goodness to me, but I am a bruised creature, and shrink even from the tenderest touch' (III, 346). Other letters follow.
13 Agrees to correct proofs of *Such*, but only because this would have been GHL's wish, and out of consideration for Blackwood.
19 Ruminating on some kind of educational memorial to GHL.
22 Reads through GHL's journals. Tells Cross, 'Some time, if I live, I shall be able to see you – perhaps sooner than anyone else – but not yet' (III, 347).
28 Acknowledges cheque from Blackwood for £777.
30 Again declines to see even Cross: 'When I said "some time" I meant still a distant time' (III, 347). Attack of renal pain.
31 Visited by Sir James Paget.

February
4 (Tues) Reports improved health to Georgiana Burne-Jones, but the onset of a mental winter.
6 Tells Barbara Bodichon she does not feel able to go away with her.
8 Orders carriage for first time.
9 Tells Cross, 'In a week or two I think I shall want to see you' (III, 348).
11 Depressed by inability to complete vol. III of *Problems*.
20 Asks Allbutt to write an article on the effect of GHL's work,

also mentioning idea of endowing an academic post in his memory.

23   Sees Cross, but refuses Spencer. Declines Cross's invitation to move for a time to Weybridge. Returns proof of *Such*.

25   Tells Blackwood that, though she will continue to correct proofs, publication of *Such* must be postponed.

March

3   (Mon) Death of W. K. Clifford (GE subsequently contributed to fund for his widow).

5   Requests revise proof of *Such*. Tells Barbara Bodichon that she is now driving out on most days.

8   Gertrude Lewes brings the grand-children to tea.

9   Henry Sidgwick discusses plans for the establishment of the GHL Studentship. GE authorises D'Albert's translation of *Scenes*.

13   Michael Foster suggests trustees for the Studentship.

16   Trübner discusses the printing of *Problems*.

17   Reads Problem II in volume v of *Problems*.

18   Signs her will. Visited by Cross, whose services become increasingly necessary and accepted.

19   Sees Maria Congreve – an indication of the gradual return towards light social engagements.

20   Moves back into the bedroom once shared with GHL. Call from Spencer, seeking advice on his *Autobiography*. Invites Georgiana Burne-Jones to visit her.

21   Blackwood sends revise proof of *Such*.

22   Asks Blackwood to supervise arrangements for foreign editions of *Such*.

23   Sends volume IV of *Problems* to printer.

25   So dissatisfied with *Such* that she writes to tell Blackwood of her decision to suppress it.

April

Begins to reread the *Iliad*.

1   (Tues) Tells Cara Bray that she will receive an annuity in her will.

5   Agrees to Blackwood's suggestion of publishing *Such* in May. Visits Charles Lewes's house for the first time.

7   Diary records, 'A mental crisis. Occupied with his writings' (*Letters*, VII, 130).

8 Invites the Harrisons to call. Visited by Elma Stuart. Explains the idea of the GHL Studentship in a letter to Barbara Bodichon: 'That there should always, in consequence of his having lived, be a young man working in the way he would have liked to work, is a memorial of him that comes nearest my feeling' (III, 355).

9 Tells Blackwood she is now taking a drive every day.

10 Letter to Harriet Beecher Stowe tells of struggle in coming to terms with bereavement: 'Formerly everything was easy because the supreme human blessing of perfect love was always with me. Now everything seems difficult. And yet I feel as if I were blaspheming to write that – for the Past is not dead, and in all I do, it is a living influence' (*Letters*, VII, 132).

17 Letter to David Kaufman is one of several of this period regretting 'our having been betrayed into an unjustifiable war in South Africa' (III, 358).

22 Requests Cross's immediate advice on whether to lend Bessie Belloc £500: loan refused. Blackwood specifies 3000 copies for first edition of *Such*.

23 Queries the royalties for *Such*.

26 Visited by the Bullock-Halls.

28 Eliza Lewes and her children return to London from South Africa, and on the 29th are entertained at The Priory. But GE tells Eliza that the family may not live there, and informs Edith Simcox that the 'morbid time of repulsion' is over 'for ever' (*Letters*, IX, 267).

May

Increased contact with Cross this month, chiefly in order to read Dante together. Other reading includes Chaucer, Shakespeare, and Wordsworth. *Such* published.

2 (Fri) Advises William Blackwood on terms for foreign editions and translations of *Such*. Correspondence on this subject continues over the first two-thirds of this month.

6 Visited by the Calls, and Eleanor and Florence Cross.

8 Burne-Jones calls.

13 Andrew Clark makes recommendations for the GHL Studentship.

16 GE's diary records a 'Crisis' – cause unknown.

19 Receives *Such*, and volume IV of *Problems*.

21 Sees Trollope.

22 Leaves for Witley, where Cross visits her once or twice a week, and they continue to study Dante.
26 Badly afflicted by further renal pain.
27 Plays piano for first time since GHL's death.
28 Hears that *Such* is going into second impression. Advises James Sully on GHL's contributions to periodicals.

June
5 (Thurs) Visited by Barbara Bodichon, who reports to her sister an enormous improvement in GE's spirits: 'In fact, I think she will do more for us than ever' (III, 367).
12 Thanks William Blackwood for sending details of foreign sales, and tells anecdotes about the reception of her books.
17 Confined to bed for three days, the complaint not finally lifting until the beginning of August.
20 Tells Blackwood, 'Yesterday I was in more acute pain than I have ever known in my life before' (III, 367). Much gratified by the public reception of *Such*.
29 Tells Georgiana Burne-Jones that 'there is a devoted friend who is backwards and forwards continually to see that I lack nothing' (III, 369). Thanks Blackwood for sending *The Ethics of George Eliot* by J. C. Brown.

July
Weight decreases to 7 stone $5^{1}/_{2}$ pounds during this month.
15 (Tues) Blackwood reports the continued success of *Such*.
16 Reports, 'The weather is a greater calamity even than the Zulu war' (*Letters*, VII, 183) – the exceptionally poor summer does little to aid her recovery.
25 Reports to Charles Lewes taking her first drive 'for a long while' (*Letters*, VII, 188).

August
7 (Thurs) Thanks James Sully for his continued help with GHL's *Problems*.
11 Invites Georgiana Burne-Jones to visit her at Witley. Thanks G. J. Holyoake for *The History of Co-operation in England*, which she has been reading.
19 Reports to Clementia Taylor that she hopes she is now fully recovered from her eight-week illness.
21 Probably refuses proposal from Cross.

September

2 (Tues) GHL Studentship at Cambridge inaugurated.

3 Tells William Blackwood of her continued delight at the quick sales of *Such*, asks for news of the translation of Kaufman's pamphlet on *Deronda*, and recommends a schoolfriend, Bradley Jenkins, if ever Blackwood should require French translations. Invites Barbara Bodichon to stay.

10 Suggests alterations in James Sully's article on GHL, especially recommending omission of GHL's criticism of Browning's obscurity.

29 Barbara Bodichon begins four-day visit to The Heights. Sends off the last proofs of *Problems*.

October

3 (Fri) William Blackwood, revealing that his uncle has had to retire on medical grounds, reports over 6000 copies of *Such* sold, and offers an extra lump sum.

7 Appreciates gift from Anna Merritt of her *Henry Merritt: Art Criticism and Romance*.

16 GE sends letter to Cross, signing herself Beatrice, and admitting her feelings for him.

18 Delighted at the success of Charles Smart Roy's application for the GHL Studentship.

27 Hears of Blackwood's severe illness, telling Charles Lewes, 'He has been bound up with what I most cared for in my life for more than twenty years; and his good qualities have made many things easy to me that, without him, would often have been difficult' (III, 383).

29 Death of Blackwood. Rejects W. L. Bicknell's request to dramatise *Romola*.

31 Visits the Crosses.

November

1 (Sat) Returns to The Priory; reading there with Cross includes Dante, Chaucer, Shakespeare, Wordsworth, and Sainte-Beuve's *Causeries*.

4 Suggests new format for *Sayings* to William Blackwood.

9 Reading Jowett's Thucydides.

22 Sixtieth birthday.

25 'Another turning-point' (*Letters*, VII, 91).

28 Visits GHL's grave.

29   Reads GHL's letters, packing them together to be buried with her.

December
5   (Fri) Answers query on the word 'adust' for James Murray's *New English Dictionary*.
9   Vol. v of *Problems* published.
17   Acknowledges receipt of the bound manuscript of *Such*, and counsels William Blackwood against the inclusion of too much easily written criticism in his magazine.
24   Tells Elma Stuart she would rather not have a portrait or bust of GHL: 'I am afraid of outward images lest they should corrupt the inward' (*Letters*, vii, 235). Eliza Lewes and children to lunch.
26   Requests Edith Simcox to stop calling her 'Mother', and discusses politics with her.
30   Jowett sends her New Year wishes and literary encouragement: 'you must not throw this precious trust away' (*Letters*, ix, 286).

1880

Cross reports, 'As the year went on, George Eliot began to see all her old friends again. But her life was nevertheless a life of heart-loneliness. Accustomed as she had been for so many years to solitude *à deux*, the want of close companionship continued to be very bitterly felt. She was in the habit of going with me very frequently to the National Gallery, and to other exhibitions. . . . This constant association engrossed me completely, and was a new interest to her . . .' (iii, 387).

January
4   (Sun) Congratulates Edward Clodd on his *Jesus of Nazareth*, whilst also expressing differences. Bret Harte introduced.
5   Thanks Clementia Taylor for her New Year greetings, mentioning that public calamities, such as the war in Afghanistan, have helped place her personal sorrow in perspective, and that she is now seeing several friends.
8   Reading the *Odyssey*, and C. P. Tiele's *Outlines of the History of Religion*.

9   Congratulates Myers on his engagement.
13 Reading Chaucer's General Prologue to the *Canterbury Tales*.
29 Pays second visit of the month to the Grosvenor Gallery.
30 Consults Croom Robertson about disposition of library.

February
1   (Sun) Declines permission for Sydney M. Samuel to dramatise *Deronda*.
13 George Smith discusses de luxe edition of *Romola*, to whose publication GE assents.
14 Expresses satisfaction with new edition of *Sayings*.

March
9   (Tues) Reveals in an interview with Edith Simcox that she has never cared as deeply for women as for men.
14 Sunday callers include Barbara Bodichon, Spencer, and the Harrisons.
28 Begins two-day visit to Weybridge.
30 Presides at sixth birthday party of GHL's grand-daughter Maud.

April
9   (Fri) Tells Paget of Cross's third proposal. Accepts Paget's advice, and consents in the evening. Cross reports, 'It was finally decided that our marriage should take place as soon, and as privately, as might be found practicable' (III, 387).
10 GE and Cross inspect 4 Cheyne Walk, soon to become their residence.
13 Tells Eleanor Cross, 'I quail a little in facing what has to be gone through – the hurting of many whom I care for. . . . The springs of affection are reopened in me' (III, 388).
19 Discusses Wordsworth in letter to Harrison, recommending Moxon's one-volume edition, and regretting some omissions in Arnold's selection from the poet.
22 Resignation of Beaconsfield following general election.
23 Tells Georgiana Burne-Jones that she is 'tired of being set on a pedestal and expected to vent wisdom' (Haight, p. 537).
24 Begins three-day visit to Weybridge. Thanks Lady Lytton for sending her photograph, speculating on the events which have contrived to make her look sadder, and assuring her of continual friendship.

26 Thanks James Sully for his sympathetic review of vol. v of GHL's *Problems* in the *Academy*.
28 Gladstone's second Ministry formed.
30 Much gratified by the sensitive feelings displayed by Charles Lewes in a long interview. He undertakes to break the news of the marriage to Edith Simcox and others.

May
 3 (Mon) Charles Bradlaugh, atheist MP, refuses to take the oath of allegiance.
 5 Writes to Georgiana Burne-Jones: 'A great momentous change is taking place in my life – a sort of miracle in which I could never have believed' (*Letters*, VII, 269). Letters also sent to William Blackwood, Barbara Bodichon, Cara Bray and Maria Congreve.
 6 Journal records, 'Married this day at 10.15 to John Walter Cross at St George's Hanover Square. Present, Charles, who gave me away, Mr and Mrs Druce, Mr Hall, William, Eleanor, and Florence Cross. We went back to The Priory, where we signed our wills. Then we started for Dover, and arrived there a little after five o'clock' (III, 393). Subsequent honeymoon takes them to France, Italy and Germany. Congratulations sent by William Blackwood and Frederic Harrison.
 9 Sends Eleanor Cross an account of their honeymoon travels, a 'chronicle of our happy married life, three days long' (III, 394).
12 Newman created Cardinal.
14 Henry James sends wedding congratulations.
17 Isaac Evans sends wedding congratulations, breaking a silence of 23 years.
21 Writes to Charles Lewes from Grenoble, 'I had but one regret in seeing the sublime beauty of the Grande Chartreuse. It was that the Pater had not seen it. I would still give up my own life willingly if he could have the happiness instead of me. But marriage has seemed to restore me to my old self' (III, 396).
25 Tells Florence Cross, 'I have been uninterruptedly well, and feel quite strong with all sorts of strength except strong-mindedness' (III, 397).
26 Replies to her brother's letter, 'Our long silence has never

broken the affection for you which began when we were little ones' (III, 398).

27 See Rossi in *Hamlet*. GE even less impressed than in London.
28 Gives Charles Lewes details of the rest of their proposed itinerary.

June
1 (Tues) Explains to Barbara Bodichon the odd circumstances of her wedding: 'I really did not finally, absolutely decide – I was in a state of doubt and struggle – until only a fortnight before the event took place, so that at last everything was done in the utmost haste' (III, 401).
2 Begin three weeks in Venice.
9 Tells Charles Lewes they are reading Ruskin, 'using his knowledge gratefully, and shutting our ears to his wrathful innuendoes against the whole modern world' (III, 405).
10 Again writes to Maria Congreve about her marriage: 'The whole history is something like a miracle-legend' (III, 406).
16 Cross suffers mental derangement in Venice, jumping into the Grand Canal. GE horrified. See III, 407–8; and, more satisfactorily, Haight, p. 544.
17 Telegraphs for William Cross.
23 GE and Cross move to Verona.

July
8 (Thurs) GE and Cross move to Wildbad, 'which, we hope, will put the finishing-touch to J.'s recovery of his usual health', GE tells Charles Lewes (III, 408).
26 Return to Witley. Reading on their journey home included novels by Daudet and Sand.

August
1 (Sun) Sends Barbara Bodichon an account of Cross's illness.
2 Apologises to Clementia Taylor for failing to send advance warning of her marriage.
3 Asks Alice Helps to send news of herself.
12 Tells Charles Lewes, 'Our life has had no more important events than calls from neighbours and our calls in return' (III, 413).
13 William Blackwood sends a report of sales, and congratulations on Charles Lewes's début in *Blackwood's Magazine*.

18   Re-establishes contact with Elma Stuart.
20   Writes to Anna Druce with details of the weight of the human brain.
24   Acknowledges gift of Elizabeth Phelps's *Sealed Orders*.

September
Visit the Otters at Ranby, Nottinghamshire, and the Bullock-Halls at Six Mile Bottom, meeting Henry and Eleanor Sidgwick with the latter, and seeing also Ely, Peterborough and Lincoln Cathedrals.
 7   (Tues) New burial law, permitting Dissenters to have their own services in churchyards, receives royal assent.
14   Tells Barbara Bodichon, 'Our only bugbear – it is a very little one – is the having to make preliminary arrangements towards settling ourselves in the new house. . . . I am become so lazy that I shrink from all such practical work' (III, 416).
19   Tells Charles Lewes, 'We supply the want of regular lawn tennis by in-door battledore and shuttlecock, at which I am becoming an expert . . .' (*Letters*, VII, 325).
22   Calls doctor, 'my ailments being no better' (*Letters*, VII, 326).
23   George Smith sends six copies of a (limited) de luxe edition of *Romola*, and an honorarium of £100.
29   Cross takes GE to Brighton for 10 days in attempt to clear renal trouble: 'The first effects of the sea breezes were encouraging, but the improvement was not maintained' (III, 416–17).

October
Reading with Cross at this time includes the Bible, Shakespeare, Milton, Wordsworth, Scott and Lamb.
15   (Fri) Smith publishes de luxe edition of *Romola*.
16   War breaks out with the Transvaal.
17   Taken seriously ill, and confined to bed. Asks Cross to read Bridges's translation of Comte's *Discours préliminaire* to her: 'This volume was one of her especial favourites, and she delighted in making me acquainted with it' (III, 419).
22   Andrew Clark comes to Witley to examine GE.

November
Cross supervises transfer of furniture and books from The Priory to Cheyne Walk during much of this month. GE takes a keen interest in the setting up of Newnham College. Cambridge.
 1   (Mon) Recovered sufficiently to play the piano.

15 Sends condolences to D'Albert on the death of his wife.
22 GE's sixty-first birthday.
24 Reads Comte and begins Goethe's *Hermann und Dorothea*.
28 Sends news of herself to Cara Bray, though conceding 'It is difficult to give you materials for imagining my "world"' (III, 434–5).
29 Leave Witley for temporary stay in a London hotel, where reading includes Comte, and Tennyson's *Ballads and Other Poems* (1880), in which 'The First Quarrel' is particularly admired.

December
 3 (Fri) Move to Cheyne Walk.
 4 Attend their first Pops Concert together, hearing Neruda and Piatti.
 6 Invites Maria Congreve to visit them at Cheyne Walk.
17 Attend a performance of Aeschylus's *Agamemnon* by Oxford undergraduates.
18 Attend Pops Concert at St James's Hall.
19 Visited by Spencer and Edith Simcox. Suddenly taken ill.
22 Dies at Cheyne Walk.
23 Cross tells Elma Stuart, 'I am left alone in this new House we meant to be so happy in' (*Letters*, VII, 351).
26 Cross sends GE's last, unfinished, letter to Lady Jane Strachey.
29 Funeral at Highgate. Cross remarks, 'Her spirit joined that choir invisible "whose music is the gladness of this world"' (III, 439).

Bibliography

'Why an exhaustive bibliography of George Eliot's work has not been written is to me quite incomprehensible', M. L. Parrish wrote in *Victorian Lady Novelists* in 1933. Over 50 years later, Eliot scholars are little better off. Since all editions of Eliot's novels were newer than their predecessors and most cheaper, the terms 'new' and 'cheap' which so frequently occur in Eliot's correspondence and on Blackwood's title pages are seldom instructive. The ensuing Bibliography therefore pays some attention to reprints of Eliot's prose fiction, listing all those published in Great Britain during the author's lifetime, whilst affording less space to the essays, letters, poems, notebooks and translations. All editions of the novels were published by Blackwood unless otherwise stated, and the reader may find it helpful to remember that this firm made three attempts at providing complete editions, referred to in this volume as the Cheap, the Stereotyped and the Cabinet. A list of other works consulted is also provided.

A. Works by George Eliot

I. PROSE FICTION

Scenes of Clerical Life
Serial: *Blackwood's Magazine*, 1857
   (1) 'The Sad Fortunes of the Reverend Amos Barton' (Jan–Feb)
   (2) 'Mr Gilfil's Love Story' (Mar–June)
   (3) 'Janet's Repentance' (July–Nov)
1st edition, 2 vols, 21s., 5 Jan 1858
2nd edition, 2 vols, 12s., 29 July 1859
3rd edition, 2 vols, 12s., 7 April 1860
Cheap edition (with *Marner*), 1 vol., 6s., Apr 1863
Stereotyped edition, 1 vol., 3s. 6d., Nov 1868
Cabinet edition, 2 vols, 10s., June and July 1878

Adam Bede
1st edition, 3 vols, 31s. 6d., 1 Feb 1859
2nd edition, 3 vols, 31s. 6d., Mar 1859

3rd edition, 2 vols, 12*s.*, 20 June 1859
4th edition, 2 vols, 12*s.*, July 1859
Cheap edition, 1 vol., 6*s.*, 15 Feb 1862
Stereotyped edition, 1 vol., 3*s. 6d.*, Apr 1867
Cabinet edition, 2 vols, 10*s.*, Apr and May 1878

'The Lifted Veil'
Blackwood's Magazine, July 1859
Cabinet edition (with *Marner* and 'Brother Jacob'), 1 vol., 5*s.*, Mar
    1878

The Mill on the Floss
1st edition, 3 vols, 31*s. 6d.*, 4 Apr 1860
2nd edition, 2 vols, 12*s.*, 24 November 1860
Cheap edition, 1 vol., 6*s.*, 8 Dec 1862
Stereotyped edition, 1 vol., 3*s. 6d.*, 1 Nov 1867
Cabinet edition, 2 vols, 10*s.*, Aug and Sep 1878

Silas Marner, the Weaver of Raveloe
1st edition, 2 vols, 12*s.*, 2 Apr 1861
2nd edition, 1 vol., 6*s.*, Dec 1861
Cheap edition (with *Scenes*), 1 vol., 6*s.*, Apr 1863
Stereotyped edition, 1 vol., 3*s. 6d.*, 1868
Cabinet edition (with 'Brother Jacob' and 'The Lifted Veil') 1 vol.,
    5*s.*, Mar 1878

Romola
Serial: *Cornhill Magazine*, July 1862 – Aug 1863 [Smith]
1st edition, 3 vols, 31*s. 6d.*, 6 July 1863 [Smith]
2nd edition, 3 vols, 31*s. 6d.*, late July 1863 [Smith]
Illustrated edition, 1 vol., 6*s.*, printed 1 Sep 1865 [Smith]
New edition, 1 vol., 2*s. 6d.*, 1871 [Smith]
Stereotyped edition, 1 vol., 3*s. 6d.*, 1878
Cabinet edition, 2 vols, 10*s.*, Jan and Feb 1878
De luxe edition, 2 vols, 15 Oct 1880 [Smith]

'Brother Jacob'
Cornhill Magazine, July 1864
Cabinet edition (with *Marner* and 'The Lifted Veil'), 1 vol., 5*s.*, Mar
    1878

Felix Holt, the Radical
1st edition, 3 vols, 31s. 6d., 14 June 1866
2nd edition, 2 vols, 12s., 11 Dec 1866
Stereotyped edition, 1 vol., ?3s. 6d., Jan 1869
Cabinet edition, 2 vols., 10s., Oct and Nov 1878

Middlemarch
1st edition, 8 parts, 5s. each, 1 Dec 1871 – 1 Dec 1872
Guinea edition, 4 vols, 21s., ?Feb/Mar 1873
One Volume edition, 1 vol., 7s. 6d., printed May 1874
Cabinet edition, 3 vols, 15s., ?Dec 1878

Daniel Deronda
1st edition, 8 parts, 5s. each, Feb–Sep 1876
Guinea edition, 4 vols, 21s., 16 Dec 1876
One Volume edition, 1 vol., 7s. 6d., Oct 1877
Cabinet edition, 3 vols, 15s., ?Dec 1878

II. ESSAYS

Essays of George Eliot, ed. Thomas Pinney (London, 1963). This selection provides in Appendix A a complete listing of articles which may definitely be attributed to Eliot, all of which have been included in this *Chronology*. Pinney's Appendix B discusses articles wrongly or doubtfully attributed to Eliot, and these have been included, with a *caveat*, where appropriate. For further attributions, on stylistic grounds alone, the reader is directed to Gordon S. Haight's standard article 'George Eliot's Theory of Fiction', *Victorian Newsletter*, x (1956) 1–3.

III. LETTERS

The George Eliot Letters, ed. Gordon S. Haight, 9 vols (New Haven, Conn., and London, 1954–78)

IV. NOTEBOOKS

Middlemarch Notebooks: A Transcription, ed. John Clark Pratt and Victor A. Neufeldt (Berkeley, Calif., 1979)

Some George Eliot Notebooks: An Edition of the Carl H. Pforzheimer Library's George Eliot Holograph Notebooks MSS 707, 708, 709, 710, 711, ed. William Baker, vol. I: MS 707 (Salzburg, 1976)

A Writer's Notebook, 1854–1879, and Uncollected Writings, ed. Joseph Wiesenfarth (Charlottesville, Va, 1981)

V. POEMS

The Legend of Jubal, and Other Poems
1st edition, May 1874, containing
   'The Legend of Jubal' (previously published in *Macmillan's Magazine*, May 1870)
   'Agatha' (previously published in *Atlantic Monthly*, August 1869)
   'Armgart' (previously published in *Macmillan's Magazine* and *Atlantic Monthly*, July 1871)
   'How Lisa Loved the King' (previously published in *Blackwood's Magazine*, 5 May 1869)
   'A Minor Prophet'
   'Brother and Sister' (privately printed, 1869)
   'Stradivarius'
   'Two Lovers'
   'Arion'
   'O May I Join the Choir Invisible'
Cabinet edition, 1879, containing the above, plus
   'A College Breakfast Party' (previously published in *Macmillan's Magazine*, July 1878)
   'Self and Life'
   'Sweet Evenings Come and Go'
   'Love'
   'The Death of Moses'

The Spanish Gypsy
1st edition, 25 May 1868
Four subsequent editions, 1868–75
Cabinet edition, 1879

VI. TRANSLATIONS

The Life of Jesus Critically Examined. By D. F. Strauss, 15 June 1846

The Essence of Christianity. By Ludwig Feuerbach, July 1854

VII. MISCELLANEOUS

'Address to Working Men, by Felix Holt', *Blackwood's Magazine*, Jan 1868

Impressions of Theophrastus Such
1st edition, May 1879
Cabinet edition, 1880

B. Other Works Consulted

Baker, William, *The George Eliot – George Henry Lewes Library: An Annotated Catalogue* (New York, 1977)
Beaty, Jerome, *Middlemarch: From Notebook to Novel* (Urbana, Ill., 1960)
Blind, Matthilde, *George Eliot* (London, 1883)
Browning, Oscar, *George Eliot* (London, 1890)
Bullett, Gerald, *George Eliot: Her Life and Books* (London, 1947)
Cooke, George Willis, *George Eliot: A Critical Study* (London, 1883)
Cross, J. W., *George Eliot's Life as Related in her Letters and Journals*, 'New edition' 3 vols (London, 1885)
Haight, Gordon S., *George Eliot: A Biography* (Oxford, 1968)
——, *George Eliot and John Chapman, with Chapman's Diaries* (New Haven, Conn., 1940)
Keller, Helen Rex, *The Dictionary of Dates*, 2 vols (New York, 1934)
Redinger, Ruby V., *George Eliot: The Emergent Self* (New York, 1975)
Steinberg, S. H., *Historical Tables*, 10th edition (London, 1979)
Summers, Alfred Leonard, 'The Homes of George Eliot' (London, 1926)
Williams, Blanche C., *George Eliot: A Biography* (New York, 1936)
Williams, David, *Mr George Eliot: A Biography of G. H. Lewes* (London, 1983)

Index

Abbotsford, 16
Aberdeen, Lord, 4th Earl (1784–1860), statesman, 34, 43
Abyssinia, 103
Academy, The, 134, 166
Acton, Sir John, (1834–1902), historian, 156
Aeschylus (525–456 BC), dramatist, 55, 57–8, 83, 91, 93, 169
Afghanistan, 164
Aguilar, Emanuel, pianist, 31
Albert, Prince Consort (1819–61), 5, 31, 78
Alexandria, 130
Alison, General Sir Archibald (1826–1907), soldier and writer, 47
Allbutt, Sir Thomas Clifford (1836–1925), physician, 106–7, 132, 159
Allingham, Helen (1848–1926), artist, 149–50
Allingham, William (1824–89), poet, 135, 150–2
All the Year Round, 68
Altenburg, the, 41
Ambleside, 33
America, 80, 88
Ancelot, Marguerite (1792–1875), writer, 36
Anderson, Elizabeth Garrett (1836–1917), physician, 123, 130
Anders, the Revd Henry Smith, 64
Antwerp, 41, 96
Appleton, Charles Edward (1841–79), editor, 134
Arbury, 1, 4
Aristophanes, (c. 448–c. 388 BC), dramatist, 113
Aristotle (384–322 BC), philosopher, 32, 92, 131
Arnold, Mary Augusta, *see* Ward, Mrs Humphry
Arnold, Matthew (1822–88), poet and critic, 45, 110, 138, 149, 165

Arnold, Thomas (1795–1842), educationalist, 12
Arnott, Neil (1788–1874), physician, 26, 36, 38
Athenaeum, The, 63, 66
Atkinson, Henry George, phrenologist, 29
Atlantic Monthly, 110–12, 121
Attleborough, 1, 46
Austen, Jane (1775–1817), novelist, 31, 51, 53, 136–7, 142
Australia, 36
Austria, 116
Aytoun, William Edmonstoune (1813–65), poet, 102

Bach, J. S. (1685–1750), composer, 82
Bagehot, Walter (1826–77), economist and journalist, 150
Baginton, 8, 15
Balzac, Honoré de (1799–1850), novelist, 68, 117
Bamford, Samuel (1788–1872), poet, weaver and radical, 92
Bancroft, George, American Ambassador, 137
Bank of England, 138
Barclay, Jessie, 5
Bateman, Kate (1842–1917), actress, 87
Bath, 49
Bayswater, 44
Beaumont, Francis (1584–1616) and Fletcher, John (1579–1625), dramatists, 82
à Beckett, Gilbert Arthur (1837–91), comic writer, 18
Beesley, Edward Spencer, Positivist, 94
Beethoven, Ludwig van (1770–1827), composer, 43, 75, 95, 150
Belgium, 96

Bellini, Vincenzo (1801–35), composer, 19, 31
Benson, Edmund and Mrs, 101
Benzon, Elizabeth (née Lehmann), 143, 150
Berlin, 42–3, 102, 116
Berlioz, Hector (1803–69) composer, 36, 43
Berne, 76
Bethnal Green Museum, 127
Biarritz, 100
Bicknell, W. L., 163
Birmingham, 7, 11, 16, 89
Blackbrook, 131–3
Blackwood, James, 123
Blackwood, John (1818–79), publisher
  Comments on GE:
  generally, 59, 65–6, 68–9, 95, 147
  on GE's writing, 50–4, 59, 61, 64–6, 69, 74–5, 95, 101, 103, 105, 110, 117, 120–2, 124, 126, 135, 141, 143–6, 158
  on reception of GE's writing, 52–3, 55, 97, 106, 162
  on sales, 65, 76, 82–3, 86, 88, 98–101, 106–8, 123–4, 130, 133, 137, 139, 145–6, 154–5
  communication with GE, 51–163 *passim*
  communication with GHL, 50–3, 55–62, 64, 66–70, 72–4, 76, 95, 97, 109, 114, 118, 120, 122, 124, 129–31, 134, 136, 141–4, 144–6, 148, 150, 152
  death, 163
Blackwood, John (Jack), 123, 146
Blackwood, Julia, 59
Blackwood, Major William, publisher, 52, 57, 61, 65–6, 68–9, 71, 75
Blackwood, William (Willie) publisher, 96, 100, 116, 122, 131, 137, 140, 144, 146–7, 156–7, 161–4, 166–7
Blackwood's Edinburgh Magazine, 51–6, 66, 103–4, 111, 127, 167
Blanc, Louis (1811–82), statesman and writer, 21, 31

Blandford Square, 73, 84
Boccaccio (1313–75), poet, 77, 82
Bodichon, Barbara (née Leigh Smith), 31, 35–6, 39, 47, 49, 55, 61, 64–6, 69, 72–5, 79, 81–2, 84, 86, 88, 91, 94, 99, 100, 103, 105, 107, 109–16, 118–20, 122–3, 125, 129–30, 133–5, 137–8, 142, 145, 147, 151, 155–6, 158–63, 165–8
Bodichon, Eugene, 55
Bohlen, Peter von (1796–1840), philologist and theologian, 47
Bohn, Henry George (1796–1884), publisher, 49
Bologna, 71
Bolton, Charles, 81
Bond, Sir Edward Augustus (1815–98), librarian and editor, 135
Bonham Carter, Joanna Hilary, 32, 93
Booksellers' Association, 31
Borrowdale, 33
Bottesini, Giovanni (1821–89), double-bass player, 76
Boucicault, Dion (1820?–1890), actor and dramatist, 156
Bouterwek, Frederic (1765–1828), philosopher, 98
Brabant, Elizabeth, 14
Brabant, Elizabeth (Rufa), *see* Hennell, Elizabeth
Brabant, Dr Robert, 14, 18, 20, 41
Bracebridge, Charles Holte, 67
Bradbury & Evans, publishers, 68
Bradlaugh, Charles (1833–91), free-thinker and politician, 166
Bray, Caroline (Cara), 9, 11–17, 20, 22–38, 40–2, 45, 59, 62–3, 66, 68, 75, 79, 81, 86–8, 91, 93, 96, 100–1, 103, 105, 112–14, 116, 118–22, 125, 130–5, 138, 141, 144, 147–50, 156–7, 160, 166, 169
Bray, Charles (1811–84), writer, 9, 11–16, 18–21, 23–36, 38–42, 44–9, 56–7, 59, 61–2, 66–8, 71–2, 75, 84, 90, 108
Bray, Elinor Mary, 91

Bremer, Frederika (1801–65), author, 28
Brezzi, Joseph, 4
Bridges, Anna Maria, 120
Bridges, John Henry (1832–1906), positivist philosopher, 64, 69, 140, 168
Bright, John (1811–89), orator and statesman, 109–10
Brighton, 20, 133, 137, 158, 168
Bristol, 13
British Museum, 44, 78, 80, 130
Brittany, 93
Broadstairs, 32
Brockhaus, Heinrich (1804–74), publisher, 61
Brontë, Charlotte (1816–55), novelist, 21, 27, 35, 53–4
Brown, John (1810–82), essayist, 63
Brown, John Crombie, 162
Brown, Samuel (1817–56), chemist, 34
Browning, Elizabeth Barrett (1806–61), poet, 51, 76, 80, 93
Browning, Oscar (1837–1923), historian, 101, 109, 114–16, 129, 140
Browning, Robert (1812–89), poet, 46, 82, 85, 93, 103, 108, 110–11, 130, 134, 163
Brussels, 41, 43, 137
Buchanan, Robert Williams (1841–1901), poet and novelist, 87–8
Bucheim, Carl, writer, 105
Buckingham, James Silk (1786–1855), author and traveller, 45
Buckland, William (1784–1856), geologist, 8
Bullock-Hall, Henry, 126–7, 137, 145, 147, 152–3, 156, 158, 161, 166, 168
Bulwer-Lytton, Edith, see Lytton, Countess of
Bulwer-Lytton, Edward George, 1st Baron (1803–73), novelist, 53, 64, 70, 72, 77, 97, 129
Bulwer-Lytton, Edward Robert, 1st Earl (1831–91), statesman and poet, 111, 117, 124–5, 137, 140, 144
Bulwer-Lytton, Rowland, 121
Bunyan, John (1628–88), writer, 68
Burke, Edmund (1729–97), statesman, 51
Burne-Jones, Sir Edward (1833–98), painter, 124, 129–30, 145, 151, 154, 159, 161
Burne-Jones, Lady (née Georgiana MacDonald), 117, 150, 155, 157, 159–60, 162, 165–6
Burton, Sir Frederic (1816–1900), painter, 88–90, 93–4, 101, 109
Byron, Lord George Gordon (1788–1824), poet, 1–2, 6, 31, 109, 113

Call, Elizabeth (Rufa), see Hennell, Elizabeth
Call, William, 28, 56, 59, 100, 161
Camaldoli, 76
Cambridge, 104, 130–1, 151, 163
Cambridge scholarships, 141
Cambridge Street, 37–8
Cameron, Julia Margaret (1815–79), photographer, 119
Canning, George (1770–1827), statesman, 1–2
Carlyle, Jane (née Welsh) (1801–66), writer, 58, 63
Carlyle, Thomas (1795–1881), essayist and historian, 10, 18, 29, 42, 45–6, 51, 61, 74, 115
Carmichael, Charlotte, 154
Caroline, Queen (1768–1821), 1
Carpenter, William Benjamin (1813–85), physiologist, 46
Carus, Julius Viktor (1823–1903), Professor of Anatomy, 60
Cash, Mary (née Sibree), 15, 19, 24, 28, 54, 86, 105, 150
Cassel, 102
Cervantes, Miquel (1547–1616), writer, 7
Chalmers, Thomas (1780–1847), theologian, 9
Chambers, Robert (1802–71), writer, publisher, 42

Chapman, Frederic (1823–95), publisher, 70
Chapman, John (1822–94), author and publisher, 18–19, 25–9, 31–6, 38–45, 48–52, 54–6, 58, 60–3, 70, 130
Chapman, Susanna, 27–8
Chapman, Thomas, 56
Chapman & Hall, publishers, 130
Chartres, 93
Chatrian, Alexandre (1826–90), playwright, 123
Chatterton, Thomas (1752–70), poet, 48
Chaucer, Geoffrey (1340?–1400), poet, 98, 161, 163, 165
Cheyne Walk, 165, 168–9
Chilvers/Coton, 1, 3, 23
Cicero (106–43 BC), orator, 78
Clapton, 15, 17
Clark, Sir Andrew (1826–93), physician, 149, 161, 168
Clark, Sir James (1788–1870), physician, 36, 38
Clark, William George (1821–78), Shakespearean scholar, 97, 114
Clarke, Catherine (Katie, GE's niece, 1851–60), 70
Clarke, Christiana (Chrissey *née* Evans, GE's sister, 1814–59), 1, 3, 8, 25, 34, 36, 38, 46, 63–4
Clarke, Edward (GE's brother-in-law, 1809–52), 3, 10, 12, 16, 34
Clarke, Emily (GE's niece, 1844–1924), 133, 137, 141, 147, 156
Clarke, Frances (GE's niece 1849–57), 53
Clarke, Leonard (GE's nephew), 20
Clifford, Lucy (née Lane), 160
Clifford, William Kingdon (1845–79), mathematician, 160
Clodd, Edward (1840–1930), banker and author, 164
Clough, Arthur Hugh (1819–61), poet, 78, 80, 109
Cobbett, William (1762–1835), politician and essayist, 155
Cobden, Richard (1804–65), statesman, 30

Colenso, Bishop John William (1814–83), 86
Coleridge, Samuel Taylor (1772–1834), writer, 3
Collins, William Wilkie (1824–89), novelist, 61, 78, 81
Cologne, 41, 43, 59
Colville, Lady Frances, 135
Colville, Sir James (1810–80), judge, 135
Combe, Cecilia, 33, 36–7, 40
Combe, George (1788–1858), phrenologist, 28–9, 32–4, 36–42
Comte, Auguste (1798–1853), philosopher, 28, 30, 38, 61, 77, 88, 90, 99, 106, 118, 140, 168, 169
Congreve, Caroline, 20
Congreve, Maria (née Bury), 73–4, 68–70, 73–4, 79, 83–4, 86–7, 90–4, 96–7, 99–101, 104–5, 107–8, 111, 113, 115–16, 121, 126, 128, 131, 166–7, 169
Congreve, Richard (1818–99), Positivist, 63–4, 68–9, 83, 87, 91–2, 97, 100–1, 105, 107
Contemporary Review, 126, 144, 149
Co-operative Building Society, 33
Cornelius, Peter von (1783–1867), artist, 41
Cornhill Magazine, 80–1, 85, 88–9, 101
Cornwallis, Caroline Frances (1786–1858), writer, 36
Courbet, Gustave (1819–77), painter, 94
Cousin, Victor (1792–1867), philosopher and politician, 41
Covent Garden, 30, 88, 92
Coventry, 2, 4, 7, 8, 14, 15, 34, 40
Coventry *Herald*, 18–19, 20, 40
Cowper, William (1731–1800), poet, 2
Cox, Dr Abram, 36
Cox, Robert (1810–72), editor, 33
Crabbe, George (1754–1832), poet, 135
Craigcrook, 33
Craig, Isa (1831–1903), poetical writer, 86

Crimean War, 39, 47
Cromer, 117
Crompton, Caroline, *see* Robertson, Caroline
Crompton, Lucy, 140
Cross, Anna (1813–78), 111, 123–5, 127–8, 132, 135–6, 142, 149, 154, 159
Cross, Eleanor (1847–95), 161, 165–6
Cross, Emily, *see* Otter, Emily
Cross family, 102, 113, 131, 133, 135, 163
Cross, Florence Nightingale (1857–1915), 161, 166
Cross, John Walter (1840–1924), 11–12, 48, 52, 111, 113, 128, 132, 134, 136, 138, 140, 142, 147–8, 152–3, 156, 159–69
Cross, Mary Finlay (1843–1902), 121, 136
Cross, William (b. 1838), 166–7
Crystal Palace, 40, 65, 88, 125
Cullen, Professor William (1710–90), physician, 113
Cumming, Dr John (1807–81), divine, 44, 46
Curtis, George William, 109
Curtius, Ernst (1814–96), philologist and historian, 130

Daily Telegraph, 125
D'Albert-Durade, François, 24–5, 68–9, 72, 74, 79, 81–2, 84–6, 89–90, 94, 98, 100, 104, 119–20, 122, 124, 127, 130, 132, 140, 142, 147, 154, 157, 160, 169
D'Albert-Durade, Julie, 169
Daly, John Augustin (1838–99), American theatrical manager and dramatist, 87
Dante, Alighieri (1265–1321), poet, 161–3
Darwin, Charles Robert (1809–82), naturalist, 68–9, 105–8, 130, 132, 134
Darwin, Erasmus (1731–1802), physician, 134
d'Aubigné, Theodore-Agrippa (1552–1630), poet, 109

Daudet, Alphonse (1840–97), novelist and dramatist, 167
Davies, Emily (1803–1921), promoter of women's education, 103, 107, 113, 147
Delane, John (1817–79), editor, 57
de Ludwigsdorff, Madame, 24
de Medici, Lorenzo (1448–92), patron of arts, 79
de Morgan, Augustus (1806–71), mathematician, 125
Depping, 98
De Quincey, Thomas (1785–1859), writer, 37
Derbyshire, 1
Deschamps Gallery, 144
de Tocqueville, Alexis (1805–59), politician and writer, 61
Deutsch, Emanuel (1829–73), semitic scholar, 102–3, 106, 110–11, 118, 130
de Vallière, Madame, 23
Devizes, 14, 138
Dickens, Charles (1812–70), novelist, 18, 31, 58, 63, 66, 68, 115, 117, 142
Dickens, Mary, 145
Disraeli, Benjamin, 1st Earl of Beaconsfield (1804–81), statesman and author, 16, 18, 20, 103–4, 108, 135, 165
Donizetti, Gaetano (1797–1848), composer, 30, 55, 96
Donne, John (1573–1631) poet, 159
Donovan, Cornelius, phrenologist, 14
Dorking, 79, 80, 83–4, 96
Dorset, 67
Dover, 18, 43, 166
Dowden, Edward (1843–1913), critic, 126, 146, 149–50
Dresden, 60, 102
Druce, Albert, 139, 166
Druce, Anna (née Cross), 139, 166, 168
Dumas, Alexandre (1803–70), novelist, 78, 151
du Maurier, George (1834–96), artist, 131

Eastbourne, 92
East Sheen, 44
Edgbaston, 7–8
Edinburgh, 16, 33, 72–3, 121
Edinburgh Review, 100, 107
Eisenach, 102
Eliot, George, 2, 26, 31, 39–40, 60, 81, 88–9, 100–1, 105, 107, 110, 127, 129, 144–5, 150–1, 156, 164, 165

General:
current affairs and politics, 5, 13, 15, 21, 22, 30, 34, 80, 86, 88, 95, 103–6, 108, 117–19, 129, 134–6, 149, 157–8, 161–2, 164; languages: German, 6, 15; Italian, 4, 6; Spanish, 89; for Greek and Latin, *see* reading classics; music, 2, 4, 7, 19, 30–1, 41–2, 65, 70, 73, 76–8, 80, 82–3, 94, 107, 110, 115–16, 124, 135, 144, 150, 155, 162, 168–9; opera, 19, 30–1, 36, 39, 41–3, 55, 60, 71, 81, 85, 88, 92, 96, 151; personal appearance, 3, 31, 39, 111; philosophy, 56, 73, 93, 142–3, 147, 154–6; for positivism, *see* religion; phrenology, 10, 14–15, 28, 33, 45; portraits, 25, 70, 72, 75, 88–90, 93, 101; pseudonym and identity as author, 7, 40, 52–5, 57–9, 61, 64–6, 68–9

Published works:
Essays:
'The Antigone and its Moral', 47
'The Art and Artists of Greece', 48
'The Art of the Ancients', 43
'*Blithedale Romance*, by Hawthorne', 33 (attrib.)
'Christianity in its Various Aspects, by Quinet' (review), 18
'Church History of the Nineteenth Century, 48

'Comic History of England, by Gilbert A'Beckett' (review), 18
'The Court of Austria', 48
'*The Creed of Christendom*, by W. R. Greg' (review), 27–8
'Evangelical Teaching: Dr Cumming', 46
'Futile Falsehoods', 92
'The Future of German Philosophy', 45
'German Mythology and Legend', 45
'German Wit: Heinrich Heine', 46
'The Grammar of Ornament', 92
'Heine's Poems', 45
'History of German Protestantism', 47
'The Influence of Rationalism', 92
'Introduction to Genesis', 47
'*The Jesuits*, by Quinet and Michelet', 18
'*Life and Opinions of Milton*', 45
'*Life of Goethe*, by George Henry Lewes', 46
'*Life of Sterling*, by Carlyle' (review), 29
'Liszt, Wagner and Weimar', 45
'Lord Brougham's Literature', 45
'Love in the Drama', 45
'Margaret Fuller and Mary Wollstonecraft', 46
'Margaret Fuller's Letters from Italy', 48
'Memoirs of Margaret Fuller' (attrib.), 30
'Memoirs of the Court of Austria', 43
'Menander and the Greek Comedy', 44
'Michelet on the Reformation', 45
'The Morality of Wilhelm Meister', 45
'*Nemesis of Faith*, by J. A. Froude' (review), 22–3
'Pictures of Life in French Novels', 48
'Poetry and Prose, from the Notebook of an Eccentric', 19

Eliot George – *continued*
Published works – *continued*
'The Poets and Poetry of America', 47
'Priests, Women, and Families by Michelet', 18
'Progress of the Intellect, by R. W. Mackay' (review), 26
'*Rachel Gray*, by Julia Kavanagh', 46–7
'Romantic School of Music', 42
'Servants' Logic', 91
'*The Shaving of Shagpat*, by Meredith', 46–7
'Story of a Blue-Bottle', 48
'Thomas Carlyle', 46
'Three Months in Weimar', 43–4
'Translations and Translators', 46
'Vice and Sausages', 19
'Who Wrote the Waverley Novels?' 48
'Woman in France: Madame de Sablé', 41–2
'A Word for the Germans', 91
'Worldliness and Other-Worldliness: The Poet Young', 48, 51

Miscellaneous:
'Address to Working Men' by Felix Holt', 103–4
Impressions of Theophrastus Such, 158–63

Poetry:
'As o'er the Fields', 5
Legend of Jubal, and Other Poems, 109, 114–16, 135–7, 143, 157: 'Agatha', 106, 109, 111–12; 'Armgart', 118, 120, 121; 'Brother and Sister', 112; 'College Breakfast Party, A', 152, 154, 157; 'How Lisa Loved the King', 109–11; 'Minor Prophet, A', 90–1; 'O May I Join the Choir Invisible', 101, 157, 169
Spanish Gypsy, The, 89–91, 98, 100–8, 110, 117, 122, 128, 131, 134, 137, 143

Prose fiction:
Adam Bede, 4, 55–6, 58–70, 73–4, 77–9, 88, 100–1, 156
'Brother Jacob', 72, 88–9, 155
Daniel Deronda, 60, 127, 130–1, 133, 136–49, 151–4, 156–8, 163, 165
Felix Holt, 2, 92–100, 103, 109, 158
'The Lifted Veil', 60, 64–6, 129, 155
Middlemarch, 10, 14, 109–10, 112–13, 115–16, 118–34, 136–7, 139, 143–4, 146, 148, 158
The Mill on the Floss, 63, 65–74, 77, 82, 84, 102, 113, 157–8
Romola, 71–2, 75–88, 93, 119, 121, 149–50, 154–5, 163, 165, 168
Scenes of Clerical Life, 53, 55–62, 64, 66, 71, 73, 79, 83–4, 107, 156: 'Amos Barton', 48, 50–3, 65, 160; 'Mr Gilfil', 51–3, 160; 'Janet's Repentance', 2, 53–6, 157, 160
Silas Marner, 73–9, 81–4, 104, 129, 147, 155

Translation:
Feuerbach, *The Essence of Christianity*, 38–41
Strauss, *Life of Jesus*, 14–18, 27, 36, 40

Unpublished and unfinished works:
3–6, 16, 22, 24, 36, 87, 109

Reading:
generally, 41, 43–4, 77, 157
art, 47
biography, 29, 37, 45, 48, 53–4, 61–3, 74, 102, 104, 113, 118, 123–4, 132–3, 138, 150, 152
classics, 12, 18, 32, 44, 50–3, 55–8, 64, 78, 91–3, 95, 102, 106, 112–13, 118, 130–1, 160, 163–4
drama, 2, 7, 18, 31, 36–7, 42–4, 82, 92, 101, 109, 113, 145, 147, 159, 161, 163, 168

Eliot, George – *continued*
Reading – *continued*
history, 5, 51, 56, 67, 75, 77–8, 85, 89, 92, 94–5, 98, 99, 102, 106, 107, 109, 115, 118, 130, 133, 137, 140, 151, 155, 162
law, 95
literary criticism, 9, 37, 91, 107, 112, 114, 138, 158
music, 98
novels, 1, 7, 16, 18, 20–1, 31, 33, 35, 42, 44, 51, 53–4, 68, 70, 77–9, 81, 84, 86, 100, 112, 115, 117–18, 121, 129, 136–7, 140, 142, 151, 167, 169
philosophy, 73, 77, 93–5, 103, 105–7, 112, 114–15, 118, 131, 134, 140, 143, 153, 168–9
phrenology, 46
poetry, 2, 4–7, 18, 31–2, 37–8, 43, 51, 71, 77, 80, 82, 84, 89, 98–9, 101–2, 106, 109–10, 112–13, 116–18, 122, 136, 150, 152–3, 159, 161–3, 165, 167–9
politics, 33, 92, 94, 101, 105, 109, 110, 112, 162
religion, 3–11, 13, 18, 20, 23, 29, 37, 39, 68, 72–3, 85–7, 89, 93–4, 102, 126, 131, 133, 138, 149, 164, 168
science, 8–9, 37, 46–8, 53, 68, 74, 86, 99, 113–14, 134
social welfare and reform, 4, 8, 32, 45, 94, 133

Religion:
views on Christianity, generally, 12, 71, 83, 85, 89, 94, 96, 97, 116, 118, 132, 138–9, 149, 156, 164; early evangelical influence, 2–8; attends church, 3–4, 8, 11–12, 25, 115, 119; onset of unbelief, 6, 9, 10–12, 14, 16, 20–1, 82, 91, 106, 150, 153
views on other religions, 50, 132, 138
Judaism, 20, 102, 106, 131, 133, 145, 147–9, 151–2
views on positivism, 68, 88, 97, 99–101, 105–8, 115, 152

reading, *see* Reading: religion
translations, *see* published works

School, 1–5

Science, 29, 34, 36, 48, 53, 59–60, 73–4, 77, 107, 128, 145

Self:
ambition, 4
career, 2, 11, 26
comments on, generally, 7, 10, 12, 18, 21–4, 28, 34, 40, 47, 57, 80, 85, 88, 91, 95, 99, 108–9, 112, 114–15, 119, 134, 139, 148, 154, 156, 158–61, 165–6, 169; self-critically, 9, 11, 16, 22, 56, 76, 119
comments on writing, generally, 48, 50, 52, 55, 57–8, 62, 64, 67–9, 72–4, 76, 78–9, 84, 97, 105, 107–8, 110, 116, 124, 134, 141, 144, 149, 157; distress over writing, 16–17, 67, 77–80, 82, 90, 93–4, 96, 126, 142–3; criticism of intellectual and creative ability, 6, 9, 47, 49–50, 53, 57, 59, 66, 68, 70, 72, 76, 80, 89, 92, 103, 105–6, 111, 134, 137, 139
happiness, 41–2, 49, 54, 57, 62, 70, 73, 79, 83, 85, 87, 98, 104, 119, 128, 133, 149
health, 6, 21–4, 32, 35, 38–40, 45–6, 48–9, 65, 70, 73–4, 76, 79, 87–8, 90, 95–6, 98, 103–4, 108–9, 111–12, 114, 116, 120, 122–3, 125, 128–9, 133–4, 140–2, 144–6, 148, 150, 153, 156, 158–9, 162, 166, 168
home and family, 3, 5–12, 17–18, 21–3, 25, 34, 36, 54–5, 64, 67, 87, 97, 107, 136
home and GHL's family, 47–8, 66–7, 72–3, 76, 81, 84, 86, 88–9, 91–2, 98, 102, 104, 111–17, 119, 121, 125, 128, 142, 153–4, 160, 162–3, 165–8
insecurity and craving for affection, 6–7, 9, 33

Eliot, George – *continued*
Self – *continued*
romance, 6, 15–16; *see also* Brabant, Chapman, Cross, D'Albert, GHL, Spencer

Social welfare and reform:
generally, 6, 8–9, 21, 31, 33, 90, 95, 103, 118
position of women, 47, 101, 103–5, 112, 114, 123, 128–30, 136, 139, 147, 151, 155, 168

Theatre, 4, 16, 29, 77–8, 85, 87–8, 90–1, 96, 123, 135, 140–1, 156, 167, 169
Elliotson, Professor John (1791–1868), physician, 38
Ely, 168
Emerson, Ralph Waldo (1802–82), philosopher, 21–2, 72, 116, 130
England, 25, 43
Englefield Green, 80
'English Men of Letters' series, 153, 158
English Woman's Journal, 58
Eton, 101, 140
Evans, Christiana (née Pearson, GE's mother, 1788?–1836), 1, 3
Evans, Christiana ('Chrissey'), *see* Clarke, Christiana
Evans, Elizabeth (née Tomlinson, wife of Samuel Evans, 1766–1849), 4, 6–7, 67
Evans, Frances ('Fanny'), *see* Houghton, Frances
Evans, Isaac (GE's brother, 1816–90), 1, 4, 7–11, 13, 54–5, 66, 166
Evans, Jane (née Attenborough, wife of Robert II), 87–8
Evans, Robert (GE's father, 1773–1849), 1, 3, 5–13, 17–18, 20–3, 67, 107
Evans, Robert II (GE's half-brother, 1802–64), 1, 87–8
Evans, Robert III (son of Robert II, 1832–1911), 87, 97, 137
Evans, Samuel (GE's uncle, 1777–1858), 5–9

Evans, Sarah (née Rawlins, GE's sister-in-law, 1806–81), 7, 8
Evans, Thomas (GE's brother, b.1821), 1
Evans, William (GE's brother, b.1821), 1
Evans, William (GE's uncle, 1769–1847), 6
Exeter, 48
Exeter Hall, 19, 30, 34, 75, 94

Faithfull, Emily, 84, 132
Faraday, Michael (1791–1867), scientist, 26, 58
Faucit, Helen, actress, *see* Martin, Lady Helen
Fawcett, Henry (1833–84), statesman and writer, 94
Fechter, Charles Albert (1824–79), actor, 77–8
Feuerbach, Ludwig Andreas (1804–72), philosopher, 38
Fielding, Henry (1707–54), novelist, 115
Fields, Annie, 136
Fields, James Thomas (1817–81), American publisher, 111
Fields, Osgood, publishers, 111
Finsbury, 14
Fiske, John, 132–3
Florence, 30, 71, 75–6, 78, 110
Foleshill, 1, 8, 10–13, 17
Fontainbleau, 131
Forster, George, 50
Forster, William Edward (1812–76), historian and biographer, 123–4
Fortnightly Review, 90–2, 98, 103, 123–4, 144
Fourier, Charles (1772–1837), philosopher, 112
Fox, W. J. (1786–1864), writer, 13, 29, 32
Foxton, Frederick J., 36
France, 49, 66, 73, 76, 80
Frankfurt, 41, 59
Franklin, the Misses, 2, 3, 11, 131
Fraser's Magazine, 43–5, 58

Frederick, William, Crown Prince of Germany (1831–88), 156

Froude, James Anthony (1818–94), historian, 23, 58, 61, 63, 118

Fuller, Margaret (1810–50), writer, 46, 48

Gall, François-Joseph (1758–1828), phrenologist, 46

Garibaldi, Giuseppi (1807–82), patriot, 88

Gaskell, Elizabeth Cleghorn (1810–65), novelist, 35, 53, 64–5, 68, 84, 94

Geneva, 23–5, 72, 76

George III (1738–1820), 1

George IV (1762–1830), 1–2

George Henry Lewes Studentship, 159–61, 163

Germany, 47, 96, 101, 104, 106, 116, 131, 166

Gibbon, Edward (1737–1794), historian, 89

Gilbert, Sir William Schwenck (1836–1911), dramatist, 147

Gilchrist, Anne (née Burrows, 1828–85), writer, 120

Gillies, Mary, 117

Girton College, Cambridge, 103, 114, 151

Gissing, George Robert (1857–1903), novelist, 56

Gladstone, William Ewart (1809–98), statesman and author, 31, 95, 108, 129, 134, 166

Glasgow, 16, 88

Gluck, Christoph Willibald von (1714–87), composer, 43

Goderich, Viscount (1782–1859), statesman, 2

Godwin, Mary (née Wollstonecraft, 1759–97), author, 46

Goethe, Johann Wolfgang von (1749–1832), poet, 18, 31, 37, 41–2, 45–7, 118, 169

Goschen, Lord, 1st Viscount (1831–1907), statesman, 151, 156

Gosse, Edmund (1849–1928), poet and man of letters, 24

Gosse, Philip Henry (1810–88), zoologist, 48

Gounod, Charles François (1818–93), composer, 85, 92

Grande Chartreuse, 166

Greece, 129

Green, John Richard (1837–83), historian, 155

Greenwich, 76

Greg, William Rathbone (1809–81), essayist, 27, 31, 33

Grenoble, 166

Gresley, William (1801–76), divine, 5

Grey, Charles, 2nd Earl (1764–1845), statesman, 2–3

Griff, 1, 4, 5, 7, 8, 11, 25, 136

Griffiths, Edith (née Evans, Isaac's daughter, GE's niece), 135–6

Griffiths, the Revd William, 135

Groombridge, publisher, 51

Grosvenor Gallery, 165

Grote, George (1794–1871), historian, 106

Grove, Sir George (1820–1900), musicologist, 145

Grüner, Joan, 151

Gruppe, Professor Otto Friedrich, writer and polymath, 42

Guedalla, Haim, 147

Gurney, Edmund (1847–88), philosophical writer, 131

Guthrie, Thomas (1803–73), preacher and philanthropist, 39

Gwyther, the Revd John, 65

Halévy, Jacques François (1799–1862), composer, 31

Hallam, Henry (1777–1859), historian, 9, 94

Hallé, Sir Charles (1819–95), conductor, 95

Hamilton, P. G., 157

Hamley, Sir Edward Bruce (1824–93), soldier, writer, 119

Handel, G. F. (1685–1759), composer, 7, 65, 83, 94

Hanover, 102

Hanover Square Rooms, 31

Harper's Weekly, 70, 123, 144–5

Harpur, Henry, 3

Harris, John (1802–56), theologian, 7

Harrison, Eliza, 117, 120, 161, 164

Harrison, Ethel, 125, 161, 165

Harrison, Frederic (1831–1923), Positivist, author, lawyer, 94–7, 100, 102, 106–7, 110, 112, 115, 124, 131, 139–41, 152, 162, 165–6

Harrogate, 89, 117

Harte, Francis Bret (1839–1902), novelist, 164

Hastings, 37, 75, 115

Hatfield, 112–13

Hawthorne, Nathaniel (1804–64), novelist, 33, 53

Haydn, Franz Joseph (1732–1809), composer, 30

Heine, Heinrich (1797–1856), poet, 45–6, 48–9, 155

Helps, Alice (daughter of Sir Arthur), 135, 141, 143, 167

Helps, Sir Arthur (1813–75), writer, 38, 41–2, 51, 57, 73, 101, 104

Helyot, Pierre, historian, 77

Hemans, Felicia Dorothea (née Browne) (1793–1835), poet, 7

Hennell, Charles, 4, 10–15, 20–1, 26–7, 116

Hennell, Elizabeth (Rufa) (née Brabant), 12–14, 44, 59, 61, 100, 125, 161

Hennell, Mary, 13

Hennell, Sara, 12–15, 17–25, 28–30, 33–6, 38–42, 46–7, 49–58, 60–1, 63–8, 71–7, 79–80, 82–3, 85–93, 95, 97–9, 101–3, 105, 108, 110, 113–14, 116, 118–19, 123–5, 127, 134–5, 138, 143, 151, 154

Henschel, Sir George (1850–1934), musician, 155

Her Majesty's Theatre, 19

Herschel, Sir John Frederick William (1792–1871), astronomer, 88

Hertfordshire, 142

Highgate Cemetry, 169

Hill, Emily, 125

Hill, Octavia (1838–1912), philanthropist, 118, 135, 141

Hitchin, 114

Hofmann, Professor A. W. (1818–92), chemist, 73

Hofwyl, 49–50, 55, 60, 72, 76

Holbeche, Vincent, 54

Holland, 96

Holland, Queen of, 141

Holland, Sir Henry, 1st Bt (1788–1873), physician, 109

Holland, Sir Henry, 1st Viscount Knutsford (1825–1914), politician, 152

Holland, Lady Margaret (née Trevelyan), 152–3

Hollingshead, John (1827–1904), journalist and theatrical manager, 129

Holmwood Common, 137

Holyoake, George Jacob (1817–1906), writer, rationalist and reformer, 141, 162

Homburg, 126–7

Homer, epic poet, 44, 102, 106, 160, 161

Hoppus, John (1789–1878), ecclesiastical writer, 5

Horace, poet, 64

Houghton, Frances ('Fanny', née Evans, GE's half-sister, 1805–82), 1, 8, 21–2, 24–5, 38, 137

Houghton, Lord (Richard Monckton Milnes, 1809–85), writer and politician, 89, 116, 131, 152, 156

Houlton, Louise, writer, 155

Housman, A. E. (1859–1936), writer, 64

Howard, George James, 9th Earl of Carlisle (1843–1911), artist and politician, 120

Hughes, Thomas (1822–96), author, 68

Hugo, Victor (1802–85), poet, 112

Hume, David (1711–1776), philosopher, 115

Hume, Mary, writer, 37

Hunt, James Henry Leigh (1784–1859), writer, 37
Hunt, Thornton Leigh, 27, 42, 51, 131
Hunt, William Holman (1827–1910), painter, 40, 89, 105
Huskisson, William (1770–1830), statesman, 2
Hutton, Richard Holt (1826–97), man of letters, 85
Huxley, Thomas Henry (1825–95), scientist, 35, 38, 94
Hyde Park, 37

Ilfracombe, 48
Ilmenau, 102
India, 144
Ireland, 17, 105
Irving, Sir Henry (1838–1905), actor, 123, 145, 156
Isle of Wight, 20, 64, 85, 101
Italy, 23, 71, 73, 75, 87–9, 110, 116

Jackson, Martha, 4–8, 10, 12, 15–16, 25
James, G. P. R. (1799–1860), writer, 5
James, Henry (1843–1916), novelist, 111, 158, 166
Jameson, Anna (1794–1860), 5, 77
Jebb, Sir Richard Claverhouse (1841–1905), Greek scholar, 131
Jeffrey, Lord Francis (1773–1850), man of letters, 33
Jenkins, Bradley, 163
Jersey, 53, 55
Joachim, Joseph (1831–1907), violinist, 80, 82, 95, 130, 135, 150, 155
Johnson, Andrew, 31
Jones, the Revd John Edmund, 2
Jones, Thomas Rymer (1810–80), zoologist, 47
Jones, the Revd William Pitman, 55
Jonson, Benjamin (1573–1637), dramatist, 109

Jowett, Benjamin (1817–93), academic, 117, 131, 140, 146, 151, 153, 156, 163, 169

Karlsruhe, 127
Kaufman, David, reviewer, 151–3, 161, 163
Kavanagh, Julia (1824–77) writer, 46–7
Keats, John (1795–1821), poet, 71, 152
Keble, John (1792–1866), divine, 2, 6
Keightley, Thomas (1789–1872), writer, 45
Keller, Gottfried (1819–90), novelist, 121
Kempis, Thomas à (1379–1471), mystic, 68
Kenilworth, 8
Kenny, Courtney Stanhope (1847–1930), legal scholar, 127
Kew Gardens, 32, 139
Kingslake, Alexander William (1809–1891), historian, 107, 140
Kingsley, Charles (1819–75), author, 33, 63, 139
Kingston, 36
Kittermaster, Edith, 6
Klein, Julius Leopold, writer, 91

La Bruyère, Jean de (1645–1696), moralist, 155
Lake District, 8, 15
Lamb, Charles (1775–1834), essayist, 168
Landseer, Sir Edwin Henry (1802–73), painter, 132
Langford, Joseph, 66, 68, 75
Lathom, Miss, 1
Laurence, Samuel (1812–84), painter, 70, 72, 75, 101
La Vernia, 76
Layard, Sir Austen Henry (1817–94), archaeologist, 67
Leader, The, 28, 30, 36, 39, 42–9, 52, 63
Leamington, 11

Lecky, William Edward Hartpole (1838–1903), historian and essayist, 92, 114, 155

Lecouvreur, Adrienne (1692–1730), actress, 36

Lee, Charlotte, 113

Leeds, 107

Legouvé, Ernest (1807–1903), dramatist, 36

Lehmann, Frederick, 88, 96, 145

Lehmann, Nina, 88, 90, 99, 145

Leighton, Lord Frederic (1830–96), artist, 81, 88, 150

Leighton, Robert (1611–84), divine, 4

Leipzig, 60

Le Mans, 93

Leopold II, King of the Belgians (1835–1909), 146

Leroux, Pierre (1797–1871), writer, 29

Leslie, Charles Robert (1794–1859), painter, 26

Lessing, Gotthold Ephraim (1729–81), writer, 104

Lewald, Fanny, *see*, Stahr, Fanny

Lewes, Agnes, 42, 44, 51, 111

Lewes, Blanche, 126, 128

Lewes, Charles Lee, 47–9, 55, 66, 70–3, 75–6, 81, 84–7, 89, 91–2, 102, 104, 106, 115–17, 121, 125–6, 142, 146, 152, 154, 160, 162–3, 166–8

Lewes, Elinor, 152–3

Lewes, George Henry:
art, *see under* GE
death, 158
GE, relationship with generally, 28–9, 34–42, 44–7, 49, 52, 54, 63–5, 69, 76, 92, 103–4, 114, 118, 159–61, 163–4; involvement in her writing, and publishing interests, 47, 59–63, 67–71, 73–4, 76–82, 84, 87, 90–2, 95–7, 100, 105–6, 118, 120–32, 134, 136–7, 141, 143–6, 148, 150, 152–3, 156; concealment of GE's identity as author, 50, 53, 55, 57, 59, 62–

4, 66, 68; health, 39, 45, 64–5, 79, 89–90, 94–5, 99, 103, 116–17, 145, 149, 156–8

music, *see under* GE

opera, *see under* GE

philosophy, 30, 120, *and see under* GE

publications: 'Alison's History of Europe', 47; 'J. S. Buckingham', 45; 'Dickens in Relation to Criticism', 123–5; *History of Philosophy*, 120; *Life of Goethe*, 42, 45–6; 'Memoirs of Sydney Smith', 44; *Physiology of Common Life*, 57, 60, 62–3; *Problems of Life and Mind*, 104, 119, 129–31, 133–4, 136, 140, 150, 159–64, 166; 'Realism in Art: Recent German Fiction', 60–1; 'The Scilly Isles', 53; *Sea-Side Studies*, 48, 53, 58

reading, 42–3, 45, 54, 67, 75, 102, 152, 157–8

religion, 70, 72, 97, 138, *and see under* GE

science, 33, 51, 60, 73–5, 145

theatre, *see under* GE

wife and family, 42, 48–9, 51, 55, 60, 66, 70–3, 76, 86–7, 89, 91, 96, 98, 102, 109, 112–15, 125, 146

wit, 29, 119

Lewes, George Herbert, 141, 161, 164

Lewes, Gertrude, 91–2, 94, 98, 115, 119, 160

Lewes, Herbert Arthur (Bertie), 47–8, 55, 66, 71, 76, 86–7, 97–8, 117, 120, 122, 127, 141–2

Lewes, Marian Evans, 127, 161, 164

Lewes, Maud, 135, 165

Lewes, Thornton Arnott, 47–9, 55, 66–7, 70–3, 76, 82–3, 86–8, 98–9, 109, 111–15

Lewis, Maria (1800?–87), 2–10, 12, 19, 137, 143

Lichfield, 67

Liebig, Baron Justus von (1803–73), chemist, 59, 61
Liège, 41
Liggins, Joseph, 54–5, 64, 66–8
Lille, 59
Limpsfield, 114, 118
Lincoln, 168
Linton, Eliza Lynn (1822–98), writer, 26, 99, 109
Liszt, Franz (1811–86), composer and pianist, 41–2, 45, 144, 151
Littlehampton, 82
Liverpool, 16
Liverpool, Lord, 2nd Earl (1770–1828), statesman, 1
Llorente, Antonio (1756–1823), writer, 98
Loch Katrine, 16
Loch Lomond, 16
Locker, Lady Charlotte (née Bruce), 140
Locker, Elinor, *see* Tennyson, Elinor
Locker, Frederick (1821–95), poet, 117, 140
Lockhart, John Gibson (1794–1854), writer, 63, 118
Lombe, Edward, 30
London (*see also individual areas and residences*), 4–5, 9, 14–16, 19, 21, 28, 30, 32–8, 40, 42, 44, 55, 58, 66
Longfellow, Henry Wadsworth (1807–82), poet, 46
Louise, Princess (1848–1939), 151
Lowell, James Russell, poet, 109–10
Lucas, Samuel (1811–65), journalist, 58, 64
Lucerne, 66
Lucretius (98–53 BC), poet, 106, 112
Lynn, Miss, 30
Lyon, 110
Lytton, Countess of, 117, 121, 124, 135, 140, 144, 165

Macaulay, Lord Thomas (1800–59), historian, 22, 51, 69, 75, 115
MacIlwaine, the Revd William, 106
Mackay, R. W. (1803–82), philosopher and scholar, 26, 29, 38

Mackaye, James, writer, 129
Macmillan, Alexander (1818–96), publisher, 132, 138, 158
Macmillan's Magazine, 116, 121, 132, 157
Macready, William Charles (1793–1873), actor, 16
Main, Alexander, 121–30, 132–4, 136–7, 139, 143, 145, 154, 163, 165
Maine, Sir Henry James Sumner (1822–88), writer, 134
Mainz, 41
Majendie, Margaret, writer, 140
Mallock, William Hurrell (1849–1923), author, 149, 153–4
Malvern, 13, 77, 90
Manchester, 15
Manning, Cardinal Henry Edward (1808–92), 140
Manx Sun, The, 54
Manzoni, Alessandro (1785–1873), writer, 109
Marchesi, Pompeo, sculptor, 77
Marcus Aurelius (121–80), philosopher, 106, 109
Marks, Phoebe, 142
Marlborough, 138
Marseille, 110
Marshall, Mary, 88
Martin, Lady Helen (née Faucit; 1817–98), 36, 87–8, 91, 135
Martin, Sir Theodore (1816–1909), man of letters, 87, 102
Martineau, Harriet (1802–76), writer, 16, 28–30, 33, 37–8, 47, 51, 150–1
Martineau, James (1805–1900), philosopher, 15–16, 27, 30
Marylebone, 72
Masson, David (1822–1907), writer, 35, 48, 93, 138
Matlock, 107
Maurice, F. D. (1805–72), divine, 85, 88, 107
Mayall, John Edwin, photographer, 59
Mazzini, Guiseppe (1805–72), patriot, 34, 93, 124

Melbourne, Lord, 2nd Viscount (1779–1848), statesman, 3

Mendelssohn, Felix (1809–47), composer, 19, 117

Meredith, George (1828–1909), novelist, 46–7, 65

Meriden, 3, 8, 13, 25, 34, 38

Merritt, Anna, 163

Merritt, Henry (1822–77), art critic, 163

Meyerbeer, Giacomo (1791–1864), composer, 31, 42, 45

Michelangelo (1475–1564), 110

Michelet, Jules (1798–1894), historian, 18, 45, 63

Mill, John Stuart, (1806–73), philosopher, 34, 92–5, 130, 133, 138

Millais, Sir John (1829–96), painter, 31, 150

Milner, Joseph (1744–97), divine, 5

Milnes, Richard Monckton, *see* Lord Houghton

Milton, John (1608–74), poet, 2, 5, 18, 45, 106, 117, 168

Mirabeau, Marquis de (1715–89), economist, 28

Mohl, Mary (née Clarke; 1793–1883), French hostess, 32

Mommsen, Theodor (1817–1903), historian, 85, 109

Montalembert, Charles Comte de (1810–70), writer and politician, 77, 85

Montégut, Emile (1825–95), writer, 69

Monteil, writer, 56

Moore, Mrs, 1

Moore, Thomas (1779–1852), poet, 2

Morley, John, 1st Viscount (1838–1923), man of letters, 98, 101

Morris, William (1834–1906), poet, artist, socialist, 106, 115, 117

Moscheles, Charlotte, 155

Moulton, Ellen Louise (b.1835), writer, 156

Moxon, Edward (1801–58), publisher, 165

Mozart, Wolfgang Amadeus (1756–91), composer, 65

Müller, Max (1823–1900), writer, 133

Müller, Otfried (1797–1840), philologist and archaeologist, 114

Mulready, William (1786–1863), painter, 88

Munich, 59–60, 110

Murray, Sir James Augustus Henry (1837–1915), lexicographer, 164

Myers, Frederic William Henry (1843–1901), academic, 128, 131, 134, 153, 165

Namur, 41

Naples, 71, 110

Nardi, Jacopo, historian, 78

National Gallery, 164

Neal, Daniel (1678–1743), historian, 93–4

Neale, Erskine (1804–83), divine, 8

Neruda, Wilma Norman (1839–1911), violinist, 115, 144, 169

Neuberg, Joseph, 100

Newby, Thomas Cautley, publisher, 67

Newdegate, Maria, 4

Newman, Francis William (1805–97), scholar, 23, 26, 31, 56, 58

Newman, John Henry (1801–90), divine, 16, 29, 89, 166

Newmarket, 147

Newnham College, Cambridge, 142, 168

Newton, Sir Charles (1816–94), archaeologist, 32

New York Century, The, 67

Nightingale, Florence (1820–1910), reformer, 32

Nisand, Desiré (1809–39), writer, 112

Noel, Edward, writer, 119

Normandy, 93

North British, The, 33

North Wales, 67

Norton, Charles Eliot (1827–1908), author, 109

Norton, Susan, 109–10

Nuneaton, 2, 10
Nuremberg, 59

Oberammergau, Passion Play, 96–7
Ockley, 36
O'Connell, Daniel (1775–1847), Irish
    politician, 2, 15
Oliphant,   Margaret   (1828–97),
    novelist, 80–1
Once a Week, 64
Osgood Ticknor & Co., publishers,
    120–1, 123
Otter, Emily (née Cross; 1848–1907),
    134, 139, 168
Otter, Francis, 139–68
Owen, Sir Richard (1804–92), natu-
    ralist, 63, 74
Owen,   Robert   (1771–1858),   re-
    former, 13, 112
Oxford, 117, 140, 146

Page, David (1814–79), geologist,
    134
Paget, Catherine, 151
Paget, Sir James (1814–99), surgeon,
    111, 128–9, 158–9, 165
Palgrave, F. T. (1824–97), poet and
    critic, 109, 136
Pall Mall Gallery, 40
Pall Mall Gazette, 90–2, 100
Palmerston, Lord, 3rd Viscount
    (1784–1865), statesman, 43, 65,
    93
Paris, 22, 47, 71, 75, 90, 99, 110, 137,
    146
Parker, John William (1792–1870),
    publisher, 58
Parkes, Elizabeth, 39
Parkes, Elizabeth Rayner (Bessie,
    daughter of the above), 29–33,
    35–9, 44, 47, 55–6, 58, 61, 84,
    86–7, 127, 161
Parkes, Joseph (1796–1865), politi-
    cian, 32
Pascal,   Blaise   (1623–62),   philo-
    sopher, 155
Pater,   Walter   (1839–94),   critic,
    117

Pattison,   Emilia,   109–10,   113–17,
    120, 124, 128, 133–4, 139, 141–
    2, 145
Pattison, Mark (1813–84), academic,
    110, 112, 116–17, 120, 134, 139,
    143
Pau, 99
Payne, John Burnell, writer, 110
Payne, Dr Joseph Frank (1840–
    1910), physician, 144
Pears, Elizabeth, 9–11, 23
Peel, Sir Robert (1788–1850), states-
    man, 3, 9, 18, 26
Pembroke, 13
Percy, Thomas (1729–1811), editor,
    102
Peterborough, 168
Petersthal, 106
Petrarch (1304–74), poet, 78
Petri,   Henri   Willem,   musician,
    150
Phelps, Elizabeth, 130, 142, 149,
    153, 168
Phrenological Journal, 33
Piatti, Alfredo Carlo (1822–1901),
    cellist, 95, 135, 150, 155, 169
Pierce, Harriet (1836–1923), journal-
    ist, 98
Pigott, Edward Frederick Smyth,
    49, 70, 77, 130
Plato (429–347 BC), philosopher,
    112, 117
Pompeii, 71, 110
Ponsonby, Elizabeth, the Hon. Mrs,
    129, 138–40, 142, 153
Pope, Alexander (1688–1744), poet,
    2
Pops concerts, 73, 82, 110, 144, 150,
    169
Portsmouth, Countess of, 146
Prague, 60
Prescott, William Hickling (1796–
    1859), historian, 102
Priory, The, 84–7, 89, 109–10, 114,
    120, 122, 124, 128, 132, 134,
    136–7, 142, 145, 147, 150, 153,
    159, 161, 163, 166
Proctor, Adelaide, 87
Prospective Review, 18, 37

Proudhon, Pierre-Joseph (1809–65), political writer, 94

Quarterly Review, 29, 38, 102
Quinet, Edgar (1803–75), writer, 18

Raff, Joachim (1822–82), composer, 41
Ragatz, 146
Ranby, 168
Raphael (1483–1520), painter, 60
Reade, Charles (1814–84), novelist and dramatist, 97, 151
Redford, George, writer, 70, 77
Redhill, 125, 135–7
Reigate, 130
Renan, Ernest (1823–92), historian, 85–6, 98–100
Renouard, George Cecil (1780–1867), scholar, 113
Reybaud, Louis (1799–1879), economist, 112
Rhône, River, 110
Richardson, Samuel (1689–1761), novelist, 20, 151
Richmond, 46, 49, 51, 57, 60, 61, 63, 86, 139
Rickmansworth, 141–2
Riehl, Wilhelm Heinrich von (1823–97), writer, 48–9, 57
Ritter, Charles, writer, 126, 129, 152, 157
Robertson, Caroline (née Crompton), 126, 129
Robertson, Professor George Groom (1842–92), philosopher, 126, 129, 165
Rome, 71, 110–11
Romilly, Lord John (1802–74), lawyer, 140
Rossetti, Dante Gabriel (1828–82), painter and poet, 82, 110, 115–17
Rossi, actor, 167
Rossini, Gioachino (1792–1868), composer, 30, 36, 39, 60, 71, 88
Rosslyn Hill Unitarian Chapel, 115, 153

Rousseau, Jean-Jacques (1712–78), writer, 18, 22
Roy, Charles Stuart, 163
Royal Academy, 40, 81, 101, 130, 151, 156
Royal Academy of Music, 155
Rubinstein, Anton Gregor (1830–94), pianist, 145
Ruskin, John (1819–1900), critic, 40, 47, 49, 58, 61, 134, 167
Russell, Lord John, 1st Earl (1792–1878), statesman, 18, 26, 94, 156
Russell, J. R., writer, 113
Russia, 48, 114
Ryland, John (1753–1825), Baptist minister, 4

St Bride's Church, 4
St George's Church, Hanover Square, 166
St James's Hall, 65, 73, 80, 95, 115, 144, 169
St Leonard's, 21, 37
St Märgen, 106
St Paul's Cathedral, 4, 31, 63
Sainte-Beuve, Charles Augustin (1804–69), critic, 163
Salisbury, 138
Salvini, Tommaso (1830–1915), actor, 140
Salzburg, 116
Samuel, Sydney M., writer, 165
Sand, George (1803–76), writer, 18, 20, 22, 31, 167
San Marco, 71
Saturday Review, 47, 48, 50, 60
Sauppe, Hedwig, 87
Savanarola, Jerome (1452–98), monk, 71–2, 75, 79
Savill & Edwards, printers, 37
Scarborough, 89
Schade, Dr, 41
Scheffer, Ary (1795–1858), painter, 40, 51
Scheldt, River, 110
Schiller, Friedrich (1759–1805), poet, 7, 37
Schleswig-Holstein, Princess Christian of (1846–1923), 155

Schumann, Clara (1819–96), pianist, 110
Scilly Isles, 53
Scotland, 8, 16, 157
Scott, Sir Walter (1771–1832), writer, 1, 21, 44–5, 63, 69, 78, 121, 151, 168
Scott, William Bell (1811–90), poet and painter, 149
Scribe, Eugène (1791–1861), dramatist, 36
Scribners, American magazine, 118
Scrope, William (1772–1852), artist and sportsman, 5
Senior, Jane Elizabeth, 99, 101, 104, 113–14, 126, 129, 136, 146
Senior, Nassau John, 119
Seymour, Henry, 90
Shaftesbury, Lord, 7th Earl (1801–85), philanthropist, 3
Shakespeare, William (1554–1616) writer, 2, 18, 31, 37, 42–4, 78, 91–2, 101, 112–13, 153, 156, 159, 161, 163, 167–8
Sheard, Henry, 68, 70
Shedden-Ralston, William (1828–89), Russian scholar, 107
Sheffield, 107
Shelley, Percy Bysshe (1792–1822), poet, 7, 41, 147
Shere, 128
Sheridan, Richard Brinsley (1751–1816), dramatist, 135
Shottermill, 120–1
Sibree, John, 20–1, 47, 150
Sibree, Mary, *see* Cash, Mary
Sidgwick, Eleanor (1845–1936), 151, 168
Sidgwick, Henry (1838–1900), philosopher and academic, 131, 151, 160, 168
Sidney, Edwin, writer, 5
Siebold, Karl Theodor Ernst von (1804–85), anatomist, 59–60
Simcox, Edith Jemima (1844–1901), 128, 134, 149, 153–7, 159, 161, 164–6, 169
Simpson, George, publisher, 128
Simpson, Mary, 129

Sismondi, Jean Charles (1773–1842), historian, 98
Six Mile Bottom, 126, 137, 147, 153, 168
Skeat, Walter William (1835–1912), philologist, 124
Smiles, Samuel (1812–1904), author, 54
Smith, Albert (1816–60), author, 58
Smith, Benjamin Leigh, 72
Smith, George (1824–1901), publisher, 79–82, 84, 88, 90, 99, 101, 139, 165, 168
Smith, John Pye (1774–1851), Non-Conformist divine, 9
Smith, Lucy, 127–30, 134, 136, 141, 147
Smith, Mary, 32
Smith, William Henry (1808–72), philosopher and poet, 40, 134
Smollett, Tobias, George (1721–71), novelist, 70
Sophocles (497–405 BC), dramatist, 50–3, 55–6
South Africa, 86, 88, 97–9, 111, 141, 155, 161–2, 168
Southey, Robert (1774–1843), writer, 2
Southfields, 63, 66–8, 72
South Kensington, 81, 88, 100
Spain, 99–100, 106
Spectator, 41, 47, 106, 110
Spence, Catherine, 147
Spencer, Herbert, 28–33, 37, 46–8, 52, 58, 61, 63–4, 67–8, 73, 88, 92, 94, 102–3, 108, 110, 114, 116, 124, 127, 133–4, 138, 154, 160, 165, 169
Spencer, William, 32, 87
Spenser, Edmund (1552?–99), poet, 7, 109
Spinoza (1632–77), philosopher, 13, 22, 24, 42–3, 47, 49
Spring Hill College, 11
Spurgeon, Charles Haddon (1834–92), preacher, 61, 118
Staffordshire, 1
Stahr, Adolf Wilhelm Theodor, historian, 43

Stahr, Fanny (née Lewald), 43
Stanford, Sir Charles Villiers (1852–1924), musician, 117, 131
Stanley, Lord, 14th Earl (1799–1869), statesman, 26, 30, 34, 59, 97, 104
Stephen, Harriet, 133
Stephen, Sir James Fitzjames (1829–94), judge and writer, 131
Stephen, Sir Leslie (1832–1904), writer, 141, 154
Stephenson, George (1781–1848), inventor, 22
Sterne, Laurence (1713–68), novelist, 129, 142
Stirling, 16
Stowe, Harriet Beecher (1812–96), author, 35, 111–12, 115, 124–5, 137, 145, 148, 161
Strachey, Jane Maria, 169
Strand (142, the Strand, London), 31
Stratford, 13, 22
Strauss, David Friedrich (1808–74), theologian, 17, 41, 60–1, 94, 126
Strauss, Ludwig (1835–99), violinist, 155
Stuart, Elvorilda Eliza Maria (Elma), 124, 132, 135, 137–40, 142–3, 145–7, 149–52, 154–5, 158, 161, 164, 168, 169
Stuart, Roland, 137
Stuttgart, 127
Sully, James, reviewer, 149, 162–3, 166
Surrey, 74, 102
Swanmore, 119
Swansea, 13, 49
Swiss Cottage, 141
Switzerland, 23, 37, 48, 66, 106, 146–7
Sydenham 29, 31, 36, 40, 88
Syme, Ebenezer (1826–60), critic, 32

Tasso, Torquato (1544–95), poet, 7
Tauchnitz, Baron Christian Bernhard (1816–95), publisher, 60, 69

Taylor, Clementia, 29–31, 35–6, 75, 83, 85, 87–8, 93, 101, 124, 133, 136, 139, 142, 151, 157, 162, 164, 167
Taylor, Edward Burnett, writer, 137
Taylor, Peter Alfred (1819–91), radical politician, 29, 151
Taylor, Isaac (1787–1865) writer, 7–8
Tenby, 13, 49
Tennyson, Alfred Lord (1809–92), poet, 32, 46, 58, 89, 101, 121–2, 145, 150, 152–3, 155–7, 159, 169
Tennyson, Elinor (née Locker), 155
Tennyson, Lionel, 155
Thackeray, William Makepeace (1811–63), novelist, 18, 33, 52, 58–9, 63, 84, 87
Theocritus (c.300 BC), poet, 95
Thierry, Augustin (1797–1873), historian, 61
Thomson, James (1834–82), poet, 136
Thoreau, Henry David (1817–62), writer, 46
Thucydides (c.460–c.400 BC), historian, 163
Ticknor, George (1791–1871), critic, 98
Tiele, Cornelius Petrus (1830–1902), theologian, 164
Times, The, 40, 57–8, 64, 69, 71, 97, 106, 119
Tolstoy, Leo (1828–1910), novelist, 67
Tonbridge, 130
Torquay, 104–5
Tours, 93
Trench, Richard Chenevix (1807–86), divine, 48
Trent, River, 67
Trinity College, Cambridge, 131
Trollope, Anthony (1815–82) novelist, 72–3, 77, 79, 81–2, 84–7, 94–5, 97–8, 117, 124, 136, 151, 155, 161
Trollope, Theodosia (1825–65), author, 71, 89, 110, 157

Trollope, Thomas Adolphus (1810–92), author, 76–7, 81, 84, 110, 157

Trübner, Nikolaus (1817–84), publisher, 131, 134, 151, 160

Tunbridge Wells, 37, 99, 104

Turgenev, Ivan (1818–83), novelist, 119, 121, 142, 151, 158

Turner, J. M. W. (1789–1862), painter, 26

Tyrol, the, 60

Ullathorne, William Bernard (1806–89), Roman Catholic bishop, 12

Varnhagen von Ense, Karl August (1785–1858), biographer, 51

Vehse, Karl Eduard, writer, 43

Venice, 71–2, 89, 167

Verdi, Guiseppe (1813–1901), composer, 81, 107

Vernon Hill, 51, 57–8

Verona, 167

Vice, John, 19

Victoria Magazine, 84

Victoria Printing Press, 132

Victoria, Princess Royal (1840–1901), 156

Victoria, Queen (1819–1901), 3, 5, 40, 70, 80, 104, 145, 149

Vienna, 60, 116

Villiers, Edith, *see* Lytton, Countess of

Villiers, George William Frederick, 4th Earl of Clarendon (1800–70), 117

Villiers, Henry Montague (1813–61), divine, 8

Vinet, Rudolph Alexandre (1797–1847), theologian, 11

Wagner, Cosima, 151

Wagner, Richard (1813–83), composer, 42, 45, 151

Wales, 142

Walford, Edward (1823–97), writer, 76

Walker, Frederick (1840–75), painter, 144–5

Wallington, Mrs, 2

Ward, Mrs Humphry (née Arnold; 1851–1920), author, 117

Watford, 113

Watson, W. F., 34

Watts, the Revd Professor Francis, 11–12

Watts, Isaac (1674–1748), hymn writer, 2

Waverley Journal, 55

Wedgwood, Frances Julia, 111

Weimar, 41–2, 45, 87

Wellington, Alice, 129

Wellington, Duke of (1769–1852), soldier and statesman, 2, 22

Westminster Review, 26–30, 32–9, 41, 43–7, 49–51, 58, 61

Wetzlar, 102

Weybridge, 113, 120, 123, 135, 145, 160, 165

Weymouth, 67

Whitby, 117

Whitman, Walt (1819–92), poet, 145

Whittem family, 8

Wilberforce, the Revd Robert Isaac (1809–57), 4

Wilberforce, Bishop Samuel (1805–73), 4

Wildbad, 167

William IV (1765–1837), 2–3

Williams & Norgate, publishers, 62

Willim, Mrs, 75, 96, 102, 116, 119

Wilson, Andrew (1831–81), author, 142

Wiltshire, 138

Wimbledon, 83, 92

Windus, B. Godfrey, art collector, 26

Wingate, David, poet, 80

Wirksworth, 6

Wiseman, Nicholas Patrick Stephen, Cardinal Archbishop, 84, 91

Witley, 148, 151–3, 156, 158, 162–3, 167–9

Wittgenstein, Princess, 41, 46

Wolf, Auguste, (1759–1824), philosopher, 118

Wollstonecraft, Mary, *see* Godwin Mary

Woolner, Thomas (1825–92), sculptor and poet, 131

Worcester, 13

Wordsworth, Christopher (1807–85), divine, 80

Wordsworth, William (1770–1850), poet, 5, 7, 18, 25, 31, 74, 161, 163, 165, 168

Worthing, 45, 85

Xenophon (?427–353 BC), historian, 18

Yorkshire, 89

Young, Edward (1683–1765), poet, 2, 48, 51

Zola, Emile (1840–1902), novelist, 152

Zoological Gardens, 36, 48, 74, 107